Z

Z
An Introduction to Formal Methods

Antoni Diller

School of Computer Science
University of Birmingham

JOHN WILEY & SONS
Chichester · New York · Brisbane · Toronto · Singapore

Wiley Editorial Offices

John Wiley & Sons Ltd., Baffins Lane,
Chichester, West Sussex PO19 1UD, England

John Wiley & Sons, Inc., 605 Third Avenue,
New York, NY 10158-0012, USA

Jacaranda Wiley Ltd, G.P.O. Box 859, Brisbane,
Queensland 4001, Australia

John Wiley & Sons (Canada) Ltd, 22 Worcester Road,
Rexdale, Ontario M9W 1L1, Canada

John Wiley & Sons (SEA) Pte Ltd, 37 Jalan Pemimpin 05-04,
Block B, Union Industrial Building, Singapore 2057

Library of Congress Cataloguing-in-Publication Data:

Diller, Antoni.
    Z : an introduction to formal methods / Antoni Diller.
     p. cm.
    Includes bibliographical references and index.
    ISBN 0 471 92489 X
    1. Z (Computer program language.   I. Title.
  QA76.73.Z2D55   1990
  005.13′3 – dc20
                             90-35819
                             CIP

British Library Cataloguing in Publication Data:

Diller Antoni
    Z. : an introduction to formal methods.
    1. Computer systems. Programming languages. Z language
    I. Title
    005.133

    ISBN 0 471 92489 X

Printed and Bound by Courier International Limited, East Kilbride

This book is dedicated
to my niece, Laura Diller.

Contents

List of Figures

Preface

This book is about the formal specification language **Z**. It is based on two lecture courses given in the School of Computer Science at the University of Birmingham. The first is a second-year course that I have now given three times, namely in the autumn term of the 1987–1988 academic year and in the spring terms of the 1988–1989 and the 1989–1990 academic years.[1] The second is a first-year course given for the first time in the autumn term of the 1989–1990 academic year. (This latter course was delivered jointly by my colleague Tom Axford and myself.) Needless to say, the material presented here has undergone much revision and elaboration during the process of turning it into book form.

Given its origins this book can be used as a textbook for courses on **Z** and formal methods at first- and second-year undergraduate level. In my second-year course I present most of the material contained in parts I, II and IV. The first-year course covers less material, but what it does contain is drawn from those same parts.

There is a growing interest in formal methods outside the academic world and—although this book is primarily designed as a textbook to be used in a university or polytechnic environment—programmers and system designers working in industry should also find it useful. In fact, much of the material in part III—about reasoning about specifications—was presented as part of a very successful and well-attended post-experience course, called "**Z** for Engineers", which was organized jointly by John Miller, of the School of Electronic and Electrical Engineering at the University of Birmingham, and myself and which took place in July 1989. This course is likely to become an annual event.

Recently, a reference manual for **Z** has been published, namely Spivey (1989b), and I have used this standard **Z** notation throughout this book. The first part of the index contained at the end of this book lists all the standard **Z** symbols that I make use of. **Z** is, however, an *extendible* language in that it contains as part of itself definition mechanisms for extending itself. On a small number of occasions I have used **Z**'s abbreviation definition, axiomatic description and generic constant introduction constructs in order to define additional symbols in order to present specifications in a more structured and better organized fashion. Every symbol introduced in this way is contained in the second part of the index to this book, as are some commonly used standard mathematical meta-linguistic symbols.

---

[1] The first two times I gave this course it was of fifteen hours duration. The third time it had grown to twenty hours.

This book is divided into seven parts. Part I contains a single chapter in which I try to briefly explain what **Z** is and why it is a good method for specifying software components.

Part II is a tutorial introduction to **Z** which covers the basic mathematical toolkit of **Z** and the fundamental ideas of the schema calculus. Many exercises are provided and—to help people using this book on their own in order to learn **Z**—answers are provided in part VII to *every* exercise set. Personally, I find it annoying when textbooks which contain exercises either contain no answers or only answers to selected exercises; therefore, I have included answers to all the exercises.

Part III looks at methods of reasoning. As well as looking at both formal and rigorous proof, I also thoroughly cover the important issues of data refinement or reification and operation decomposition. These topics are crucial to the use of **Z** for the specification of large software systems and yet none of the other textbooks on **Z**, namely Ince (1988a) and Woodcock and Loomes (1988), give any account of them whatsoever.

Part IV contains four specification case studies: two small ones and two fairly large ones. The two small ones are of the bill of materials problem and of a simple route planner. (The route planner specification was suggested to me by my colleague Tom Axford.) The two large case studies are of a display-orientated text-editor— based on Sufrin's specification—and of Wing's library problem. One of the distinctive features of this book is the large number of case studies provided. In addition to the four contained in this part of the book, no less than nine others are included in other parts. These range in size from the 22-page specification of the library problem down to a half-page specification of the problem of finding square roots. Most of the specifications contained in this book are original, but I have also included some well-known favourites like the classroom specification, the bill of materials problem and an updated and revamped version of Sufrin's editor specification. In part II of the book whenever a new **Z** data type is introduced, it is illustrated by means of a case study. Thus, a telephone number database is used to illustrate relations, a weather map to illustrate functions, sorting to illustrate both sequences and bags, a vending machine to illustrate bags and a theorem-checker and theorem-prover to illustrate sequences and free types (in this case, trees).

In part V I look at how a **Z** specification can be animated using a high-level modern functional programming language and Prolog. With the increasing use of formal methods in industry I believe that specification animation will become a useful aid to help ensure that a specification is correct and behaves as the customer wants.

Part VI is a reference manual of all the most frequently used **Z** notations and part VII consists of two appendices as well as an annotated bibliography which contains many pointers into the ever-increasing literature on **Z**. I have concentrated on recent books and articles written on **Z**, especially those written in the past three years. Appendix A contains a list of the functions to which I put all the single-letter identifiers used in this book. (I would urge other authors to follow my example in providing such useful information.) Appendix B contains answers to all the exercises set in this book.

Having mentioned the reference section I would just like to repeat here what I said earlier, namely that I have used standard **Z** notation where a standard exists and I have taken Spivey (1989b) to define what standard **Z** is. Where I have needed to use a notation for a concept not mentioned in Spivey (1989b) I have used standard mathematical symbols and conventions. My guiding principle has been not to create notations unnecessarily. One example of this is that in presenting formal proofs in the propositional and predicate calculuses I have used the most widely used format—found, for example, in Lemmon (1965) and Newton-Smith (1985)—rather than inventing a proof-architecture of my own. One of the main disadvantages of Woodcock and Loomes (1988) and Woodcock (1989b) is that the authors ignore standard practice in presenting proofs and develop their own highly idiosyncratic format for proofs. The deficiencies of this—and the strengths of the standard format—are detailed in Diller (1990b). Another advantage of the notation for proofs used in this book is that it is based on that found in Sufrin (1986b), which is the earlier **Z** standard on which Spivey (1989b) is based. I find it difficult to see why Woodcock has chosen to ignore this and has decided rather to re-invent the wheel in the area of proof-architecture. I am confident that the standard notation used here will become universally accepted. A further disadvantage that Woodcock and Loomes (1988) suffers from is that its treatment of first-order logic does not use a *typed* predicate calculus. The treatment of the predicate calculus given on pp. 42–72 of that book uses formulas of the form $\forall x \bullet P$ and $\exists x \bullet P$, which are simply not part of standard **Z**. My book is the first book on **Z** to present a proof-theory, in chapter 10, for **Z**'s typed predicate calculus.

Antoni Diller
Birmingham
February 1990

Acknowledgements

The following trademarks are used in this book. 'Miranda' is a trademark of Research Software Ltd. 'IBM' is a registered trademark of International Business Machines Corporation. 'TEX' is a trademark of the American Mathematical Society. 'Unix' is a trademark of AT & T Bell Laboratories. 'Ada' is a registered trademark of the US Government (Ada Joint Program Office).

As mentioned in the preface this book grew out of lecture courses that I have given in the University of Birmingham. I am grateful to my students for helping to "debug" the material I taught them and, in particular, to Richard Billington, an MSc student, who found several mistakes in my initial specification of Wing's library problem.

This book was typeset using LaTeX and I am grateful to Mike Spivey for giving me a copy of the TEX macros he wrote for producing the various boxes and notations used in Z. I am also grateful to Tom Axford for the \enclose macro used on p. 97. Although I think that LaTeX is—on the whole—a very good package of TEX macros, there are certain design decisions made by Lamport that I disagree with. In particular, throughout this book I use the TEX commands \eqalign and \eqalignno in preference to LaTeX's \eqnarray.

I am indebted to a large number of people for my knowledge of Z and for many of the ideas contained in this book. I initially learnt Z from Bernard Sufrin and Ib Sørensen of Oxford University's Programming Research Group and I am grateful to them—and Mike Spivey—for answering many questions about Z. I am grateful to my colleague Rachid Anane for reading chapter 1 and pointing out some errors in an earlier draft and to Tom Axford for suggesting the route planner problem and for several useful conversations about it. Peter Greenfield and Peter Hammond have helped in my understanding of Prolog. I am especially grateful to Antony Wilson, Mark Tarver, Francine Wright and Karl Laing for reading through earlier drafts of this book and for providing many helpful suggestions. I apologise for any omissions of acknowledgement and will correct them when the opportunity arises if they are drawn to my attention. Needless to say, any mistakes contained in this book are my own responsibility.

Part I

The Philosophy of Formal Methods

Chapter 1

What is Z?

1.1 Introduction

This is a book about the formal specification language **Z**. This notation was developed at Oxford University's Programming Research Group in the late seventies and early eighties by Jean-Raymond Abrial, Bernard Sufrin and Ib Sørensen. It is not, however, an academic plaything, because from a very early stage in its development **Z** was used in the real world. In particular, it was taken up by IBM Hursley where it has been used in the re-specification of their very successful Customer Information Control System (CICS).[1] This has had beneficial effects on the development of **Z**. The language has grown and developed as a result of actually being used to specify large software systems in an industrial environment. After a certain amount of experimentation and theoretical investigation, a standard core language has been defined and this can be found in Spivey (1989b). This book makes use of that standard **Z** notation, although additional symbols and operators have been defined when appropriate to do so. This is perfectly legitimate as **Z** contains within itself mechanisms for carrying out abbreviation definitions. Such definitions help structure specifications and make them more perspicuous; therefore, it is important for the user of **Z** to know how and when to employ them.

In this introductory chapter I explain what it means to say that **Z** is both a *formal* language and a *specification* language, then I discuss the two fundamental abstraction methods used in constructing formal specifications, namely *procedural* and *representational* abstraction, and to conclude I briefly state some of the advantages of using **Z** in software engineering.

1.1.1 Z is a Formal Language

The **Z** language is based on the mathematical disciplines of first-order logic and set theory.[2] The use of mathematics for specification purposes has many advantages. For

---

[1] For more information about CICS, see Hayes (1985a, 1987a, 1987b).

[2] Unlike some rival specification methods, **Z** uses classical two-valued logic. At various places in this book I mention some of the differences between classical logic and intuitionistic logic—which is also used for specification purposes—and also between it and the three-valued logic that is used in VDM.

example, it leads to concise, unambiguous and exact specifications that are easy to reason about. The more I use and teach **Z** the more I am convinced that it is the fact that you can reason mathematically about **Z** specifications and prove results about them that is its main advantage over alternative specification methods. The construction of a *theory* about a piece of software—involving theorems, lemmas and proofs—in addition to a descriptive specification quickly reveals gaps and inconsistencies in that specification, if they exist, and if they do not, then it greatly increases your understanding of that piece of software and your confidence that it will behave as you—or your client—wants it to behave. In this book, therefore, a great deal of emphasis is placed on proving results about specifications and this has necessitated the inclusion of a fairly detailed treatment of both formal and rigorous methods of proof.

1.1.2 Z is a Specification Language

One of the key ideas involved in calling **Z** a specification language is that specification and implementation should be kept separate. The specification should precisely state *what* the eventual piece of software is supposed to do and not *how* it is to go about achieving its task. Separating specification and implementation results in a separation of the often conflicting tasks of correctly solving the problem in hand and that of building an efficient piece of software. Something that is very important to realise is that writing a formal specification is very different from writing a computer program. What you are about in producing a formal specification is a *functional description* of what the eventual program is going to do. That is to say, an account of *what* the program is going to do and not *how* it is going to go about doing it.

One way of looking at the methodology underlying the use of **Z** is that it stresses the primacy of *declarative* thinking over *procedural* or *imperative* thinking. One of the things that people find most difficult to do when they start writing formal specifications is to stop thinking *procedurally*. The goal is to describe what a program is going to do, so you should not be concerned about efficiency or even implementability. Thus, operations are specified by giving their preconditions and postconditions, and not by giving a procedure for how those operations are to be carried out. The technique of ignoring the computational or procedural difficulties associated with a problem and only concentrating on its functional specification is known as *procedural* or *operational abstraction*.

1.1.3 Formal Methods

Another term that you are likely to have come across is *formal methods*. Formal methods comprises two things, namely *formal specification* and *verified design*.[3] This division is shown in Fig. 1.1. The methodology underlying formal methods is that you first precisely specify the behaviour of a piece of software, then that software is written and then you prove whether or not that actual implementation meets its specification. This final aspect of formal methods is known as *verified design*. This term applies to the relation between a formal specification and the software component that is written

---

[3]This division is taken from Jones (1986a), p. xiv.

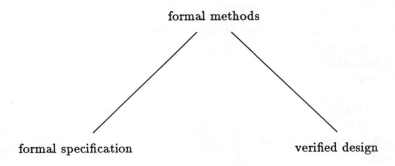

Figure 1.1: The branches of formal methods.

to meet that specification. Clearly, we want the software component to satisfy its specification and proof techniques have been developed to enable someone to prove that a software component meets its specification.[4]

This account should not make you think that programs are written independently of the specification that they are supposed to satisfy and only then are correctness proofs attempted. Although it is, in general, impossible to mechanically derive a program from a specification, various heuristic methods have been developed which offer guidelines as to how to write an algorithm to carry out a specified task. Furthermore, the derivation of the program and the construction of the correctness proof also usually go hand-in-hand as well.

1.1.4 A Simple Example

In order to illustrate the above discussion, consider the problem of finding the non-negative real square root of a given real number. The specification of this problem is as follows:

$$radicand? \geq 0 \land squareroot!^2 = radicand? \land squareroot! \geq 0, \qquad (1.1)$$

where *radicand?* and *squareroot!* are both real numbers, *radicand?* being the number whose square root we are trying to find and *squareroot!* being the square root that we are after. Conventionally, inputs in **Z** are written with a final question mark and outputs with a final exclamation mark. The question mark and the exclamation mark are to be considered as parts of the identifiers themselves. The wedge $\land$ is just a symbolic way of representing the word 'and'. It is known as logical conjunction.

---

[4]One of the commonest approaches makes use of Hoare logics—see Hoare (1969), Gries (1981), Backhouse (1986), Baber (1987), Gumb (1989) and Dromey (1989)—but other approaches are currently the subject of much fruitful research. See, for example, the collection of papers in Morgan, Robinson and Gardiner (1988).

The precondition of the specification (1.1) is the single predicate *radicand?* ≥ 0. Only non-negative real numbers have real square roots. (1.1) is an example of a functional specification. It does not tell you how to calculate square roots. A Pascal function which does that is the following:

```
function SquareRoot (radicand: real): real;
   const epsilon = 0.0001;
   var guess: real;
begin
   guess := 1.0;
   while abs (radicand − (guess ∗ guess)) > epsilon do
      guess := (guess + (radicand/guess))/2;
   SquareRoot := guess;
end;
```

This function makes use of Newton's method for calculating square roots.

A Foretaste of Schema

To give you a brief foretaste of what the schema language—which is fully discussed later—looks like, I will now write the square root specification in it. The schema language is just a graphical extension of **Z**.

$$
\begin{array}{|l}
\underline{\quad SquareRootSpec \quad\rule{0pt}{0pt}}\\
\quad radicand?, squareroot!: \mathbf{R}\\
\hline
\quad radicand? \geq 0\\
\quad squareroot!^2 = radicand?\\
\quad squareroot! \geq 0\\
\end{array}
$$

The box with part of one side missing is the *schema box*. The identifier at the top, namely *SquareRootSpec*, is the *name* of the schema. Above the horizontal line there are a number of declarations. Here, the identifiers *radicand?* and *squareroot!* are both declared to be real numbers. The central horizontal line can be read 'such that' and below it there are a number of predicates. Predicates appearing on separate lines are assumed to be conjoined together, that is to say, linked with the truth-functional connective $\wedge$.

1.2   Fundamental Abstraction Methods

1.2.1   Procedural Abstraction

In explaining what it means to say that **Z** is a specification language I talked about *procedural* or *operational abstraction* and this was illustrated by means of the square root specification. Using procedural abstraction we ignore issues relating to *how* a task is to be carried out and just concentrate on accurately stating *what* has to be done.

6

Another way of expressing this facet of the methodology inherent in the use of formal methods is that it stresses the primacy of *declarative* thinking over *imperative* or *procedural* thinking and in this respect it is diametrically opposed to the approach advocated, for example, by Abelson and Sussman (1985), p. xvi:

> Underlying our approach to this subject is our conviction that "computer science" is not a science and that its significance has little to do with computers. The computer revolution is a revolution in the way we think and in the way we express what we think. The essence of this change is the emergence of what might best be called *procedural epistemology*—the study of the structure of knowledge from an imperative point of view, as opposed to the more declarative point of view taken by classical mathematical subjects. Mathematics provides a framework for dealing precisely with notions of "what is." Computation provides a framework for dealing precisely with notions of "how to."

In our present state of knowledge it is impossible to say whether the attitude of Abelson and Sussman or that inherent in the use of formal specification methods is the best, though the tide of opinion seems to be swinging in the direction of the primacy of declarative methods in computing; not only **Z**, but also logic programming and functional programming make extensive use of declarative methods.

1.2.2 Representational Abstraction

Procedural abstraction is one of the two main ways in which abstraction is used in **Z** in order to manage the complexity of the problem of correctly specifying a piece of software. The other main abstraction technique is *representational abstraction*. This involves using high-level mathematical structures—like arbitrary sets, relations, functions, sequences, bags, trees and so on—in the specification of software systems without worrying about how these are going to be eventually implemented. This has the beneficial consequence that in solving a specific problem we are allowed to think using structures most suited to the problem in hand, rather than being forced at a premature stage to think in terms of the baroque data structures available in most programming languages.[5]

1.3 The Advantages of Z

1.3.1 Introduction

Some of the advantages of **Z** were mentioned in section 1.1, namely those that follow from the fact that **Z** is a *mathematical* notation. For example, specifications written in **Z** are precise, unambiguous, concise and amenable to proof. In this section some further advantages of **Z** will be mentioned, relating to how **Z** fits into our modern understanding of software engineering.

---

[5]This is just another example of the value of the divide-and-conquer problem-solving strategy.

1.3.2   Z and Software Engineering

Hoare (1983) has argued that programming is an engineering discipline and many people talk about software engineering, but how seriously do they take the word 'engineering' in the phrase 'software engineering'? Consider the following quotation from Darlington (1987), p. 71:

> Is programming a craft or a science? Most professional (and amateur) programmers would like to claim that what they do is scientific, but compared with the standards attained in other, more mature, engineering disciplines such as aeronautical or civil engineering, programming has a long way to go. If one were asked to build a bridge I doubt that it would be acceptable to construct an initial version, try it out and when it fell down correct the mistakes made in the design, and then repeat the process until the bridge stood up. This is, however, the paradigm that most practicing programmers follow as they debug their programs towards a working state. At present, programming suffers from a lack of notations for building models or initial specifications of systems and any criteria for judging the correctness of solutions to such specifications.

Z is an attempt—and a pretty successful attempt at that—to devise a notation for building models of software systems and for proving that programs meet their specifications. The comparison between *software* engineering and *civil* engineering is fitting because—as Hoare has argued—programming is an engineering profession. You would find it very strange if people built a bridge without using sophisticated mathematical techniques, if they just specified the problem in natural language. Therefore, you should expect software engineers to be using mathematical techniques in the specification and development of computer programs. One of the differences between civil engineering and software engineering is in the parts of mathematics that are used. In civil engineering it is things like mechanics and dynamics, whereas the branches of mathematics that are used in specifying computer systems are discrete mathematics, set theory and mathematical logic.

1.4   Conclusion

In this brief introductory chapter I have tried to impart something of the "feel" of formal methods in general and Z in particular. I think that it would be out of place in a textbook on Z to spend an inordinately large amount of space arguing for the use of formal methods—several books and papers that do this are mentioned in the annotated bibliography—and so I have kept this chapter short.

Part II

Tutorial Introduction

Chapter 2

First-order Logic

2.1 Introduction

Z is based on the languages of logic and set theory. In this chapter I look at the language of logic. I begin with the propositional calculus and then go on to discuss the predicate calculus with identity.

Logic is the study of *inference*, of what *follows* from what, of what can be *deduced* from a given set of assumptions. Typically, inferences and deductions are expressed in the form of *arguments*. An example of such an argument is this:[1] 'If Britain leaves the EC or if the trade deficit is reduced, then the price of butter will fall. If Britain stays in the EC, then exports will not increase. The trade deficit will increase unless exports are increased. Therefore, the price of butter will not fall.' It is the presence of the word 'therefore' that tells us that we are dealing with an argument. This word signals that an inference is being drawn. Other words—like 'so', 'because' and 'since'—can also perform this task. The premises or assumptions of this argument are the three propositions 'If Britain leaves the EC or if the trade deficit is reduced, then the price of butter will fall', 'If Britain stays in the EC, then exports will not increase' and 'The trade deficit will increase unless exports are increased'. The conclusion is the sentence 'The price of butter will not fall'.

It is a logical problem to decide whether or not this argument is valid, that is to say, whether or not the conclusion follows from the premises. (In the case of this example I will answer that question later on in this chapter—on p. 19—after I have introduced the main ideas of the propositional calculus.)

Formal logic is the application of rigorous mathematical methods to the study of such notions as *inference*, *argument* and *validity*. In presenting a formal logical argument or inference we want to be certain that our inference is correct or valid. There are two main ways of studying any logical system, namely the semantic and the proof-theoretic. In formal semantics we are concerned with notions related to truth and falsity and in proof-theory we are concerned with axioms and rules of inference. The proof theory of first-order logic is dealt with in chapter 10.

---

[1] This example is borrowed—with a number of minor changes—from Stewart and Tall (1977), p. 131, where it is exercise 6(b).

2.2 Propositional Logic

2.2.1 Introduction

Z uses the classical, two-valued propositional calculus in which every proposition is considered to be either true or false, but not both.[2] In this section I present the basic facts about the propositional calculus. Although **Z** uses classical logic, various other logical systems are used in computing—particularly for specification purposes—and so I try to point out some of the distinctive features of classical logic with respect to other logical systems and I give a few references to other works that treat those systems in more detail.

2.2.2 Model-theory

There are two main ways of studying any logical system, namely the *proof-theoretic* and the *model-theoretic*. Model-theory or formal semantics deals with concepts like truth, interpretation and satisfiability, whereas proof-theory deals with axioms, rules of inference and proofs. In this section I describe the model-theory of the propositional calculus and in chapter 10 I discuss its proof-theory.

As already mentioned, **Z** uses the classical, two-valued propositional calculus in which every proposition is considered to be either true or false, but not both.[3] Not surprisingly, the propositional calculus is the study of propositions. A proposition is something that can be either true or false. No third truth-value is permitted, nor is it allowed for a proposition to lack a truth-value.[4] The only two truth-values permitted are truth and falsity. In this chapter these will be represented by t and f, respectively. The following are examples of propositions:

$$2 + 7 = 9, \tag{2.1}$$

$$3 > 9, \tag{2.2}$$

$$\text{The moon is made of green cheese.} \tag{2.3}$$

Proposition (2.1) is true, (2.2) is false and (2.3) is also false.

In discussions of natural language propositions are contrasted with commands (imperatives) and also with questions (interrogatives). Examples of commands are sentences like 'Close the door!' and 'Shut the window!' and examples of questions are sentences like 'Is Paris the capital of France?' and 'Who murdered John Lennon?'

---

[2]This claim is known as the law of bivalence.

[3]Philosophers argue about whether logic deals with sentences—thought of as linguistic entities—or propositions—considered as semantic entities, that is to say, the alleged meanings of sentences—or statements, which are sentences uttered at a particular time and in a particular place. Such discussions—though necessary for a correct philosophical understanding of logic—are irrelevant to us as computer scientists. The *word* 'proposition', however, is very useful and I shall use it as an alternative to '(indicative) sentence'. In books on **Z** the word 'predicate' is also used for a proposition and I shall also use that at times for variety.

[4]It is possible to devise n-valued logics which have n truth-values. The specification language of VDM, for example, uses a 3-valued logic. In using **Z**, however, you should always be aware that it is based on classical logic.

Although logics have been created which can cope with the logical relations that exist between these kinds of sentences, they are not necessary for specification purposes and so will not be mentioned again here.[5]

Propositional Connectives and Constants

The letters P, Q and R, sometimes with subscripts, are used consistently in this book to stand for arbitrary propositions. They are not used for any other purpose. (Appendix A contains details about how all single-letter identifiers are consistently used in this book.)

Negation   You cannot do very much with just propositions, you also need some propositional connectives (also known as truth-functional connectives). The simplest of these is negation, which is represented by the sign $\neg$. This makes a proposition out of a proposition. Thus, applying negation to (2.1) and (2.2), respectively, yields the two propositions:

$$\neg(2 + 7 = 9), \tag{2.4}$$
$$\neg(3 > 9). \tag{2.5}$$

(2.4) is false and (2.5) is true. The meaning of negation is fully determined by the following truth-table:

P	$\neg P$
t	f
f	t

A proposition $\neg P$ is false if and only if P is true and $\neg P$ is true if and only if P is false. The phrase 'if and only if' occurs so frequently in discussions of logic that it is usually abbreviated to 'iff'.

Conjunction   The first two-place propositional connective that I consider is conjunction. This is the logical name for the word 'and' and it is represented by the symbol $\wedge$. This makes a proposition out of two other propositions. Thus,

$$(2 + 7 = 9) \wedge (3 > 9)$$

is a proposition, which is referred to as a *conjunctive* proposition or simply as a *conjunction*. The two constituent propositions of a conjunction are known as *conjuncts*. The meaning of conjunction is completely given by this truth-table:

---

[5]The study of the logical relations that hold between imperatives is known as *deontic* logic and the study of questions is known as *erotetic* logic. For more information about erotetic logic see Prior and Prior (1955).

P	Q	$P \wedge Q$
t	t	t
t	f	f
f	t	f
f	f	f

This says that a conjunction is true iff both of its conjuncts are true.

Disjunction Disjunction is another two-place propositional connective. Disjunction is the logical name for the word 'or' and it is represented by the symbol $\vee$. Thus, the following is a proposition:

$$(2 + 7 = 9) \vee (3 > 9).$$

The constituent propositions are known as *disjuncts*. Another example of a disjunctive proposition is:

The trade deficit will increase unless exports are increased,

although this does not contain the word 'or'. This is because logically 'unless' behaves as disjunction. The meaning of disjunction is given by the following truth-table:

P	Q	$P \vee Q$
t	t	t
t	f	t
f	t	t
f	f	f

Thus, a disjunction is only false when both its constituent disjuncts are false. Such a disjunction is known as *non-exclusive* or *inclusive* disjunction. Philosophers wonder if the natural language word 'or' is used in its inclusive or exclusive sense,[6] but for specification purposes that problem can be ignored. Inclusive disjunction is more useful.

Implication Implication is symbolized by an arrow $\Rightarrow$; thus the following is an example of a conditional proposition:

$$(9 > 5) \Rightarrow (2 > 4).$$

This can be read as either '9 > 5 implies (that) 2 > 4' or as 'If 9 > 5, then 2 > 4'. Such a proposition is known either as a *conditional* or as an *implication*. The first component proposition, namely '9 > 5', is known as the *antecedent* or the *protasis* of

---

[6]Inclusive disjunction *includes* the situation in which both P and Q are true, that is to say, considers it true; exclusive disjunction *excludes* this possibility, that is to say, treats it as false.

the implication and the second component proposition, namely '2 > 4', is known as the *consequent* or the *apodosis* of the conditional. The meaning of implication is fully determined by the following truth-table:

P	Q	$P \Rightarrow Q$
t	t	t
t	f	f
f	t	t
f	f	t

A conditional proposition is false only if its antecedent is true and its consequent is false; otherwise it is true. This has the consequence that all of the following propositions are true:[7]

1. If President Lincoln is alive today, then walnuts grow on banana trees.

2. If President Lincoln is alive today, then walnuts do not grow on banana trees.

3. If President Lincoln is not alive today, then walnuts do not grow on banana trees.

Many people find it distinctly odd to think of such propositions as being true and philosophers agonize over whether 'if' in ordinary speech is ever used in this way, but their worries can be ignored for specification purposes, since this form of implication is all that is needed in mathematics. This kind of implication is known as the *material conditional* in order to distinguish it from other sorts of implication, such as *strict* implication which I will not go into here.[8]

Bi-implication Bi-implication is also known as the *bi-conditional* or *material equivalence*. An example of its use is:

$$x = 1 \Longleftrightarrow (x^2 = 1 \land x > 0).$$

This is read as '$x = 1$ if and only if $x^2 = 1$ and $x > 0$'. The meaning of the bi-conditional is fully determined by the following truth-table:

P	Q	$P \Longleftrightarrow Q$
t	t	t
t	f	f
f	t	f
f	f	t

---

[7]These sentences are from Prior (1962), p. 19.

[8]Logical systems which study notions like strict implication, necessity and possibility are known as *modal logics*. They have their uses in computing, but they are not needed for many specification tasks and so will not be mentioned again. For more information about strict implication and modal logics see Lewis and Langford (1959) and Hughes and Cresswell (1968, 1984).

The Always True and the Always False Propositions   Z also contains two constant propositions, namely the always true and the always false propositions. The former of these is symbolized by *true* and the latter by *false*. The constant propositions *true* and *false* should be carefully distinguished from the truth-values t and f. The latter are used to give meaning to propositions. The relation between a proposition and its truth-value is similar to that which holds between a name and its bearer. I am different from the name 'Antoni Diller', but my name stands for or denotes or refers to me—similarly with propositions and their truth-values. The proposition '$2 + 3 = 5$' refers to the truth-value t.

Another difference is that the constant propositions can be combined with the truth-functional connectives—for example, *true* $\Rightarrow 2 + 3 = 5$—but t and f cannot be used in this way. They belong to the meta-language we use to talk about the propositional calculus and are not part of that language themselves.

Precedence and Associativity of the Connectives

Negation binds most strongly, so $\neg P \vee Q$ means $(\neg P) \vee Q$ and not $\neg (P \vee Q)$. Conjunction binds more strongly than any truth-functional connective except negation, and then come disjunction, implication and bi-implication, in that order. So, $P \vee Q \wedge R \Rightarrow P$ means $(P \vee (Q \wedge R)) \Rightarrow P$. Implication $\Rightarrow$ associates to the right, whereas $\wedge$, $\vee$ and $\Longleftrightarrow$ all associate to the left. So, $P \wedge Q \wedge R \Rightarrow P \Rightarrow R$ means $((P \wedge Q) \wedge R) \Rightarrow (P \Rightarrow R)$.

It is a straightforward task to write a grammar for the propositional calculus which embodies all the information contained in this section and any reader who would find such a grammar useful is encouraged to construct it for him or herself.

Tautologies

A *tautology* is a proposition that is true irrespective of the truth-values of its constituent propositions. One of the simplest tautologies is $P \vee \neg P$. This is true—in classical logic—no matter what the truth-value of P is.[9] This can be straightforwardly shown by constructing a truth-table, thus:

P	P	$\vee$	$\neg P$
t	t	t	f
f	f	t	t

---

[9]This tautology is known as *the law of the excluded middle*. Mathematicians and logicians of the intuitionistic school do not accept that it is logically valid. Intuitionistic ideas will not be pursued here—though they have their uses in computing. See Dummett (1977) and Martin-Löf (1984) for more information.

16

Another simple tautology is $P \Rightarrow P$. This can be proved like this:

P	P	$\Rightarrow$	P
t	t	t	t
f	f	t	f

Another example of a tautology is the proposition $(P \Rightarrow Q) \vee (Q \Rightarrow P)$. That this is a tautology is rather surprising, but the following truth-table proves that it is:

P	Q	$(P \Rightarrow Q)$	$\vee$	$(Q \Rightarrow P)$
t	t	t	t	t
t	f	f	t	t
f	t	t	t	f
f	f	t	t	t

Truth-tables can also be used to show that a proposition is not a tautology. Consider, for example, the truth-table of the proposition $(P \Rightarrow Q) \Rightarrow (Q \Rightarrow P)$:

P	Q	$(P \Rightarrow Q)$	$\Rightarrow$	$(Q \Rightarrow P)$
t	t	t	t	t
t	f	f	t	t
f	t	t	f	f
f	f	t	t	t

When P is false and Q is true, then $(P \Rightarrow Q) \Rightarrow (Q \Rightarrow P)$ is false. Thus, it is not a tautology. It is not necessary to draw the entire truth-table in order to show that a proposition is not a tautology; it is sufficient to give the truth-values of P and Q that serve as a counter-example, that is to say, make the proposition false.

The final example of a truth-table that I give is one that involves three constituent propositions. The following truth-table shows that the proposition $(P \Rightarrow Q) \vee (Q \Rightarrow R)$ is a tautology:

P	Q	R	$(P \Rightarrow Q)$	$\vee$	$(Q \Rightarrow R)$
t	t	t	t	t	t
t	t	f	t	t	f
t	f	t	f	t	t
t	f	f	f	t	t
f	t	t	t	t	t
f	t	f	t	t	f
f	f	t	t	t	t
f	f	f	t	t	t

The Semantic Turnstile

To show that a proposition P is a tautology we write $\models P$. Thus,

$$\models P \vee \neg P$$

says that $P \vee \neg P$ is a tautology. The sign $\models$ is, in fact, a relation between a—possibly empty—set of propositions and a proposition. To say that the *semantic sequent*,

$$P_1, P_2, \ldots, P_n \models Q,$$

is *valid* means that it is impossible for Q to be false when all of the P_i are true. The sign $\models$ can be read as 'therefore', though some mathematicians prefer the reading 'models'. Note that the curly brackets { } which normally indicate the presence of a set are usually omitted when writing sequents. The propositions $P_1, P_2, \ldots, P_n$ are known as the *premises* of the sequent and the proposition Q is its *conclusion*. $P, P \Rightarrow Q \models Q$, is an example of a valid sequent. That this is indeed valid is proved as follows. First, we draw up a truth-table:

P	Q	P	$P \Rightarrow Q$	$\models$	Q
t	t	t	t		t
t	f	t	f		f
f	t	f	t		t
f	f	f	t		f

Note that we do not write anything in the semantic turnstile column. This is because $\models$ is not a truth-functional connective. It is, rather, a relation between a set of propositions and a single proposition. It is a symbol in the meta-language that we use to talk about the propositional calculus.

The way we use this truth-table is to look at those rows in which the conclusion of the sequent, namely Q, is false. In neither of these are all the premises true; hence the sequent is valid.

It is now possible for me to answer the question whether or not the natural language argument given on p. 11 above is valid. First, we have to represent it as a sequent. In order to do this we use the following key:

proposition	symbol
Britain leaves the EC	P_1
The trade deficit is reduced	P_2
The price of butter falls	P_3
Exports increase	P_4

The required sequent is then:

$$P_1 \vee P_2 \Rightarrow P_3, \ \neg P_1 \Rightarrow \neg P_4, \ \neg P_2 \vee P_4 \models \neg P_3.$$

18

This is invalid. It is possible to draw up the complete truth-table for this sequent, but in order to demonstrate invalidity we just need to know the assignment of truth-values that make the conclusion false and all the premises true. For this example, the following suffices: both P_1 and P_3 are true and both P_2 and P_4 are false.

The Relation between Implication and the Semantic Turnstile There is a close connection between $\models$ (models) and $\Rightarrow$ (material implication). We have that $P \models Q$ iff $\models P \Rightarrow Q$. The proof is straightforward. It splits into two cases.

1. To show that if $P \models Q$ then $\models P \Rightarrow Q$ we argue as follows: Assume $P \models Q$; that is to say, it is impossible for Q to be false and for P to be true. Hence, $P \Rightarrow Q$ must be true; that is to say, it is a tautology and this is written $\models P \Rightarrow Q$.

2. To show that if $\models P \Rightarrow Q$ then $P \models Q$ we argue as follows: Assume $\models P \Rightarrow Q$; that is to say, $P \Rightarrow Q$ is a tautology. In other words, it is always true. So, it is impossible for Q to be false and for P to be true; that is to say, $P \models Q$.

In general, we have:

$$P_1, P_2, \ldots, P_n \models Q \quad \text{iff} \quad P_1, P_2, \ldots, P_{n-1} \models P_n \Rightarrow Q.$$

Semantic Equivalence

The notation $P \models\!\mid\!= Q$ means that both $P \models Q$ and $Q \models P$ are valid. Only single propositions can be written either side of $=\!\mid\!\models$. An example of the use of $=\!\mid\!\models$ is the following:

$$P \Rightarrow Q \ =\!\mid\!\models\ \neg P \vee Q.$$

To prove this we split it into two cases. First, we show $P \Rightarrow Q \models \neg P \vee Q$. This is established by considering the following truth-table:

P	Q	$P \Rightarrow Q$	$\models$	$\neg P \vee Q$
t	t	t		t
t	f	f		f
f	t	t		t
f	f	t		t

The row to consider is that in which the conclusion $\neg P \vee Q$ is false. In this case the premise $P \Rightarrow Q$ is not true; therefore the sequent is valid.

Next, we show $\neg P \vee Q \models P \Rightarrow Q$. This is established by considering the following truth-table:

P	Q	$\neg P \vee Q$	$\models$	$P \Rightarrow Q$
t	t	t		t
t	f	f		f
f	t	t		t
f	f	t		t

The row to consider is that in which the conclusion $P \Rightarrow Q$ is false. In this case the premise $\neg P \lor Q$ is not true; therefore the sequent is valid. Combining these two arguments proves what we set out to prove.

Ways of Defining the Connectives

So far I have introduced just five truth-functional connectives and given the meaning of each one of them independently of the others, but is is possible to define all of these connectives using only a subset of them. For example, we can take negation and disjunction as primitive and define all the other connectives like this:

$$P \land Q \mathrel{==} \neg(\neg P \lor \neg Q),$$
$$P \Rightarrow Q \mathrel{==} \neg P \lor Q,$$
$$P \Longleftrightarrow Q \mathrel{==} (P \Rightarrow Q) \land (Q \Rightarrow P),$$
$$\mathrel{==} (\neg P \lor Q) \land (\neg Q \lor P),$$
$$\mathrel{==} \neg(\neg(\neg P \lor Q) \lor \neg(\neg Q \lor P)).$$

The sign $==$ used here is the **Z** notation for an abbreviation definition. The left-hand side is being defined to mean the same as the right-hand side.[10]

In fact, there exist connectives in terms of which all the others can be defined. One example of such a connective is Sheffer's stroke, which has the following truth-table:

P	Q	$P \mid Q$
t	t	f
t	f	t
f	t	t
f	f	t

It is possible to define $\neg$, $\land$, $\lor$, $\Rightarrow$ and $\Longleftrightarrow$ in terms of $\mid$. First, we define $\neg$ and $\lor$ like this:

$$\neg P \mathrel{==} P \mid P,$$
$$P \lor Q \mathrel{==} (P \mid P) \mid (Q \mid Q).$$

Then, we use the previous definitions.

This shows that there is nothing absolute about what is a primitive truth-functional connective and what is a defined one.

An Interesting Sequent

Consider the following valid sequent:[11]

$$(P \land Q) \lor (\neg P \land R) \mathrel{=\!\!\mid\!\!\mid\!\!=} (P \Rightarrow Q) \land (\neg P \Rightarrow R).$$

---

[10]See chapter 19 below and Spivey (1989b), pp. 52 and 79, for more information about abbreviation definitions.

[11]Note that in the 3-valued logic of VDM the formula $(P \land Q) \lor (\neg P \land R)$ is *not* a valid consequence of the formula $(P \Rightarrow Q) \land (\neg P \Rightarrow R)$.

This is useful in writing specifications. Consider the problem of specifying the fact that r is the absolute value of i, where r and i are both integers. There are at least two approaches to this:

$$(i < 0 \land r = -i) \lor (i \geq 0 \land r = i), \qquad (2.6)$$

$$(i < 0 \Rightarrow r = -i) \land (i \geq 0 \Rightarrow r = i). \qquad (2.7)$$

From the above valid sequent we have that (2.6) $\dashv\vdash$ (2.7).

A Pascal command which satisfies this specification is:

$$\textbf{if } i < 0 \textbf{ then } r := -i \textbf{ else } r := i \qquad (2.8)$$

Notice that neither (2.6) nor (2.7) tell you *how* to calculate the absolute value of i. (2.8) is a (trivial) algorithm for doing this. To show that (2.8) meets its specification—either (2.6) or (2.7)—is the problem of *verified design*. For that you need what are known as *Hoare logics*. I do not discuss Hoare logics in this book, but there are some excellent books available on the subject.[12]

2.3 Predicate Calculus

2.3.1 Introduction

Types

One of the distinctive features of **Z** is that it is a typed language. A *type* is just a collection of objects. There are a number of standard types that can always be used, like **N**—the type of all non-negative natural numbers, $\textbf{N}_1$—the type of all positive whole numbers, **Z**—the type of all integers (negative numbers, zero and positive numbers) and **R**—the type of all real numbers. It is also possible to introduce your own types. In this chapter I use—for illustrative purposes—the type *Europe*, which is the collection of all European states.

Signatures

To indicate an object's type, say that x is a natural number, we write $x : \textbf{N}$. This can be read as either 'x is a natural number' or 'The type of x is **N**'. To say that France is a European state we write *france* : *Europe*. Such type assigning phrases are known as *declarations*. Another example of a declaration is $y : \textbf{Z}$. A collection of declarations is known as a *signature*. An example is:

$$x : \textbf{N}; \textit{france} : \textit{Europe}; y : \textbf{Z} \,.$$

When declaring two or more variables of the same type, rather than writing:

$$x : X; y : X; z : X,$$

we can simply write:

$$x, y, z : X.$$

---

[12]For example, Gries (1981), Backhouse (1986), Baber (1987), Gumb (1989) and Dromey (1989). Hoare logics were first introduced in Hoare (1969).

Quantifiers

Restricted Quantifiers Using the truth-functional operators defined earlier in this chapter we can write things like:

$$1 < 11 \wedge 2 < 11 \wedge 4 < 11 \wedge 7 < 11 \wedge 8 < 11. \tag{2.9}$$

But this is very cumbersome. The predicate $\_ < 11$ appears five times. (Note the use of the underscore to indicate the "gap" in the predicate.) This violates our desire for abstraction. We should avoid requiring something to be stated more than once. We should factor out the recurring pattern. Luckily in **Z** there is a more concise way of expressing (2.9). We can use the *restricted universal quantifier* as follows:

$$\forall x : \mathbf{N} \mid x \in \{1, 2, 4, 7, 8\} \bullet x < 11.$$

This can be read as 'Every natural number which is in the set $\{1, 2, 4, 7, 8\}$ is (such that it is) less than 11'. The letter x here is a variable. Because **Z** is a typed language, whenever we introduce a variable we have to give its type. So, following the symbol $\forall$—known as the *universal quantifier*—there occurs a declaration. The occurrence of x in the declaration is called its *binding* occurrence. The remaining occurrences of x in this formula are *bound* occurrences. They are *bound by* the binding occurrence. If a variable other than x occurred in the predicates of this formula, then they would be said to be *free*.[13]

The sentence 'Every European state which has a common border with Albania also has a common border with Bulgaria' can be translated into the following **Z** predicate:

$$\forall x : \textit{Europe} \mid x \textit{ borders albania} \bullet x \textit{ borders bulgaria},$$

where $\_ \textit{ borders } \_$ means $\_$ has a common border with $\_$. My knowledge of geography is so poor that I do not know if this is true or false.

The restricted universal quantifier applies to *all* things of some type which have a particular property. There is another quantifier which only applies to *some* things. This is the *restricted existential quantifier*, which applies to *some* things which have a particular property. If we wanted to say in **Z** that some natural number less than or equal to 5 is equal to its square, then—without the restricted existential quantifier—we would have to write:

$$0 = 0 * 0 \vee 1 = 1 * 1 \vee 2 = 2 * 2 \vee 3 = 3 * 3 \vee 4 = 4 * 4 \vee 5 = 5 * 5.$$

This is cumbersome and the same pattern of expression is used six times. A better way of writing it is:

$$\exists x : \mathbf{N} \mid x \leq 5 \bullet x = x * x,$$

and this is read as 'There exists some natural number (which is) less than or equal to 5 such that it is equal to its own square'.

---

[13]This terminology is defined more rigorously in section 10.2.1 below.

The sentence 'Some European state which has a common border with Albania is a member of the EC' can be translated into **Z** as:

$$\exists x: Europe \mid x \; borders \; albania \bullet ec \; x,$$

where $ec \_$ means $\_$ is a member of the European Community.

Unrestricted Quantifiers In **Z** we often want to say things about *all* numbers without restriction or about *all* things belonging to some other type. For this purpose we use unrestricted quantifiers. For example, the sentence 'Every natural number is equal to itself' gets translated into:

$$\forall x: \mathbf{N} \bullet x = x.$$

This predicate makes use of the *unrestricted universal quantifier* and to translate the sentence 'Some natural number is equal to its own square' into **Z** you need to make use of the *unrestricted existential quantifier* as follows:

$$\exists x: \mathbf{N} \bullet x = x * x.$$

The **Z** translation of 'Every European state is a member of the Warsaw Pact' is:

$$\forall x: Europe \bullet pact \; x,$$

where $pact \_$ means $\_$ is a member of the Warsaw Pact. The translation of 'Some European state has a common border with Iceland' into **Z** is:

$$\exists x: Europe \bullet x \; borders \; iceland.$$

Connection between Restricted and Unrestricted Quantifiers

Let J be a signature and P and Q predicates. Then we have the following two equivalences:

$$(\forall J \mid P \bullet Q) \Longleftrightarrow (\forall J \bullet P \Rightarrow Q),$$
$$(\exists J \mid P \bullet Q) \Longleftrightarrow (\exists J \bullet P \wedge Q).$$

Unique Quantifiers

The symbol $\exists_1$ represents the *unique existential quantifier* and the notation:

$$\exists_1 x: X \mid P \bullet Q,$$

is used to mean that there exists exactly one x of type X which has the property P such that Q is also true. Let J be a signature and P and Q predicates. Then we have the following equivalence:

$$(\exists_1 J \mid P \bullet Q) \Longleftrightarrow (\exists_1 J \bullet P \wedge Q).$$

The unique quantifier satisfies the following equivalence:

$$(\exists_1 x: X \bullet P'x) \Longleftrightarrow (\exists x: X \bullet (Px \wedge (\forall y: X \bullet Py \Rightarrow x = y))).$$

The notation Px means that the variable x can occur free in the predicate P. If Px and Py both occur in the same context, then Py is the same as Px, except that y has been substituted for all free occurrences of x in Px.

2.4 Exercises

2.1) Draw up truth-tables for the following formulas in order to ascertain which are and which are not tautologies.

a) $P \wedge P$.

b) $P \wedge \neg Q$.

c) $(P \Rightarrow Q) \Rightarrow P$.

d) $P \Rightarrow (Q \Rightarrow P)$.

e) $P \Rightarrow (Q \Rightarrow (P \Rightarrow P))$.

f) $(P \wedge Q) \Rightarrow P$.

g) $P \Rightarrow (P \wedge Q)$.

h) $((P \wedge Q) \Rightarrow R) \Longleftrightarrow ((P \Rightarrow R) \vee (Q \Rightarrow R))$.

2.2) Construct truth-tables in order to ascertain whether or not the following semantic sequents are valid.

a) $\neg P \Rightarrow P \models P$.

b) $P \models Q \Rightarrow (P \wedge Q)$.

c) $P \Rightarrow Q, P \Rightarrow \neg Q \models \neg P$.

d) $(P \wedge Q) \Longleftrightarrow P \models P \Rightarrow Q$.

e) $Q \Rightarrow R \models (P \vee Q) \Rightarrow (P \vee R)$.

f) $P_1 \Rightarrow P_2, P_3 \Rightarrow P_4 \models (P_1 \vee P_3) \Rightarrow (P_2 \vee P_4)$.

2.3) Define the truth-functional connectives $\vee$, $\Rightarrow$ and $\Longleftrightarrow$ in terms of $\neg$ and $\wedge$.

2.4) The connective $\downarrow$ has the following truth-table:

P	Q	$P \downarrow Q$
t	t	f
t	f	f
f	t	f
f	f	t

Define the connectives $\neg$, $\vee$, $\wedge$, $\Rightarrow$ and $\Longleftrightarrow$ in terms of $\downarrow$.

2.5) Express the following propositions using restricted quantifiers:

a) $2 + 3 = 4 \wedge 2 + 3 = 5 \wedge 2 + 3 = 7 \wedge 2 + 3 = 19$.

b) $2 + 3 = 4 \vee 2 + 3 = 5 \vee 2 + 3 = 7 \vee 2 + 3 = 19$.

24

2.6) Translate the following English sentences into **Z**:

a) Every natural number strictly less than 3 is not equal to 7.

b) Some natural number strictly less than 3 is not equal to 7.

c) Every even natural number less than 9 is not odd.

d) Some European state which is a member of the EC has a common border with Belgium.

e) Every European state which is a member of the EC is not a member of the Warsaw Pact.

Chapter 3

Set Theory

3.1 Ways of Making Sets

A set or class is a collection of objects which satisfy some property. There are two main ways of making sets in **Z** and they are by *enumeration* and by *comprehension*.

3.1.1 Enumeration

Some sets can be specified by writing down all their elements. This is specifying a set *extensionally* or by *enumeration*. This method of making sets is only feasible for small finite sets. The elements of the set are simply listed or enumerated. Thus, the set of the first seven prime numbers can be enumerated as follows:

$$\{2, 3, 5, 7, 11, 13, 17\}.$$

Another notation is also sometimes used for the introduction of sets by enumeration, especially sets of messages in a specification, and that is the following:

$$Report ::= \text{'Okay'}$$
$$| \text{ 'At top of document'}$$
$$| \text{ 'At bottom of document'}$$

This is just a restricted use of **Z**'s notation for introducing *free* types. The definition of *Report* just given is equivalent in every way to the following:[1]

$$Report == \{\text{'Okay', 'At top of document', 'At bottom of document'}\}.$$

The notation $\_ \ldots \_$ is used for number ranges. Thus,

$$89 \ldots 94 = \{89, 90, 91, 92, 93, 94\}.$$

---

[1] This equivalence follows from the way in which free types are treated in **Z**. It is fully justified in section 9.3 below. The whole of chapter 9 is devoted to the topic of free types and their use in specifications.

3.1.2 Set Comprehension

Set comprehension allows us to make a set from other sets. For example, the set comprehension term:

$$\{n:\mathbf{N} \mid n \neq 0 \wedge n \bmod 2 = 0 \bullet n\},$$

defines the set of all positive even numbers.[2] ($\mathbf{N}$ is the set of all the non-negative whole numbers and mod is $\mathbf{Z}$'s remainder operator.) Note that this set comprehension has three main parts to it and these are separated by a vertical line $\mid$ and a bullet $\bullet$. The part to the left of the vertical line is a signature, the part between the vertical line and the bullet is a predicate and the part to the right of the bullet is a term:

$$\{ \; \overbrace{n:\mathbf{N}}^{\text{signature}} \; \mid \overbrace{n \neq 0 \wedge n \bmod 2 = 0}^{\text{predicate}} \bullet \; \overbrace{n}^{\text{term}} \; \}.$$

If the term in a set comprehension is identical to the only variable declared in the signature, then it can be omitted. In other words, if the term of a set comprehension is absent, the default value is the symbol that occurs in the signature (on the left hand side of the colon), assuming that the signature contains only a single declaration. Thus, we could define the set of even numbers like this:

$$evens == \{n:\mathbf{N} \mid n \neq 0 \wedge n \bmod 2 = 0\}.$$

In a set comprehension there is no need for the term to be a simple variable; it can be a complex expression. Thus, another way in which to specify the set of positive even numbers is:

$$\{n:\mathbf{N} \mid n \neq 0 \bullet 2 * n\}.$$

For another example, consider the following definition of the set of all the squares of the non-negative numbers:

$$squares == \{n:\mathbf{N} \mid true \bullet n * n\}.$$

Note that the predicate part of this set comprehension is the always true proposition. When this happens it is possible to abbreviate the set comprehension by leaving *true* out, like this:

$$squares == \{n:\mathbf{N} \bullet n * n\}.$$

It is possible for both these abbreviatory conventions to be used in a single set comprehension; thus the set comprehension $\{n:\mathbf{N}\}$ is short for $\{n:\mathbf{N} \mid true \bullet n\}$, and that is just a roundabout way of writing the set of natural numbers $\mathbf{N}$.

Because $\mathbf{Z}$ is a typed language, whenever you write down a set comprehension that does not violate the type discipline, you can be certain that the set corresponding to that set comprehension exists.

---

[2] Note that 0 is not thought of as an even number. This is just a convention. If you place your money on *evens* in roulette in a British casino and 0 comes up, then you lose half your bet. (The casino still has a 1.35% edge.) Clearly, casino owners are in two minds about whether 0 is even or not!

3.2 Predicates on Sets

3.2.1 Membership

To show that an object x is a member of a set X we write $x \in X$, thus:

$$3 \in \{1,3,5,7,9\},$$
$$4 \in \textit{evens},$$
$$4 \in \{n \colon \mathbf{N} \mid n < 10 \bullet n\}.$$

If a set has been introduced by enumeration, then we can establish the truth of a set membership predicate by simply going through all the enumerated objects and checking whether or not they are identical to the term of the membership predicate. For example,

$$3 \in \{1,3,5,7,9\} \Longleftrightarrow (3 = 1 \vee 3 = 3 \vee 3 = 5 \vee 3 = 7 \vee 3 = 9).$$

When a set has been introduced by comprehension, we need the following law in order to check the truth of statements involving that set comprehension:

$$x \in \{J \mid P \bullet t\} \Longleftrightarrow \exists J \mid P \bullet t = x,$$

where J is a signature, P a predicate, t a term and x a variable that is not declared in J. For example,

$$i \in \{n \colon \mathbf{N} \mid n \neq 0 \bullet 2 * n\} \Longleftrightarrow \exists n \colon \mathbf{N} \mid n \neq 0 \bullet 2 * n = i.$$

3.2.2 Equality

In a typed set theory two sets of the same type—in fact, two objects in general—are defined to be identical iff they are members of exactly the same sets:[3]

$$x = y == (\forall U \colon \mathbf{P}\, X \bullet x \in U \Longleftrightarrow y \in U),$$

where x and y are both of type X.

The way we establish whether or not two sets are the same, however, is by checking whether or not they have the same members. This procedure is justified by means of the axiom of extensionality:

$$\forall U, V \colon \mathbf{P}\, X \bullet (\forall x \colon X \bullet x \in U \Longleftrightarrow x \in V) \Rightarrow U = V.$$

Do not confuse the definition of equality in a typed set theory with the axiom of extensionality.

---

[3]This may not seem correct to those of you familiar with Zermelo–Fraenkel set theory. See Quine (1969), pp. 241–331, and Hatcher (1982), pp. 103–134, for the truth of my assertions about typed set theory.

3.2.3 Subset

Let U and V be sets of the same type $\mathbf{P}\,X$. Then U is a *subset* of V iff every member of U is also a member of V. This is written $U \subseteq V$ and can be represented in symbols as:

$$U \subseteq V \Longleftrightarrow (\forall x\colon X \bullet x \in U \Rightarrow x \in V).$$

For example,

$$\{1,2,3\} \subseteq \{1,2,3\},$$
$$\{1,2,3\} \subseteq \mathbf{N},$$
$$\{1,2,3\} \subseteq \{n\colon \mathbf{N} \mid n < 10\}.$$

Let U and V be sets of the same type $\mathbf{P}\,X$. Then U is a *proper subset* of V iff U is not the same as V and U is a subset of V. This is written as $U \subset V$ and is represented symbolically as:

$$U \subset V \Longleftrightarrow (U \neq V \wedge U \subseteq V).$$

3.3 Some Special Sets

3.3.1 Empty Sets

Intuitively you might think that there is a unique empty set, since any set which contains no members is the same as any other set which contains no members. Unfortunately, this is false in a typed set theory like $\mathbf{Z}$. Here there are an infinite number of empty sets, one for each type of set. The definition of the empty set in $\mathbf{Z}$ is, therefore, generic:

$$\{\ \}[X] == \{x\colon X \mid false\}.$$

The empty set $\{\ \}[X]$ can also be written $\emptyset[X]$. Usually the type of the empty set can be omitted, since the context makes it clear which one is being used.

3.3.2 Power Sets

If X is a set, then so is $\mathbf{P}\,X$, which is known as the *power set* of X. The fundamental property of power sets is:

$$U \in \mathbf{P}\,X \Longleftrightarrow U \subseteq X.$$

That is to say, something is a member of $\mathbf{P}\,X$ iff it is a subset of X. In other words, $\mathbf{P}\,X$ is the collection of all the subsets of X. For example,

$$\mathbf{P}(\{1,2\}) = \{\{\ \}, \{1\}, \{2\}, \{1,2\}\}.$$

The set of non-empty subsets of an arbitrary set X is represented as $\mathbf{P}_1\,X$ and is defined as:

$$\mathbf{P}_1\,X == \{U\colon \mathbf{P}\,X \mid U \neq \{\ \}[X]\}.$$

For example,

$$\mathbf{P}_1(\{1,2\}) = \{\{1\}, \{2\}, \{1,2\}\}.$$

3.4 Operations on Sets

3.4.1 Union

The union of two sets U and V of the same type is just the set obtained by pooling all their members. This is written as $U \cup V$. For example, if *available* represents the set of all the copies of books in a library that are available for borrowing and *checkedout* represents the set of all copies of books currently borrowed, then

$$available \cup checkedout,$$

represents the set of all copies of books owned by the library.

The fundamental property of set union is:

$$x \in U \cup V \Longleftrightarrow (x \in U \lor x \in V).$$

3.4.2 Intersection

If U and V are sets of the same type, then the intersection of U and V is the set which consists of everything that is both in U and in V. This is represented as $U \cap V$. For example, to show that no copy of a book in a library is both available for check out and checked out at the same time, we write:

$$available \cap checkedout = \{ \ \},$$

where $\{ \ \}$ represents the empty set which consists of no copies of books.

The fundamental property of set intersection is:

$$x \in U \cap V \Longleftrightarrow (x \in U \land x \in V).$$

3.4.3 Difference

The notation $U \setminus V$, denotes the set consisting of all those elements of U which are not in V. In other words, you take out of U everything that is in V. For example,

$$odds = \mathbf{N}_1 \setminus evens.$$

The fundamental property of set difference is:

$$x \in U \setminus V \Longleftrightarrow (x \in U \land x \notin V).$$

3.4.4 Symmetric Difference

The notation $U \bigtriangleup V$ represents the symmetric difference of the sets U and V, which must be of the same type.

$$U \bigtriangleup V == (U \setminus V) \cup (V \setminus U).$$

The fundamental property of symmetric difference is:

$$x \in U \triangle V \iff (x \in U \cup V \wedge x \notin U \cap V).$$

It should be noted that the symmetric difference operator is not part of the standard **Z** language as defined in Spivey (1989b), but it can be introduced by means of the abbreviation definition just given when it is required. The symbol $\triangle$ is the only symbol discussed in this chapter which is not part of standard **Z**.

3.5   Generalized Union and Intersection

The generalized union of a set U of sets of type $\mathbf{P}\, X$ is the set which contains all those members of X which are in at least one of the sets in U. Here, U is a set whose elements are themselves sets. The generalized union of U, represented as $\bigcup U$, is the set which consists of all those things which are members of at least one of the sets that is an element of U. For example,

$$\bigcup\{\{0,1,2\}, \{5,7,9\}, \{1,2,3,5,7,9\}, \{767,789\}\} =$$
$$\{0,1,2,3,5,7,9,767,789\}.$$

The generalized intersection of a set U of sets of $\mathbf{P}\, X$ is the set which contains all those members of X which are in all of the sets in U. For example,

$$\bigcap\{\{0,1,2\}, \{5,7,9\}, \{1,2,3,5,7,9\}, \{767,789\}\} = \{\ \},$$
$$\bigcap\{\{0,1,2\}, \{1,2,9\}, \{1,2,3,5,7,9\}, \{1,2,7\}\} = \{1,2\}.$$

3.6   Exercises

3.1) Let the sets *zer*, *low*, *eve*, *bla*, *red*, *odd* and *hig*—all of type $\mathbf{P}\,\mathbf{N}$—be defined like this:

$$zer == \{0\},$$
$$low == 1 \mathbin{..} 18,$$
$$eve == \{n \colon \mathbf{N} \mid 1 \leq n \wedge n \leq 18 \bullet 2 * n\},$$
$$bla == \{2,4,6,8,10,11,13,15,17,20,22,24,26,28,29,31,33,35\},$$
$$red == (1 \mathbin{..} 36) \setminus bla,$$
$$odd == \{n \colon \mathbf{N} \mid 0 \leq n \wedge n \leq 17 \bullet 2 * n + 1\},$$
$$hig == 19 \mathbin{..} 36.$$

Roulette players will have no difficulty recognising these sets! Let U be a set of roulette numbers. Then the probability of a number from U coming up is $\#U/37$, where $\#U$ is the size or cardinality of the set U.

a) List the elements of *red* ∩ *odd*.

b) List the elements of (*low* ∪ *eve*) ∩ *bla*.

c) List the elements of (1 .. 36) \ (*red* ∪ *eve*).

d) List the elements of *bla* △ *odd*.

e) List the elements of *low* ∩ *eve* ∩ *bla*.

f) What is the probability of a member of *low* winning?

g) What is the probability of a member of *low* ∪ *eve* winning?

h) What is the probability of a member of *bla* ∪ *red* winning?

i) What is the probability of a member of *low* ∩ *eve* ∩ *bla* winning?

h) What is the probability of a member of *bla* △ *odd* winning?

3.2) a) Let $U = \{2,3,5,7,11,13,17\}$ and $V = \{0,1,2,3,4,5\}$. Write down $U \cup V$, $U \cap V$ and $U \setminus V$.

b) Write down the sets $10..15 \cup 12..18$, $10..15 \cap 12..18$ and $10..15 \setminus 12..18$.

c) Let $U = \{x : \mathbf{N} \mid x < 27\}$. Write down the sets $U \cap \{x : \mathbf{N} \mid x \bmod 3 = 1\}$ and $U \cap \{x : \mathbf{N} \mid x \operatorname{div} 7 = 2\}$.

d) The countries *england*, *france* and *spain* are all European states, that is to say, *england*, *france*, *spain*: *Europe*. Write down all the members of the following power set $\mathbf{P}\{england, france, spain\}$.

3.3) a) Write down a set comprehension which defines all the leap years between 1900 and 2100, inclusive.

b) Write down two set comprehensions which define, respectively, the set of all European states which are members of the European Community and those which are members of the Warsaw Pact.

Chapter 4

Relations and Schemas

4.1   Cartesian Products and Relations

We are all familiar with relations in arithmetic like $n \geq m$ or n is divisible by m. Relations are used extensively in $\mathbf{Z}$ and—as is customary in mathematics—a relation is just thought of as a set of ordered pairs. If X and Y are sets, then so is $X \times Y$, their *Cartesian product* or *cross product*. An example of a cross product is:

$$\{1,3\} \times \{2,4\} = \{(1,2),(1,4),(3,2),(3,4)\}.$$

The usual way to express the fact that the ordered pair made up out of 3 and 2 is a member of this Cartesian product is like this:

$$(3,2) \in \{1,3\} \times \{2,4\},$$

but often it is clearer to write $3 \mapsto 2$ for $(3,2)$, so the above fact would be written as:

$$3 \mapsto 2 \in \{1,3\} \times \{2,4\}.$$

What is important about an ordered pair is that it is a structured object made up out of two components one of which comes first and the other second.

The Cartesian product $X \times Y$ of two sets X and Y is the set of *all* the ordered pairs whose first elements are drawn from X and whose second elements are drawn from Y. A relation F between X and Y is a subset of the Cartesian product $X \times Y$, that is to say, $F \subseteq X \times Y$. The type of *all* relations between elements drawn from X and Y is written as $X \leftrightarrow Y$. This is, in fact, just another way of writing $\mathbf{P}(X \times Y)$. The standard way of defining the type of all relations between X and Y is:

$$X \leftrightarrow Y == \mathbf{P}(X \times Y).$$

4.2   An Internal Telephone Number Database

In order to make the material about relations easier to absorb, I am going to develop the ideas and notations associated with relations in conjunction with the specification of a small internal telephone number database.[1] In order to make the example more realistic, I shall assume that the database is going to be used in a university environment. Clearly, we are going to need to be able to refer to all the people who might end up in the database and also to all the possible phone numbers that the telephone exchange can handle. So, let *Person* be the type of all the people that we might be interested in and let *Phone* be the set of all possible internal telephone numbers. Since we are engaged in writing a *specification* there is no need at this stage to consider how we are going to eventually represent people and numbers in a program. To make decisions about such issues at this time is premature.

The relation that exists between people and their internal telephone numbers I am going to denote by means of the identifier *telephones*, thus:

$$telephones: Person \leftrightarrow Phone.$$

This means—recall the definition of $\leftrightarrow$ given above—that:

$$telephones \subseteq Person \times Phone.$$

So, for example, in the case of the University of Birmingham, we have:

$$(diller, 4794) \in telephones.$$

This can be written equivalently as:

$$diller \mapsto 4794 \in telephones.$$

It is possible for one person to have more than one internal telephone. This happens, for example, if he or she is a very important person:

$$jarratt \mapsto 4936 \in telephones,$$
$$jarratt \mapsto 5317 \in telephones.$$

Similarly, if you are not very important, then you might have to share your internal telephone:

$$smith \mapsto 3174 \in telephones,$$
$$jones \mapsto 3174 \in telephones.$$

For the time being, let that be the entire state of our database:

$$
\begin{aligned}
telephones = \{ &jarratt \mapsto 4936, \\
&jarratt \mapsto 5317, \\
&diller \mapsto 4794, \\
&smith \mapsto 3174, \\
&jones \mapsto 3174 \}.
\end{aligned}
$$

This can be represented by means of a diagram as in Fig. 4.1. The type of the relation *telephones* is *Person* $\leftrightarrow$ *Phone*. The type *Person*, however, contains *every* possible person, the type *Phone* includes *every* conceivable internal telephone number and the type *Person* $\leftrightarrow$ *Phone* contains *all* the relations between *Person* and *Phone*. The small relation *telephones* is just one of these.

---

[1] This specification derives ultimately from one used by Spivey in various talks and which also appears in Spivey (1988), pp. 2–7. I have altered it, however, to better serve my purposes.

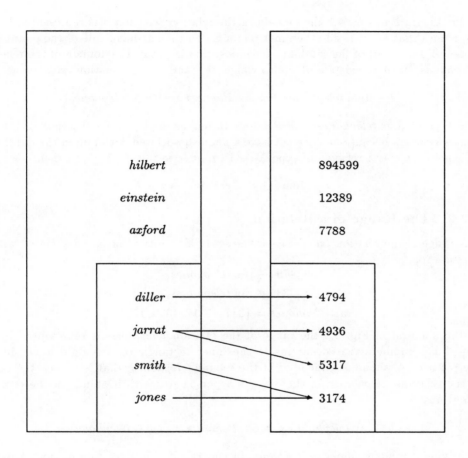

Figure 4.1: Graphical representation of *telephones*.

4.2.1   The Domain of a Relation

One thing that we might be interested in knowing is the set of people in our database. In our example, that would be the set consisting of *diller*, *jarratt*, *smith* and *jones*. The set consisting of just these four people is the *domain* of the relation *telephones* and it is written like this:

$$\text{dom } telephones = \{diller, jarratt, smith, jones\}.$$

In the diagram in Fig. 4.1 the domain of the relation *telephones* is represented by all the names that occur inside the inner rectangle on the left-hand side of the picture. A person is a member of the set dom *telephones*, that is to say, the domain of the relation *telephones*, iff there exists a phone to which he stands in the relation *telephones*:

$$x \in \text{dom } telephones \iff \exists y \colon Phone \bullet x \mapsto y \in telephones.$$

The type of dom *telephones* is **P** *Person*. In our example, *einstein* is not in the set dom *telephones* because he does not have a phone associated with him in the database. In general, if F is a relation of type $X \leftrightarrow Y$, that is to say, $F \colon X \leftrightarrow Y$, then:

$$x \in \text{dom } F \iff \exists y \colon Y \bullet x \mapsto y \in F.$$

4.2.2   The Range of a Relation

The range of the relation *telephones* is the set of all phones that are associated with a person. So,

$$4794 \in \text{ran } telephones,$$
$$833335 \notin \text{ran } telephones,$$
$$\text{ran } telephones = \{3174, 5317, 4936, 4794\}.$$

In the diagram in Fig. 4.1 the range of the relation *telephones* is represented by all the phone numbers that occur inside the inner rectangle on the right-hand side of the picture. A phone is a member of the set ran *telephones*, that is to say, the range of the relation *telephones*, iff there exists a person to which it stands in the relation *telephones*:

$$y \in \text{ran } telephones \iff \exists x \colon Person \bullet x \mapsto y \in telephones.$$

The type of ran *telephones* is **P** *Phone*. In general, if F is a relation of type $X \leftrightarrow Y$, that is to say, $F \colon X \leftrightarrow Y$, then:

$$y \in \text{ran } F \iff \exists x \colon X \bullet x \mapsto y \in F.$$

4.2.3   The Union of Two Relations

A relation is just a particular kind of set. Every relation is a set, but not every set is a relation. So, we can use the usual set-theoretic operations on relations. Things like set union, for example. Say we want to add an association between a *Person* and a *Phone*

38

to our database. The existing state of the database I have been calling *telephones* and the new state I will call *telephones'*. The prime indicates that it is the *after* state; the unprimed version is the *before* state. Suppose what we want to add is the fact that Axford can now be reached at extension 7788; that is to say, we want to add the ordered pair *axford* ↦ 7788 to our database. I am going to call such associations between people and phones *entries*. So, we have got:

$$telephones' = telephones \cup \{axford \mapsto 7788\}.$$

The new database now consists of the following entries:

$$telephones' = \{jarratt \mapsto 4936,$$
$$jarratt \mapsto 5317,$$
$$diller \mapsto 4794,$$
$$smith \mapsto 3174,$$
$$jones \mapsto 3174,$$
$$axford \mapsto 7788\}.$$

This relation is pictured in the diagram Fig. 4.2.

4.3   Schemas

Z contains a two-dimensional graphical notation—called a *schema*—for grouping together all the relevant information that belongs to a state description. The two main uses of schemas are:

1. Specifying states.

2. Specifying state transitions.

A state is just a collection of sets and objects and some predicates defined on those things. For the telephone database I will specify the state by means of the following schema:

```
┌─ PhoneDB ──────────────────────────────────
│  members: P Person
│  telephones: Person ↔ Phone
├────────────────────────────────────────────
│  dom telephones ⊆ members
└────────────────────────────────────────────
```

In order to make the example a little bit more interesting I have included the set *members* in the state. This set consists of all the members of the university whose telephone directory we are modelling.

   The name of this schema is *PhoneDB*. Above the central horizontal line in the schema box are written various declarations and below this line a predicate is placed. This predicate—in our case dom *telephones* ⊆ *members*—forms the *state invariant* of the specification. Only members of the university can have telephones.

39

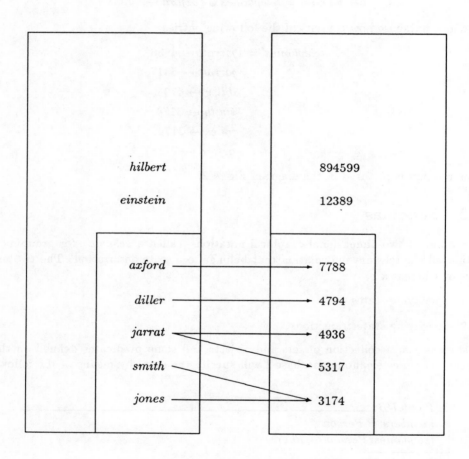

Figure 4.2: Graphical representation of *telephones'*.

4.3.1 Schema Decoration

In order to specify a state transformation we need to represent the before and after states. In **Z** the *after* state is represented by *decorating* all the variables with a prime. *PhoneDB* is the name of a schema which represents a before state. Decorating a schema name with a prime, for example, *PhoneDB'*, represents the *after* state. *PhoneDB'* is the same as *PhoneDB*, except that every *variable* has been decorated with a prime. This is an example of *schema decoration*. The schema *PhoneDB'* is, therefore:

PhoneDB'

$members'$: **P** *Person*
$telephones'$: *Person* $\leftrightarrow$ *Phone*

---
dom $telephones' \subseteq members'$

4.4 Adding an Entry to our Database

The operation of adding an entry to our database is represented by means of the following schema:

AddEntry

$members, members'$: **P** *Person*
$telephones, telephones'$: *Person* $\leftrightarrow$ *Phone*
$name?$: *Person*
$newnumber?$: *Phone*

---
dom $telephones \subseteq members$
dom $telephones' \subseteq members'$
$name? \in members$
$name? \mapsto newnumber? \notin telephones$
$telephones' = telephones \cup \{name? \mapsto newnumber?\}$
$members' = members$

Notice that question marks occur in some of the identifiers of this schema, namely *name?* and *newnumber?* This is how inputs are indicated in **Z**. The predicates:

$$name? \in members,$$

$$name? \mapsto newnumber? \notin telephones,$$

are *preconditions* of the operation *AddEntry*. You cannot add an entry involving somebody who is not a member of the university into the database and you cannot add an entry that is already in the database.

The state invariant involving only before variables, namely the predicate:

$$\text{dom } telephones \subseteq members,$$

41

is also a kind of precondition for the operation specified by means of the schema *AddEntry*. One of the differences between this state invariant and the other preconditions is that the invariant is a precondition of *every* operation defined on the telephone database. It is best to think of the (before) state invariant as a precondition to the entire specification, rather than as being specific to any one operation. (In section 12.6 I explain how to calculate the precondition schema of a schema describing a state transformation and I further discuss there the role of the before state invariant and its relation to the other preconditions of a schema.)

4.5 Schema Operations

I am going to take a short break from developing the telephone number database in order to deal with some schema operations and conventions which will greatly reduce the length of specifications. These will enable us to specify complex operations concisely and perspicuously. The schema operations and conventions that I am going to look at are:

1. Schema inclusion.

2. Linking schemas with propositional connectives.

3. The Δ and Ξ conventions.

4.5.1 Schema Inclusion

A schema name S may be included in the declaration part of another schema T. The effect of this is that the declarations of S are now considered part of T and the predicates of S and T are conjoined together, that is to say, linked with conjunction. The only restriction is that if a variable x is declared in both S and T, then it must have the same type in both of them. For example, consider the following two schemas:

$$
\begin{array}{|l}
\hline S \\
\hline x, y\colon \mathbf{N} \\
\hline x < y \\
\hline
\end{array}
\qquad
\begin{array}{|l}
\hline T \\
\hline S; z\colon \mathbf{R} \\
\hline \sqrt{x} = z \\
\hline
\end{array}
$$

Here, the schema S is included in the schema T. Expanding T we get:

$$
\begin{array}{|l}
\hline T \\
\hline x, y\colon \mathbf{N} \\
z\colon \mathbf{R} \\
\hline x < y \\
\sqrt{x} = z \\
\hline
\end{array}
$$

4.5.2 Linking Schemas with Propositional Connectives

Let S and T be two schemas. Then it is possible to write $S \wedge T$, $S \vee T$, $S \Rightarrow T$ and $S \Longleftrightarrow T$. These all have very similar meanings, so I will consider $S \heartsuit T$, where $\heartsuit$ can be any of $\wedge, \vee, \Rightarrow$ or $\Longleftrightarrow$. The schema $S \heartsuit T$ is formed by merging the declarations of S and T and by combining their predicates by means of the connective $\heartsuit$. The same condition about declarations must be respected as with schema inclusion, namely that if a variable x is declared in both S and T, then it must have the same type in both of them. Let S and T be the schemas used as examples above in discussing schema inclusion. Then the schema $Alpha \triangleq S \heartsuit T$ has the following expansion:[2]

$$\boxed{\begin{array}{l} \underline{\;Alpha\;} \\ x, y \colon \mathbf{N} \\ z \colon \mathbf{R} \\ \hline (x < y) \heartsuit (\sqrt{x} = z) \end{array}}$$

For example, if $\heartsuit$ is $\vee$, then the schema $Beta \triangleq S \vee T$ has the following expansion:

$$\boxed{\begin{array}{l} \underline{\;Beta\;} \\ x, y \colon \mathbf{N} \\ z \colon \mathbf{R} \\ \hline (x < y) \vee (\sqrt{x} = z) \end{array}}$$

Schema Normalization

In explaining schema inclusion and the linking of schemas with propositional connectives above, I said that if a variable x is declared in both of the schemas involved, then it must be of the same type in both of them. This qualification is not as straightforward as it may at first appear. This is because it is possible in $\mathbf{Z}$ to declare a variable $x \colon X$, where X is a subset of some other type, say Y. For example, we can declare $y \colon 1 \mathinner{\ldotp\ldotp} 57$ although $1 \mathinner{\ldotp\ldotp} 57 \subseteq \mathbf{Z}$. This happens, for example, in the following two schemas:

$$\boxed{\begin{array}{l} \underline{\;Gamma\;} \\ y \colon 1 \mathinner{\ldotp\ldotp} 57 \\ U \colon \mathbf{P}\,\mathbf{Z} \\ \hline y \in U \end{array}} \qquad \boxed{\begin{array}{l} \underline{\;Delta\;} \\ y \colon \mathbf{Z} \\ V \colon \mathbf{P}\,\mathbf{Z} \\ \hline y \notin V \end{array}}$$

Here, y does have the same type in both $Gamma$ and $Delta$, because the type of a variable x in a declaration $x \colon X$ is only X if X is a *maximal* type. Every specification will make use of several types and the *maximal* types of a given specification are all the types that we need which are pairwise disjoint. Thus, $1 \mathinner{\ldotp\ldotp} 57$ is not a maximal type and the type of the variable y in the declaration $y \colon 1 \mathinner{\ldotp\ldotp} 57$ is $\mathbf{Z}$.

---

[2]The symbol $\triangleq$ is used to define schemas. Here, for example, I am defining $Alpha$ to be equivalent to the schema obtained by linking S and T with the connective $\heartsuit$.

In order to combine *Gamma* and *Delta* with a propositional connective, say implication, we first have to *normalize Gamma*. That involves replacing the declaration $y: 1 \mathinner{\ldotp\ldotp} 57$ with $y: \mathbf{Z}$ and adding the predicate $y > 0 \wedge y < 58$ to the predicate part of the schema. Let *NormGamma* be the normalized version of *Gamma*. Expanding *NormGamma* gives us:

```
┌─ NormGamma ──────────────────────────────────────────
│ y: Z
│ U: P Z
├──────────────────
│ y > 0
│ y < 58
│ y ∈ U
└──────────────────────────────────────────────────────
```

Let *Epsilon* $\triangleq$ *Gamma* $\Rightarrow$ *Delta*. In order to form *Epsilon* we have to make use of the normalized version of *Gamma*. So, the expansion of *Epsilon* is:

```
┌─ Epsilon ────────────────────────────────────────────
│ y: Z
│ U, V: P Z
├──────────────────
│ (y > 0 ∧ y < 58 ∧ y ∈ U) ⇒ (y ∉ V)
└──────────────────────────────────────────────────────
```

In general, what normalizing a schema involves is replacing every set X, say, which occurs in a declaration $x: X$, with its corresponding maximal type and adding predicates to the predicate part of the schema involved to constrain the variable appropriately.

A related topic to schema normalization concerns quantified predicates and set comprehensions. In **Z** we can write $\exists x: U \bullet P$ even if U is not a maximal type. Thus, $\exists x: 1 \mathinner{\ldotp\ldotp} 57 \bullet x \in evens$, is a legitimate quantified predicate. It is, however, just an abbreviation for the following:

$$\exists x: \mathbf{Z} \bullet x \in 1 \mathinner{\ldotp\ldotp} 57 \wedge x \in evens,$$

which makes use of the maximal type **Z**. In general, $\exists x: U \bullet P$ is an abbreviation for $\exists x: X \bullet x \in U \wedge P$, where X is the maximal type such that $U \subseteq X$. Similarly, $\forall x: U \bullet P$ is short for $\forall x: X \bullet x \in U \Rightarrow P$ and the set comprehension $\{x: U \mid P \bullet t\}$ as an abbreviation for $\{x: X \mid x \in U \wedge P \bullet t\}$.

4.5.3   The Δ and Ξ Conventions

Usually, $\Delta State$ is the schema obtained by combining the before and after specifications of *State*. This can be defined using either schema inclusion as:

```
┌─ ΔState ─────────────────────────────────────────────
│ State
│ State'
└──────────────────────────────────────────────────────
```

or, alternatively, using schema conjunction, thus:

$$\Delta State \stackrel{\wedge}{=} State \wedge State'$$

In the case of the telephone number database $\Delta PhoneDB$ is:

```
┌─ ΔPhoneDB ──────────────────────────────────
│  members, members': P Person
│  telephones, telephones': Person ↔ Phone
├─────────────────────────────────────────────
│  dom telephones ⊆ members
│  dom telephones' ⊆ members'
└─────────────────────────────────────────────
```

This can be written more concisely as either:

$$\Delta PhoneDB \stackrel{\wedge}{=} PhoneDB \wedge PhoneDB'$$

or—using schema inclusion—in this way:

```
┌─ ΔPhoneDB ──────────────────────────────────
│  PhoneDB
│  PhoneDB'
└─────────────────────────────────────────────
```

This is the usual way of understanding $\Delta State$, but it is not mandatory. It is allowed to define $\Delta State$ to be whatever you want it to be, but if you do use it in a non-standard way make absolutely certain that any reader of your specification will be aware of what you are doing. Throughout this book I always use Δ schemas in the standard way explained here.

The schema $\Xi PhoneDB$ is used in the specification of operations that do not change the state of the database:

```
┌─ ΞPhoneDB ──────────────────────────────────
│  ΔPhoneDB
├─────────────────────────────────────────────
│  members = members'
│  telephones = telephones'
└─────────────────────────────────────────────
```

What I said above about the standard meaning of Δ schema also applies to Ξ schemas. They too can be redefined to suit your purposes.

4.6   A Concise Specification of Adding an Entry

Using the Δ convention it is now possible to concisely specify the operation of adding an entry to our database.

```
┌─ AddEntry ─────────────────────────────────────────────┐
│ ΔPhoneDB                                                │
│ name?: Person                                           │
│ newnumber?: Phone                                       │
├─────────────────────────────────────────────────────── │
│ name? ∈ members                                         │
│ name? ↦ newnumber? ∉ telephones                         │
│ telephones' = telephones ∪ {name? ↦ newnumber?}         │
│ members' = members                                      │
└─────────────────────────────────────────────────────────┘
```

4.6.1 Dealing with Errors

I will now look at what happens when the preconditions of the schema *AddEntry* are not fulfilled. That is to say, the cases when either of the following is true:

$$name? \mapsto newnumber? \in telephones, \qquad (4.1)$$

$$name? \notin members. \qquad (4.2)$$

When either of these two predicates is true, we want to output a suitable error message. Dealing with errors again reveals the peculiar status enjoyed by the before state invariant, since we do not have to consider what happens when dom *telephones* ⊈ *members*. This possibility can never arise.

When an error occurs we do not want the state of the database altered in any way, so the schema which deals with the situation in which (4.2) is true will include the schema Ξ*PhoneDB*. The schema in question is:

```
┌─ NotMember ────────────────────────────────────────────┐
│ ΞPhoneDB                                                │
│ name?: Person                                           │
│ rep!: Report                                            │
├─────────────────────────────────────────────────────── │
│ name? ∉ members                                         │
│ rep! = 'Not a member'                                   │
└─────────────────────────────────────────────────────────┘
```

The error situation in which (4.1) is true is dealt with by the following schema:

```
┌─ EntryAlreadyExists ───────────────────────────────────┐
│ ΞPhoneDB                                                │
│ name?: Person                                           │
│ newnumber?: Phone                                       │
│ rep!: Report                                            │
├─────────────────────────────────────────────────────── │
│ name? ↦ newnumber? ∈ telephones                         │
│ rep! = 'Entry already exists'                           │
└─────────────────────────────────────────────────────────┘
```

4.6.2 The Total Specification

The next schema I am going to introduce just outputs the message 'Okay' in order to inform the user that the transaction he requested to be carried out has in fact been successfully carried out.

```
┌─ Success ─────────────────────────────────
│ rep!: Report
├───────────────────────────────────────────
│ rep! = 'Okay'
└───────────────────────────────────────────
```

It is now possible to define the total specification of the operation of adding an entry to the database.

$$DoAddEntry \stackrel{\wedge}{=} AddEntry \wedge Success$$

$$\vee$$

$$NotMember$$

$$\vee$$

$$EntryAlreadyExists$$

In order to illustrate the utility of **Z** to concisely express quite complicated operations I will show what the schema *DoAddEntry* looks like when expanded.

```
┌─ DoAddEntry ─────────────────────────────────
│ members, members': P Person
│ telephones, telephones': Person ↔ Phone
│ name?: Person
│ newnumber?: Phone
│ rep!: Report
├──────────────────────────────────────────────
│ dom telephones ⊆ members
│ dom telephones' ⊆ members'
│ ((name? ∈ members ∧
│ name? ↦ newnumber? ∉ telephones ∧
│ telephones' = telephones ∪ {name? ↦ newnumber?} ∧
│ members' = members ∧
│ rep! = 'Okay')
│        ∨
│ (name? ∉ members ∧
│ members' = members ∧
│ telephones' = telephones ∧
│ rep! = 'Not a member')
│        ∨
│ (name? ↦ newnumber? ∈ telephones ∧
│ members' = members ∧
│ telephones' = telephones ∧
│ rep! = 'Entry already exists'))
└──────────────────────────────────────────────
```

I think that you will agree that the Δ and Ξ conventions and the linking of schemas using truth-functional connectives leads to concise and well-structured specifications.

4.7 Interrogating the Database

4.7.1 The Image of a Relation

The next operation that I want to specify concerning the telephone database is that of finding out all the telephone numbers where a particular individual can be reached. In order to do this I need to introduce the idea of a *relational image*. So, given our database and a set of elements of type *Person*, say $\{jarratt\}$, then we want this operation to return all the telephones associated with $\{jarratt\}$, that is to say, all the extensions at which he can be reached. This is known as the *relational image* of a set through a relation and it is written:

$$telephones(\!|\{jarratt\}|\!) = \{4936, 5317\}.$$

It can be defined like this:

$$F(\!|U|\!) == \{y\!:\!Y \mid (\exists x\!:\!X \bullet x \in U \wedge x \mapsto y \in F) \bullet y\},$$

where $F\!:\!X \leftrightarrow Y$ and $U\!:\!\mathbf{P}\,X$. Thus, $F(\!|U|\!)$ is the set of all those things of type Y which can be reached from U. Using the conventions that $\exists x\!:\!U \bullet P$ is short for $\exists x\!:\!X \bullet x \in U \wedge P$ if $U \subseteq X$, introduced on p. 44 above, and also that the term part of a set comprehension can be omitted if it is the same as the single variable declared in the signature part—mentioned on p. 28 above—the definition of the image of a relation can be shortened to:

$$F(\!|U|\!) == \{y\!:\!Y \mid (\exists x\!:\!U \bullet x \mapsto y \in F)\}.$$

I will now give some more examples of the use of the relational image of a set. The set of people known to our database is represented by dom *telephones*. Let us call this set *known*:

$$known == \text{dom } telephones.$$

We might want to partition the set *known* into *staff* and *proles*:[3]

$$staff \cup proles = known,$$
$$staff \cap proles = \{\ \}\,.$$

Thus, in the small database that I am using for illustrative purposes we might have:

$$staff = \{diller, jarratt\},$$
$$proles = \{smith, jones\}.$$

Given these definitions of *staff* and *proles* the set $telephones(\!|staff|\!)$ is the set of all staff telephone numbers, that is to say, the set of all extensions at which a staff member

---

[3]My students were not amused by this attempt at humour.

of the university can be reached and $telephones(\!|proles|\!)$ is the set of all prole telephone numbers, that is to say, the set of all extensions at which a non-staff member of the university can be reached. In our particular database we have:

$$telephones(\!|staff|\!) = \{4794, 4936, 5317\},$$
$$telephones(\!|proles|\!) = \{3174\}.$$

4.7.2 Interrogating the Database by Person

The operation *FindPhones* has as its input a person—represented by the identifier *name?*—and as its output it has a set of telephone numbers *numbers!* Note that outputs end conventionally with an exclamation mark. Interrogating the database does not alter it, so we have to include the predicates:

$$members' = members,$$
$$telephones' = telephones,$$

and this is done most conveniently by means of the Ξ notation.

```
┌─ FindPhones ──────────────────────────────
│ ΞPhoneDB
│ name?: Person
│ numbers!: P Phone
├──────────────────────────────
│ name? ∈ dom telephones
│ numbers! = telephones(|{name?}|)
└──────────────────────────────
```

Now I will deal with what happens when the predicate $name? \in \text{dom } telephones$ is false. In that case we want to output some sort of error message.

```
┌─ UnknownName ──────────────────────────────
│ ΞPhoneDB
│ name?: Person
│ rep!: Report
├──────────────────────────────
│ name? ∉ dom telephones
│ rep! = 'Unknown name'
└──────────────────────────────
```

Thus the complete specification of the operation to interrogate the database by person is given by means of the schema:

$$DoFindPhones \stackrel{\wedge}{=} FindPhones \wedge Success$$
$$\vee$$
$$UnknownName$$

It would be possible to give more detailed error messages by distinguishing between the case when we input a name of someone who is not a member of the university—that is to say, the case when the predicate *name?* ∈ *members* is true—and the case when the input name is of a member of the university, but one who does not have an extension. This latter possibility would hold if the predicate:

$$name? \in members \wedge name? \notin \text{dom } telephones$$

were true. This possibility, however, will not be pursued here.

4.7.3 Interrogating the Database by Number

I have just described an operation which outputs the set of telephone numbers at which a particular member of the university can be reached. Similarly, we can specify an operation which outputs all the names associated with a particular telephone number. In order to specify this operation I will have to make use of the inverse of the relation *telephones*.

4.7.4 Relational Inversion

Given any relation F you can form its inverse F^{-1}. If the type of F is $X \leftrightarrow Y$, then the type of F^{-1} is $Y \leftrightarrow X$. F^{-1} is F with each element flipped over, so:

$$y \mapsto x \in F^{-1} \Longleftrightarrow x \mapsto y \in F.$$

An example will make this idea clearer. With *telephones* as before *telephones*$^{-1}$ is the following:

$$
\begin{aligned}
telephones^{-1} = \{ &4936 \mapsto jarratt, \\
&5317 \mapsto jarratt, \\
&4794 \mapsto diller, \\
&3174 \mapsto smith, \\
&3174 \mapsto jones \}.
\end{aligned}
$$

Using the inverse of the relation *telephones* it is now possible to specify what happens when we successfully interrogate the database in order to find out all the people who can be reached at a particular extension.

FindNames _____

Ξ*PhoneDB*
names!: **P** *Person*
number?: *Phone*

---

number? ∈ ran *telephones*
names! = *telephones*$^{-1}$(|{*number?*}|)

In order to specify the total operation we have to state what happens when the precondition of the schema *FindNames* is false.

```
┌─ UnknownNumber ──────────────────────────────────────
│ ΞPhoneDB
│ number?: Phone
│ rep!: Report
├──────────────────────────────────────────────────────
│ number? ∉ ran telephones
│ rep! = 'Unknown number'
└──────────────────────────────────────────────────────
```

Now it is possible to specify the total operation of interrogating the database by number:

$$DoFindNames \triangleq FindNames \land Success$$

$$\lor$$

$$UnknownNumber$$

4.8   Removing an Entry from the Database

We need to be able to specify the operation of removing an entry from the database in order to capture what happens when somebody can no longer be reached at a particular extension. This operation is specified by the schema *RemoveEntry*:

```
┌─ RemoveEntry ────────────────────────────────────────
│ ΔPhoneDB
│ oldnumber?: Phone
│ name?: Person
├──────────────────────────────────────────────────────
│ name? ↦ oldnumber? ∈ telephones
│ telephones' = telephones \ {name? ↦ oldnumber?}
│ members' = members
└──────────────────────────────────────────────────────
```

RemoveEntry has only a single precondition, namely:

$$name? \mapsto oldnumber? \in telephones.$$

This states that you can only remove an entry from the database if that entry actually is present in the database. What happens in the case when this precondition is violated is captured by the following schema:

```
┌─ UnknownEntry ───────────────────────────────────────
│ ΞPhoneDB
│ oldnumber?: Phone
│ name?: Person
│ rep!: Report
├──────────────────────────────────────────────────────
│ name? ↦ oldnumber? ∉ telephones
│ rep! = 'Unknown entry'
└──────────────────────────────────────────────────────
```

51

The complete specification of the operation of removing an entry from the database is given by the schema *DoRemoveEntry*:

$$DoRemoveEntry \triangleq RemoveEntry \land Success$$

$$\lor$$

$$UnknownEntry$$

4.9 Adding and Removing Members

The final things that I want to specify concerning the internal telephone number database are the operations of someone leaving the university and someone joining. First, someone joining. This is specified by means of the schema *AddMember*:

```
┌─ AddMember ──────────────────────────────────────
│ ΔPhoneDB
│ name?: Person
├──────────────────────────────────────────────────
│ name? ∉ members
│ members' = members ∪ {name?}
│ telephones' = telephones
└──────────────────────────────────────────────────
```

The operation can only go wrong in one way, namely if *name?* ∈ *members*. What happens in this case is captured by means of the following schema:

```
┌─ AlreadyMember ──────────────────────────────────
│ ΞPhoneDB
│ name?: Person
│ rep!: Report
├──────────────────────────────────────────────────
│ name? ∈ members
│ rep! = 'Already a member'
└──────────────────────────────────────────────────
```

Thus, the complete specification of the operation of adding a member is:

$$DoAddMember \triangleq AddMember \land Success$$

$$\lor$$

$$AlreadyMember$$

4.9.1 Someone Leaving the University

In order to specify the operation of someone leaving the university we first need to introduce another operation on relations, namely domain corestriction. This is closely connected to domain restriction, so I will discuss both of these operations next.

52

Domain Restriction

Consider the relation *ages*: *Person* $\leftrightarrow$ **N** which associates people with their ages. An example of *ages* is:

$$ages = \{john \mapsto 23,$$
$$mary \mapsto 30,$$
$$tom \mapsto 27,$$
$$alan \mapsto 53,$$
$$alice \mapsto 21\}.$$

Say that we are only interested in the ages of males. We restrict the relation *ages* so that the first elements of all ordered pairs in the restricted relation have to be male. Let *male*: **P** *Person* and $\{john, tom, alan\} \subseteq male$. Then we have:

$$male \lhd ages = \{john \mapsto 23,$$
$$tom \mapsto 27,$$
$$alan \mapsto 53\}.$$

male $\lhd$ *ages* is a relation which is a subset of *ages*. The fundamental property of $\lhd$ is, where U: **P** X and F: $X \leftrightarrow Y$:

$$x \mapsto y \in U \lhd F \Longleftrightarrow (x \in U \land x \mapsto y \in F).$$

Domain Corestriction

Domain corestriction is also sometimes known as *domain subtraction* or *domain anti-restriction*. Say that we are interested in the ages of women. Let *female*: **P** *Person* and $\{mary, alice\} \subseteq female$. Then we have:

$$female \lhd ages = \{mary \mapsto 30,$$
$$alice \mapsto 21\}.$$

But we could also write:

$$male \ntriangleleft ages = \{mary \mapsto 30,$$
$$alice \mapsto 21\}.$$

Assuming that nobody is both male and female, that is to say, that the sets *male* and *female* partition the set *Person*:

$$male \cup female = Person,$$
$$male \cap female = \{ \ \}.$$

male $\ntriangleleft$ *ages* is a relation which is a subset of *ages*. The fundamental property of $\ntriangleleft$ is, where U: **P** X and F: $X \leftrightarrow Y$:

$$x \mapsto y \in U \ntriangleleft F \Longleftrightarrow (x \notin U \land x \mapsto y \in F).$$

53

4.9.2 Removing a Member

The operation of removing someone, and all entries in which they figure, from the database is specified by the following schema:

$$
\begin{array}{|l}
\hline
\quad RemoveMember \rule{5cm}{0pt} \\
\; \Delta PhoneDB \\
\; name?: Person \\
\hline
\; name? \in members \\
\; members' = members \setminus \{name?\} \\
\; telephones' = \{name?\} \lhd telephones \\
\hline
\end{array}
$$

This goes wrong if $name? \notin members$. This case is captured by means of the schema *NotMember*, which has already been discussed. The complete specification of this operation is given by the schema *DoRemoveMember*:

$$DoRemoveMember \mathrel{\hat=} RemoveMember \wedge Success$$

$$\vee$$

$$NotMember$$

4.10 Presenting a Formal Specification

So far in this chapter I have presented the specification of an internal telephone number database in a way that has been guided by pedagogic concerns. This is not, however, the order in which the material would be presented in a specification document. In this section I want to say a few things about the format of a **Z** specification document.

One of the most important things to remember in writing a **Z** document is that it should *not* consist solely of mathematical symbols. There should be a substantial amount of English prose. In general, there will be more English prose than **Z** notation.

It is a good idea to begin the specification document with a brief introduction which informally gives an overview of the system of which you are going to present a formal specification.

Secondly, the document should contain a list of all the user-defined types that the specification makes use of and any constants it uses. These primitive types—or *given sets*, as they are also known—occur between square brackets and are separated by commas. That is actually a piece of **Z** syntax. As well as indicating the given sets in this way you should also explain what the sets represent in ordinary English. In the case of the internal telephone number database we have the following given sets:

$$[Person, Phone, Report]$$

Thirdly, you should mention the initial state. In the case of the telephone database presented earlier the initial state is:

```
┌─ InitPhoneDB' ──────────────────────────────────────────
│  PhoneDB'
│ ─────────────
│  members' = { }
│  telephones' = { }
└─────────────────────────────────────────────────────────
```

Conventionally in **Z** the variables in the schema describing the initial state are primed. Concerning this, Woodcock and Loomes (1988), p. 113, write:

> We can regard the initialization of a system as a peculiar kind of operation that creates a state out of nothing; there is no before state, simply an after state, with its variables decorated.

Fourthly, the document should contain the specification of all the operations that can be performed on the database.

Chapter 5

More about Relations and Schemas

5.1 Introduction

In this chapter I introduce some more operations on relations and schemas that are useful in building up concise specifications. To begin with I look at the composition of two relations. **Z** contains both a forward and a backward relational composition operator. After that I introduce the important notion of a *homogeneous* relation, that is to say, a relation which obtains between objects of the same type. The identity relation is introduced as the simplest example of a homogeneous relation. Having introduced relational composition and the identity relation it is possible to define both the transitive and the reflexive-transitive closure of a homogeneous relation.

Then, in section 5.4, I explain how *schemas* can be combined using the composition operator and I illustrate the value of this schema composition operator by defining the operation—on the telephone database system—of someone changing their extension number in terms of the schemas *RemoveEntry* and *AddEntry*.

To conclude the chapter I illustrate range restriction and anti-restriction. These are similar to domain restriction and anti-restriction, except that they form a new relation from an old one by restricting its range rather than its domain.

5.2 Relational Composition

In this section I want to discuss and define the very important idea of forward relational composition. This is a way of making a relation out of two other relations.

Let *Person* be the set of all people, let *Dog* be the set of all dogs and let *Breed* be the set of all the different breeds of dog that there are. The sets *owner*, *pet* and *kind* are introduced by the following declarations:

$$owner: \mathbf{P}\ Person; pet: \mathbf{P}\ Dog; kind: \mathbf{P}\ Breed.$$

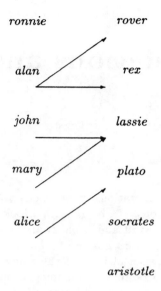

ronnie   rover

alan   rex

john   lassie

mary   plato

alice   socrates

aristotle

Figure 5.1: Graphical representation of *has*.

For illustrative purposes the sets just introduced will contain the following members:

$$owner = \{ronnie, alan, john, mary, alice\},$$
$$pet = \{rover, rex, lassie, plato, socrates, aristotle\},$$
$$kind = \{alsatian, labrador, bulldog, terrier, poodle, rottweiler\}.$$

The relation *has*: *Person* ↔ *Dog* tells us who owns which dog. It is possible for a person to own more than one dog and a dog can be jointly owned by two or more people. One example of the relation *has* is given here:

$$has = \{alan \mapsto rover,$$
$$alan \mapsto rex,$$
$$john \mapsto lassie,$$
$$mary \mapsto lassie,$$
$$alice \mapsto plato\}.$$

The relation is presented graphically in Fig. 5.1. On the left of this diagram members of the set *owners* are shown and on the right members of the set *pet* are listed. An arrow going from an owner to a pet indicates that that person owns that dog.

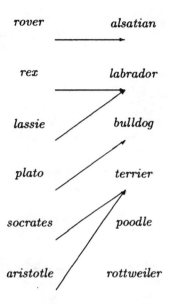

Figure 5.2: Graphical representation of *isa*.

The relation *isa*: *Dog* ↔ *Breed* tells us the breed of any particular dog. One example of the *isa* relation follows:

$$
isa = \{ rover \mapsto alsatian,
$$
$$
rex \mapsto labrador,
$$
$$
lassie \mapsto labrador,
$$
$$
plato \mapsto bulldog,
$$
$$
socrates \mapsto terrier,
$$
$$
aristotle \mapsto terrier \}.
$$

This relation is presented graphically in Fig. 5.2. On the left of this diagram members of the set *pet* are shown and on the right members of *kind* are listed. An arrow going from a pet to a kind indicates that that dog is of that breed.

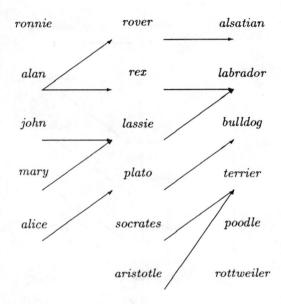

Figure 5.3: Graphical representation of *has* and *isa*.

Fig. 5.3 combines the information presented in Fig. 5.1 and Fig. 5.2. Given this information one of the things that we might be interested in is that of knowing what breed of dog any particular person owns. For example, does *ronnie* own a *bulldog* or a *terrier* or some other breed of dog, if he owns a dog at all? Clearly a person x owns a dog of breed z iff there exists a dog y such that $x \mapsto y \in has$ and $y \mapsto z \in isa$. The graphical interpretation of this is that the person x owns a dog of breed z iff we can travel along a line from x to z in Fig. 5.3. The relation that we are interested in is given extensionally as follows:

$$\{ alan \mapsto alsatian,$$
$$alan \mapsto labrador,$$
$$john \mapsto labrador,$$
$$mary \mapsto labrador,$$
$$alice \mapsto bulldog \}.$$

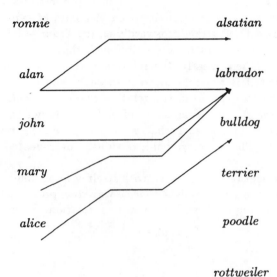

Figure 5.4: Graphical representation of $has; isa$.

The relation $has \mathbin{;} isa$ is one which holds between people and breeds iff the person in the relation owns a dog of that breed. The relation $has \mathbin{;} isa$ is known as the forward relational composition of has and isa and it is graphically represented in Fig. 5.4. Symbolically, we have:

$$x \mapsto z \in has \mathbin{;} isa \Longleftrightarrow (\exists y: Dog \bullet x \mapsto y \in has \land y \mapsto z \in isa).$$

And in general, where $F: X \leftrightarrow Y$ and $G: Y \leftrightarrow Z$, we have:

$$x \mapsto z \in F \mathbin{;} G \Longleftrightarrow (\exists y: Y \bullet x \mapsto y \in F \land y \mapsto z \in G).$$

Z also contains a backward relational composition operator which is symbolized by the sign ○ and this is defined so that $z \mapsto x \in G \circ F$ iff $x \mapsto z \in F \mathbin{;} G$.

5.3 Identity and Closures

Let $F: X \leftrightarrow Y$ be a relation. Then, if X is different from Y, then the relation F is known as a *heterogeneous* relation and if X is the same type as Y, then F is known as a *homogeneous* relation. There are situations in which homogeneous relations are very useful and in this section I discuss some of their properties.[1]

The simplest homogeneous relation between elements of type X is the *identity relation* id X, which is defined straightforwardly as $\{x: X \bullet x \mapsto x\}$.

Let *parent*: *Person* $\leftrightarrow$ *Person* be a relation such that $x \mapsto y \in parent$ iff y is a (natural) parent of x. Then, clearly, the relation *parent* is a homogeneous relation. One of the things that it is possible to do with such relations is to compose them with themselves. Thus, we can form the relation *parent* ⨾ *parent*. This is such that $x \mapsto y \in parent$ ⨾ *parent* iff x is a grandchild of y. Similarly, we can form the relation *parent* ⨾ *parent* ⨾ *parent*. This is such that $x \mapsto y \in parent$ ⨾ *parent* ⨾ *parent* iff x is a greatgrandchild of y. This process could, obviously, be repeated as many times as desired.

If a homogeneous relation is composed with itself several times, then the resulting expression becomes very big. There is a concise way to express such forms in **Z**. This is best introduced by example. Let $F: X \leftrightarrow X$ be a relation. Then. we have:

$$F^0 = \mathrm{id}\, X,$$
$$F^1 = F,$$
$$F^2 = F \mathbin{⨾} F,$$
$$F^3 = F \mathbin{⨾} F \mathbin{⨾} F,$$
$$F^4 = F \mathbin{⨾} F \mathbin{⨾} F \mathbin{⨾} F,$$

and clearly the process could be carried on indefinitely. The *transitive closure* of a homogeneous relation F is the relation obtained by forming the union of all F's iterations except F^0. It is symbolized as F^+. If *parent* is as explained above, then $x \mapsto y \in parent^+$ iff y is an ancestor of x.

The *reflexive-transitive closure* of a relation F is the relation obtained by forming the union of all F's iterations *including* F^0. It is symbolized as F^*.

5.4 Schema Composition

Schema composition is the analogue of forward relational composition in the world of schemas. It is a useful operation and it is one of several operations on schemas that allow us to build new specifications out of old ones. In order to explain it I first have to describe schema hiding and schema renaming.[2]

---

[1]The notions of a transitive and a reflexive-transitive closure illustrated in this section are used in section 14.1 where I discuss two specifications of the bill of materials problem.

[2]Schema renaming is not part of standard **Z** and so the official definition of schema composition given in Spivey (1989b), p. 77, differs from my account. However, if you follow the recipe given here for constructing the composition of two schemas you will always end up with the same thing had you used the official definition.

5.4.1 Schema Renaming

Consider the following simple schema:

```
┌─ S ──────────────────────────────────
│ x: N
│ y: P N
├──────────────
│ x ∈ y
└──────────────────────────────────────
```

Schema renaming actually means renaming the variables in the schema. The notation $S[m/x]$ means that every *free* occurrence of x in S is replaced by m. Let $T \triangleq S[m/x]$. Then, the result of expanding T is the following schema:

```
┌─ T ──────────────────────────────────
│ m: N
│ y: P N
├──────────────
│ m ∈ y
└──────────────────────────────────────
```

It might be easier to remember this if you think of it as $S[new/old]$.

5.4.2 Schema Hiding

Let S be as above. Then, the notation $S \setminus (x)$ is used to indicate the schema S with x hidden, that is to say, $S \setminus (x)$ is a schema in which x is removed from the declaration part and existentially quantified over in the predicate part. Let $T \triangleq S \setminus (x)$. Then, the result of expanding T is the following schema:

```
┌─ T ──────────────────────────────────
│ y: P N
├──────────────
│ ∃x: N • x ∈ y
└──────────────────────────────────────
```

5.4.3 Schema Composition Illustrated

Schema composition is a way of relating the after state variables of one schema with the before variables of another schema. The related variables must have the same base name. (The *base name* of a variable is what we are left with after we remove all the decorations, that is to say, the symbols !, ? and '.) Input and output variables are unaffected. For example, consider the schemas:

```
┌─ S ──────────────        ┌─ T ──────────────
│ x?, s, s', y!: N         │ x?, s, s': N
├──────────────            ├──────────────
│ s' = s − x?              │ s < x?
│ y! = s                   │ s' = s
└──────────────            └──────────────
```

In order to form $S \, \overset{\circ}{,} \, T$ we go through the following stages:

1. We rename all the after state variables in S to something entirely new, for example, s^+. That is to say, we form $S[s^+/s']$.

2. We rename all the before state variables in T to the same new thing, which—in this case—is s^+. That is to say, we form $T[s^+/s]$.

3. We form the conjunction of the two renamed schemas obtained in 1 and 2 above, that is to say, we form $S[s^+/s'] \wedge T[s^+/s]$.

4. We hide the variable—introduced in steps 1 and 2—in the schema formed in step 3, that is to say, we form the schema $(S[s^+/s'] \wedge T[s^+/s]) \setminus (s^+)$.

Let $S_1 \overset{\triangle}{=} S[s^+/s']$ and $T_1 \overset{\triangle}{=} T[s^+/s]$, that is to say, S_1 and T_1 are the schemas obtained by carrying out the transformations described in steps 1 and 2. The expanded versions of S_1 and T_1 are the following schemas:

$$
\begin{array}{|l}
\hline
\;S_1 \underline{\hspace{3cm}} \\
x?, s, s^+, y! \colon \mathbf{N} \\
\hline
s^+ = s - x? \\
y! = s \\
\hline
\end{array}
\qquad
\begin{array}{|l}
\hline
\;T_1 \underline{\hspace{3cm}} \\
x?, s^+, s' \colon \mathbf{N} \\
\hline
s^+ < x? \\
s' = s^+ \\
\hline
\end{array}
$$

The result of carrying out step 3 is the schema $Alpha \overset{\triangle}{=} S[s^+/s'] \wedge T[s^+/s]$, whose expansion is:

$$
\begin{array}{|l}
\hline
\;Alpha \underline{\hspace{5cm}} \\
x?, s, s^+, s', y! \colon \mathbf{N} \\
\hline
s^+ = s - x? \\
y! = s \\
s^+ < x? \\
s' = s^+ \\
\hline
\end{array}
$$

The composition of two schemas S and T is written $S \, \overset{\circ}{,} \, T$.

$$S \, \overset{\circ}{,} \, T \overset{\triangle}{=} (S[s^+/s'] \wedge T[s^+/s]) \setminus (s^+)$$

Carrying out the operation described in step 4 above results in the schema $Beta \overset{\triangle}{=} S \overset{\circ}{,} T$, whose expansion follows:

$$
\begin{array}{|l}
\hline
\;Beta \underline{\hspace{5cm}} \\
x?, s, s', y! \colon \mathbf{N} \\
\hline
\exists s^+ \colon \mathbf{N} \; \bullet \\
\qquad (s^+ = s - x? \; \wedge \\
\qquad y! = s \; \wedge \\
\qquad s^+ < x? \; \wedge \\
\qquad s' = s^+) \\
\hline
\end{array}
$$

The predicate that results when we form the relational composition of two schemas can usually be considerably simplified. In the case of $S \, \c{9} \, T$ the predicate is equivalent to:

$$\exists s^+ : \mathbf{N} \bullet s' = s - x? \land y! = s \land s' < x?$$

All that I have done to obtain this predicate is to substitute s' for s^+ in the first three conjuncts within the scope of the existential quantifier. As the variable s^+ now no longer occurs in the scope of the quantifier, it can be dropped.[3] Thus, the schema $S \, \c{9} \, T$ is equivalent to the following, where $Beta \mathrel{\hat{=}} S \, \c{9} \, T$:

```
┌─ Beta ──────────────────────────────
│ x?, s, s', y!: N
├─────────────────────────────────────
│ s' = s - x?
│ y! = s
│ s' < x?
└─────────────────────────────────────
```

5.4.4   The Utility of Schema Composition

Schema composition is a useful operation because it is one of several schema operations that allow us to make new specifications out of old ones. In order to illustrate this I am going to consider the internal telephone number database presented in the previous chapter and I am going to show how the operation of someone changing one of their extensions can be composed out of the operations of removing an entry from the database and adding an entry to the database. What I am going to construct is the schema $RemoveEntry \, \c{9} \, AddEntry$. In order to do this we have to go through the four stages mentioned above. Carrying out step 1 results in the schema $Alpha$ which is a short name for the schema $RemoveEntry[members^+/members'][telephones^+/telephones']$:

```
┌─ Alpha ─────────────────────────────
│ members, members⁺: P Person
│ telephones, telephones⁺: Person ↔ Phone
│ oldnumber?: Phone
│ name?: Person
├─────────────────────────────────────
│ dom telephones ⊆ members
│ dom telephones⁺ ⊆ members⁺
│ name? ↦ oldnumber? ∈ telephones
│ telephones⁺ = telephones \ {name? ↦ oldnumber?}
│ members⁺ = members
└─────────────────────────────────────
```

---

[3]These simplifications are possible because of the predicate calculus sequents $Pa \dashv\vdash \exists x : X \bullet Pa$ and $Py \dashv\vdash \exists z : X \bullet z = y \land Pz$, proved on pp. 122ff. below.

Next we have to do is to perform the operation mentioned in step 2 above. This results in the schema $Beta \,\hat{=}\, AddEntry[members^+/members][telephones^+/telephones]$:

$$
\begin{array}{|l}
\quad Beta \rule[-0.2em]{0pt}{1em} \\[-0.1em]
\hline
members^+, members': \mathbf{P}\ Person \\
telephones^+, telephones': Person \leftrightarrow Phone \\
newnumber?: Phone \\
name?: Person \\
\hline
\mathrm{dom}\ telephones^+ \subseteq members^+ \\
\mathrm{dom}\ telephones' \subseteq members' \\
name? \in members^+ \\
name? \mapsto newnumber? \notin telephones^+ \\
telephones' = telephones^+ \cup \{name? \mapsto newnumber?\} \\
members' = members^+ \\
\end{array}
$$

The next thing we have to find is:

$$RemoveEntry[members^+/members'][telephones^+/telephones']$$
$$\wedge\ AddEntry[members^+/members][telephones^+/telephones].$$

I shall call this schema $Gamma$:

$$
\begin{array}{|l}
\quad Gamma \rule[-0.2em]{0pt}{1em} \\[-0.1em]
\hline
members, members^+, members': \mathbf{P}\ Person \\
telephones, telephones^+, telephones': Person \leftrightarrow Phone \\
oldnumber?, newnumber?: Phone \\
name?: Person \\
\hline
\mathrm{dom}\ telephones \subseteq members \\
\mathrm{dom}\ telephones^+ \subseteq members^+ \\
\mathrm{dom}\ telephones' \subseteq members' \\
name? \in members^+ \\
name? \mapsto newnumber? \notin telephones^+ \\
name? \mapsto oldnumber? \in telephones \\
telephones' = telephones^+ \cup \{name? \mapsto newnumber?\} \\
telephones^+ = telephones \setminus \{name? \mapsto oldnumber?\} \\
members' = members^+ \\
members^+ = members \\
\end{array}
$$

To obtain the composition of *RemoveEntry* and *AddEntry* we just existentially quantify over the variables introduced in steps 1 and 2 above. Let $Delta \mathrel{\hat{=}} RemoveEntry \mathbin{\fatsemi} AddEntry$. Then *Delta* is the following schema:

Delta

$members, members' : \mathbf{P}\ Person$
$telephones, telephones' : Person \leftrightarrow Phone$
$oldnumber?, newnumber? : Phone$
$name? : Person$

$(\exists members^+ : \mathbf{P}\ Person;\ telephones^+ : Person \leftrightarrow Phone \bullet$
$\quad \operatorname{dom} telephones \subseteq members\ \wedge$
$\quad \operatorname{dom} telephones^+ \subseteq members^+\ \wedge$
$\quad \operatorname{dom} telephones' \subseteq members'\ \wedge$
$\quad name? \in members^+\ \wedge$
$\quad name? \mapsto newnumber? \notin telephones^+\ \wedge$
$\quad name? \mapsto oldnumber? \in telephones\ \wedge$
$\quad telephones' = telephones^+ \cup \{name? \mapsto newnumber?\}\ \wedge$
$\quad telephones^+ = telephones \setminus \{name? \mapsto oldnumber?\}\ \wedge$
$\quad members' = members^+\ \wedge$
$\quad members^+ = members)$

After simplification this turns out to be:

Delta

$\Delta PhoneDB$
$oldnumber?, newnumber? : Phone$
$name? : Person$

$name? \in members$
$name? \mapsto newnumber? \notin telephones \setminus \{name? \mapsto oldnumber?\}$
$name? \mapsto oldnumber? \in telephones$
$telephones' = telephones$
$\qquad \setminus \{name? \mapsto oldnumber?\} \cup \{name? \mapsto newnumber?\}$
$members' = members$

One of the consequences of this is that it is possible for *newname?* and *oldname?* to be the same. You might not think that this possibility should be allowed, so in defining *ChangeEntry* we exclude this possibility, thus:

$$ChangeEntry \mathrel{\hat{=}} (RemoveEntry \mathbin{\fatsemi} AddEntry) \mid newname? \neq oldname?$$

The notation $S \mid P$, where S is a schema and P a predicate, just indicates the schema obtained by adding the predicate P to the predicate part of S.

5.5   Range Restriction and Anti-restriction

Range restriction and anti-restriction are similar operations to domain restriction and anti-restriction, except that they work on the range of a relation rather than on its domain. Range anti-restriction is also known as range *corestriction* or range *subtraction*. I shall introduce these two operations by means of a simple example.

Let *Month* be the type consisting of all twelve of the months of the year and let the relation *normal*: *Month* $\leftrightarrow$ **N** be such that $x \mapsto y \in normal$ iff the month x has y days in it. I am assuming that the year in question is not a leap year. The relation *normal* can be specified extensionally as follows:

$$normal = \{jan \mapsto 31,$$
$$feb \mapsto 28,$$
$$mar \mapsto 31,$$
$$apr \mapsto 30,$$
$$may \mapsto 31,$$
$$jun \mapsto 30,$$
$$jul \mapsto 31,$$
$$aug \mapsto 31,$$
$$sep \mapsto 30,$$
$$oct \mapsto 31,$$
$$nov \mapsto 30,$$
$$dec \mapsto 31\}.$$

Range restriction is represented by the symbol $\rhd$.

$$normal \rhd \{30\} = \{apr \mapsto 30, jun \mapsto 30, sep \mapsto 30, nov \mapsto 30\}.$$

A pair $x \mapsto y$ is a member of *normal* $\rhd \{30\}$ iff its second component y is in $\{30\}$. So, the set of all months that have exactly 30 days in them is denoted by means of the expression dom(*normal* $\rhd \{30\}$).

Range anti-restriction is represented by the symbol $\rhd\!\!\!-$.

$$normal \rhd\!\!\!- \{30\} = \{jan \mapsto 31,$$
$$feb \mapsto 28,$$
$$mar \mapsto 31,$$
$$may \mapsto 31,$$
$$jul \mapsto 31,$$
$$aug \mapsto 31,$$
$$oct \mapsto 31,$$
$$dec \mapsto 31\}.$$

An ordered pair $x \mapsto y$ is a member of *normal* $\rhd\!\!\!- \{30\}$ iff its second component y is *not* in $\{30\}$. So, the set of all months that do not have 30 days in them is denoted by means of the expression dom(*normal* $\rhd\!\!\!- \{30\}$).

5.6   Exercises

5.1) Let *father*, *mother*, *brother*, *firstcousin*, *grandfather* and *greatgrandmother* all be relations of type *Person* ↔ *Person*. Furthermore, $x \mapsto y \in father$ iff y is the father of x, $x \mapsto y \in mother$ iff y is the mother of x, $x \mapsto y \in brother$ iff x and y are brothers (not half-brothers), $x \mapsto y \in firstcousin$ iff x and y are first cousins, $x \mapsto y \in grandfather$ iff y is a grandfather of x and $x \mapsto y \in greatgrandmother$ iff y is a greatgrandmother of x.

   a) Define the relation *brother* in terms of *father* and *mother*.

   b) Define the relation *firstcousin* in terms of *father* and *mother*.

   c) Give two definitions of the relation *grandfather* in terms of *father* and *mother*, one using variables and quantifiers and the other not.

   d) What are the sets $grandfather(\!|\{x\}|\!)$ and $grandfather^{-1}(\!|\{x\}|\!)$?

   e) Give two definitions of the relation *greatgrandmother* in terms of *father* and *mother*, one using variables and quantifiers and the other not.

   f) Write down an expression which represents the set of all a person x's ancestors.

5.2) Often when someone joins the university they are given a telephone extension straight away. The operation *Join* can be defined using schema composition as *AddMember* ⨟ *AddEntry*. Work out what *Join* is by calculating it as explained in this chapter.

5.3) Specify by means of a schema *Films* a database for recording information about films. The database must be capable of holding information about who directed a particular film and about the writer of the film's screenplay. Every film in the database must have a director and writer associated with it. Provision must also be made for films that are directed by several people and written by more than one person.

State what the schemas Δ*Films*, Ξ*Films* and *InitFilms'* are.

Specify the operation of adding information to the database concerning a film with only one director and only one writer.

Specify two operations which interrogate the database in order to find out all the films directed by a particular individual and all the films written by a specific person.

Chapter 6

Functions

6.1 Introduction

A function is an association between objects of some type, say X, and things of another type, say Y,[1] such that given an object of type X, there exists one and only one thing in Y associated with that object.[2] In **Z** a function is identified with a particular collection of ordered pairs. The type of all partial functions from X to Y is denoted by $X \nrightarrow Y$ and is defined in this way:

$$X \nrightarrow Y == \{F: X \leftrightarrow Y \mid (\forall x: X; y, z: Y \bullet (x \mapsto y \in F \wedge x \mapsto z \in F \Rightarrow y = z))\}.$$

That is to say, there exists only one object in Y corresponding to a single object in X. Note that if $f: X \nrightarrow Y$ is a partial function, then there may exist elements of type X which are not the first components of any ordered pair which is a member of f.

Let $f: X \nrightarrow Y$ be a partial function, let $x \in \text{dom} f$ and let y be the element of Y associated with x by f. Then, rather than writing $x \mapsto y \in f$, we often write $fx = y$. Parentheses can be placed around x if preferred, thus $f(x) = y$. Here, x is known as the *argument* of the function and y is its *value*.

I do the following things in the remainder of this chapter. In the next section I illustrate the use of partial functions in specifications by presenting a brief specification of a weather map. In the course of doing this I introduce the very important notion of function overriding—symbolized by the sign $\oplus$—which is used frequently in specifications. After that I define the type of all *total* functions in **Z** and briefly mention some of the less frequently used types of function. Then, to conclude the chapter, I explain the λ-notation that is part of **Z** and I discuss the topic of currying. Every symbol defined or explained in this chapter is part of the standard **Z** core language.

---

[1]The types X and Y need not be distinct.

[2]Functions are also known as *mappings*, *morphisms*, *transformations* and *operations*.

6.2 Specifying a Weather Map

6.2.1 Introduction

In order to illustrate the use of functions in specifications, I am going to describe a simple weather map which just records the temperature (in degrees Celcius) of various regions of some country. Let *Region* be the type of all the regions that we might need to use. Then the state of our system is given by the schema *WeatherMap*:

$$
\begin{array}{|l}
\hline
\text{\textit{WeatherMap}} \\
\hline
known: \mathbf{P}\ Region \\
temp: Region \nrightarrow \mathbf{Z} \\
\hline
\text{dom } temp = known \\
\hline
\end{array}
$$

Here, *known* is the set of all the regions whose temperature is shown on our weather map and *temp* is the temperature function which returns the temperature associated with a region, given that region as its argument. The state invariant of the schema *WeatherMap* tells us that every region in the set *known* has a temperature associated with it. For example, the set *known* might be $\{west, east, south, north\}$. An example of the state of this system—with *known* as just enumerated—is the following:

$$temp = \{west \mapsto 17, east \mapsto -3, south \mapsto 8, north \mapsto 0\}.$$

Because a function is just a special kind of relation, we can take its range and domain:

$$\text{dom } temp = \{west, east, south, north\},$$
$$\text{ran } temp = \{17, -3, 8, 0\}.$$

This is a correct example of the state of our system because the state invariant is true, as is easily verified.

The schema $\Delta WeatherMap$ and $\Xi WeatherMap$ are defined in the usual way, as is the initial state, by the following equations:

$$\Delta WeatherMap \mathrel{\widehat{=}} WeatherMap \wedge WeatherMap'$$
$$\Xi WeatherMap \mathrel{\widehat{=}} \Delta WeatherMap \mid known' = known \wedge temp' = temp$$
$$Init WeatherMap' \mathrel{\widehat{=}} WeatherMap' \mid known' = \{\ \} \wedge temp' = \{\ \}$$

6.2.2 Updating the Weather Map

In order to specify the operation of updating the weather map I need to use the function overriding operator, symbolized by $\oplus$. This is one of the most widely used operators in **Z** specifications; therefore you should become familiar with its meaning and use.

Function Overriding

The way that function overriding works is easy to grasp with the aid of an example. Let *Month* be the type of all the months and let *normal, leap*: *Month* $\nrightarrow$ N_1 be partial functions which return the number of days in a normal and a leap year, respectively. The function *normal* can be enumerated as follows:

$$normal = \{jan \mapsto 31,$$
$$feb \mapsto 28,$$
$$mar \mapsto 31,$$
$$apr \mapsto 30,$$
$$may \mapsto 31,$$
$$jun \mapsto 30,$$
$$jul \mapsto 31,$$
$$aug \mapsto 31,$$
$$sep \mapsto 30,$$
$$oct \mapsto 31,$$
$$nov \mapsto 30,$$
$$dec \mapsto 31\}.$$

The function *leap* is clearly the same as *normal* except for the number it associates with February. This is captured using function overriding as follows:

$$leap = normal \oplus \{feb \mapsto 29\}.$$

Just to make sure that you have grasped the significance of this I will spell out what *leap* is:

$$leap = \{jan \mapsto 31,$$
$$feb \mapsto 29,$$
$$mar \mapsto 31,$$
$$apr \mapsto 30,$$
$$may \mapsto 31,$$
$$jun \mapsto 30,$$
$$jul \mapsto 31,$$
$$aug \mapsto 31,$$
$$sep \mapsto 30,$$
$$oct \mapsto 31,$$
$$nov \mapsto 30,$$
$$dec \mapsto 31\}.$$

The function overriding operator $\oplus$ combines two functions of the same type to give a new function also of that type. Let $f, g: X \nrightarrow Y$ be partial functions. Then $f \oplus g$

73

is defined for an object $x\colon X$ if either $x \in \operatorname{dom} f$ or $x \in \operatorname{dom} g$. If $x \in \operatorname{dom} g$, then $(f \oplus g)x = gx$. If $x \notin \operatorname{dom} g$ but $x \in \operatorname{dom} f$, then $(f \oplus g)x = fx$. $f \oplus g$ can be read as 'f overridden by g'.

A Note about Maximal Types In discussing range restriction and anti-restriction in chapter 5 I talked about the *relation normal: Month* $\leftrightarrow$ **N** and in this chapter I have used the *partial function normal: Month* $\nrightarrow$ $\mathbf{N}_1$. Although I have used the same identifier, namely *normal*, in both cases, there is no type conflict involved. This is because the type of *normal* in both cases is $\mathbf{P}(Month \times \mathbf{Z})$. The type of all integers **Z** is the maximal type of which both **N** and $\mathbf{N}_1$ are subsets and the set $\mathbf{P}(Month \times \mathbf{Z})$ is the maximal type of which both *normal: Month* $\leftrightarrow$ **N** and *normal: Month* $\nrightarrow$ $\mathbf{N}_1$ are subsets.[3]

Specifying the Operation

Using function overriding it is easy to specify the operation of updating the weather map:

$$
\begin{array}{|l}
\underline{\ Update\ }\\
\Delta\,WeatherMap \\
r?\colon Region \\
t?\colon \mathbf{Z} \\
\hline
r? \in known \\
temp' = temp \oplus \{r? \mapsto t?\}
\end{array}
$$

To illustrate the operation of *Update*, let *temp* be as enumerated on p. 72 above and let $r? = west$ and $t? = 13$. Then, $temp'$ is given by the equation:

$$temp' = temp \oplus \{west \mapsto 13\}.$$

This has the consequence that $temp'$ is the following function:

$$temp' = \{west \mapsto 13, east \mapsto -3, south \mapsto 8, north \mapsto 0\}.$$

6.2.3 Looking up the Temperature of a Region

Another operation that we might want to specify is that of looking up the temperature of a particular region. This is done by the schema *LookUp*:

$$
\begin{array}{|l}
\underline{\ LookUp\ }\\
\Xi\,WeatherMap \\
r?\colon Region \\
t!\colon \mathbf{Z} \\
\hline
r? \in known \\
r? \mapsto t! \in temp
\end{array}
$$

---

[3]For more information about the types of relations and functions, see Spivey (1989b), p. 30.

Note that I have written $r? \mapsto t! \in temp$ here. This is done in order to emphasize the fact that in **Z** functions are just sets of ordered pairs which satisfy the property mentioned in section 6.1. It could have been written as $temp(r?) = t!$ using the notation for function application explained above.

6.3 Total Functions and Others

As already mentioned, a partial function $f: X \nrightarrow Y$ need not have a value for every member of X taken as argument. In other words, it is possible for the domain of a partial function $f: X \nrightarrow Y$ to be a *proper* subset of X. If we wish to exclude this possibility, then we have to make use of a *total* function. Let $f: X \rightarrow Y$ be a total function. Then dom $f = X$. The type of all total functions from X to Y is easy to define:

$$X \rightarrow Y == \{f: X \nrightarrow Y \mid \text{dom } f = X\}.$$

Z also contains notations for many other kinds of function—such as finite functions, injections, surjections and bijections—but these are not used very frequently. In any case, it would be confusing just to list them here. They are better explained in a context where their use is genuinely needed. Thus, I introduce the notion of a finite function on p. 78 of chapter 7 on sequences—since finite sequences are defined in terms of finite functions—and I make use of bijective functions on p. 100 of the chapter on free types and also on p. 203 of chapter 16 in which I present the specification of a display-orientated text editor. The definitions of all the different types of function to be found in standard **Z** can be found in chapter 23 of the reference part of this book.

6.4 The λ-notation

The λ-notation is a very useful way of defining functions in **Z**. In using it, however, it is important not to forget that functions in **Z** are just particular kinds of sets of ordered pairs. Do not confuse the λ-notation of **Z** with the λ-calculus. Many of the characteristic features of the λ-calculus, such as the self-application of functions, are not possible with **Z**'s λ-notation because they would violate the type discipline.

As an example of the use of the λ-notation consider the problem of defining a function *square* which squares its argument:

$$square \, 2 = 4,$$
$$square \, 7 = 49,$$
$$square \, 12 = 144,$$

and so on. We could write:

$$square == \{x: \mathbf{N} \bullet x \mapsto x * x\},$$

but using the λ-notation we obtain the more perspicuous definition:

$$square == \lambda x: \mathbf{N} \bullet x * x.$$

These two definitions are equivalent. In general we have:

$$\lambda x_1\colon X_1; \ldots; x_n\colon X_n \mid P \bullet t \iff \{x_1\colon X_1; \ldots; x_n\colon X_n \mid P \bullet (x_1, \ldots, x_n) \mapsto t\}.$$

6.5   Currying

Currying[4] is best explained by means of an example. The standard integer addition function $\_ + \_$, for example, has type $\mathbf{Z} \times \mathbf{Z} \to \mathbf{Z}$. This means that it takes a single (structured) argument, namely an ordered pair consisting of two integers, and returns an integer as its value. Sometimes it is useful to have a *curried* version of $\_ + \_$. I will call this *add*. This is a function of type $\mathbf{Z} \to (\mathbf{Z} \to \mathbf{Z})$ defined like this:

$$
\begin{array}{|l}
add\colon \mathbf{Z} \to (\mathbf{Z} \to \mathbf{Z}) \\
\hline
add = \lambda i\colon \mathbf{Z} \bullet (\lambda j\colon \mathbf{Z} \bullet i + j)
\end{array}
$$

This graphical notation is known as an *axiomatic description*. Its general form is:

$$
\begin{array}{|l}
D \\
\hline
P
\end{array}
$$

where D is a declaration which introduces one or more variables and P is an optional predicate that constrains the values taken by the variables introduced in D.

The reason why curried functions are sometimes useful is that they can be partially parameterized. For example, *add* 3 is a function of type $\mathbf{Z} \to \mathbf{Z}$ which adds 3 to its single integer argument and *add* 77 is a function of the same type which adds 77 to its argument.

---

[4]This has nothing to do with Indian cuisine. It is derived from the surname of the logician Haskell Curry.

Chapter 7

Sequences

7.1 Introduction

In this chapter I am going to look at sequences. Most of the chapter will be taken up with finite sequences and operations defined on them, but at the end I shall show how infinite sequences can be defined in **Z**. Some of the functions defined in this chapter are not part of standard **Z**, namely the subsequence forming functions after, drop, for, take and map and also the type of all finite and infinite functions and the concatenation operator defined on that type.[1] Apart from these, everything else contained in this chapter is part of standard **Z**. As **Z** is an extendible language,[2] you can define any of the non-standard operators whenever you need them. Many of the operators defined in this chapter—including the non-standard subsequence forming ones—will be used in the specification of a display-orientated text editor contained in chapter 16. Infinite sequences are used in Diller (1990a) to specify interactive processes in **Z**.

7.2 Fundamental Ideas

The type of *all* finite sequences of elements drawn from a set or type X is denoted as seq X and to show that σ is a sequence of type seq X we write σ: seq X. Sequences are written enclosed in angle brackets with their elements separated by commas, like this $\langle x_1, x_2, \ldots, x_n \rangle$. The empty sequence in **Z** is written as $\langle\ \rangle$.

Some examples should clarify and reinforce these ideas. In this chapter I make a lot of use of sequences of months for illustrative purposes, so I define the type *Month* here by enumeration:

$$Month = \{jan, feb, mar, apr, may, jun, jul, aug, sep, oct, nov, dec\}.$$

---

[1] The reason why I define drop, take and map is that often writing a specification in **Z** that involves sequences is similar to writing a program in a functional language like Miranda and those functions are used extensively in functional programming as Bird and Wadler (1988) excellently demonstrate. The functions after and for were defined in the earlier reference manual Sufrin (1986b).

[2] **Z** is an extendible language because it contains as part of itself the mechanisms of abbreviation definition (==), axiomatic description and generic definition. These are all explained in chapter 19.

The following are examples of sequences:

$$\langle feb, apr, dec, jan \rangle \in \text{seq } Month,$$

$$\langle 77, 5, 6 \rangle \in \text{seq } \mathbf{N},$$

$$\langle \langle \ \rangle, \langle feb, mar \rangle, \langle apr \rangle \rangle \in \text{seq}(\text{seq } Month),$$

$$\langle \{1, 2, 83\}, \{ \ \}, evens \rangle \in \text{seq}(\mathbf{P} \, \mathbf{N}).$$

7.3   Defining Sequences

In order to define the type of all finite sequences in **Z** we first of all need the idea of a *finite* function. The type $X \nrightarrow Y$ is the type of all finite functions from X to Y and it is defined like this, where $\mathbf{F} \, X$ is the type of all finite sets whose elements are drawn from X:

$$X \nrightarrow Y == \{f : X \nrightarrow Y \mid \text{dom } f \in \mathbf{F} \, X \bullet f\}.$$

In words, the type $X \nrightarrow Y$ consists of all those partial functions from X to Y which have a finite domain. The type of all finite sequences which have their elements drawn from X can now be defined as follows:

$$\text{seq } X == \{f : \mathbf{N} \nrightarrow X \mid \text{dom } f = 1 .. \#f \bullet f\}.$$

So, a sequence of things of type X is a finite function from the non-negative whole numbers to X whose domain consists of all the numbers between 1 and $\#f$, that is to say, whose domain is an initial segment of the natural numbers.

Earlier I had the following example of a sequence of months:

$$\langle feb, apr, dec, jan \rangle \in \text{seq } Month.$$

This sequence is just the function or set:

$$\{1 \mapsto feb, 2 \mapsto apr, 3 \mapsto dec, 4 \mapsto jan\}.$$

Because sequences are functions you can apply them to numbers. Let $\sigma : \text{seq } X$. Then, $\sigma 1$ is the first element of σ, $\sigma 2$ is the second element of σ, $\sigma 3$ is the third element of σ, and so on, assuming, of course, that they all exist. So, we have:

$$\langle feb, apr, dec, jan \rangle \, 3 = dec,$$

$$\langle feb, apr, dec, jan \rangle \, 1 = feb.$$

Because sequences are functions the empty sequence $\langle \ \rangle$ is just an alternative notation for the emptyset $\emptyset$ or $\{ \ \}$.

7.4   Sequence Manipulating Functions

Concatenation for Sequences

Given two arbitrary sequences σ and τ, $\sigma \frown \tau$ is the sequence which results from sticking the two sequences together, for example:

$$\langle jan, feb \rangle \frown \langle mar, apr, may \rangle = \langle jan, feb, mar, apr, may \rangle.$$

The formal definition of the concatenation operator is:

$$
\begin{array}{|l}
\hline [X] \\
\hline \_ \frown \_ : (\text{seq } X) \times (\text{seq } X) \to (\text{seq } X) \\
\hline \forall \sigma, \tau : \text{seq } X \; \bullet \\
\quad \sigma \frown \tau = \sigma \cup \{ n : \text{dom } \tau \; \bullet \; n + \#\sigma \mapsto (\tau n) \} \\
\hline
\end{array}
$$

The "box" used in this definition, namely:

$$
\begin{array}{|l}
\hline [X] \\
\hline x : X \\
\hline P \\
\hline
\end{array}
$$

introduces a *generic definition* in **Z**. It defines a whole family of variables x of generic type X which satisfy some predicate P. When we actually come to use x we have to supply an actual type instead of the parameter X. For example, if we were dealing with numbers we would write $x[\mathbf{N}]$ and if we were dealing with European states we would write $x[Europe]$, and so on. Often the actual type is omitted when it can be deduced from the context.

The Function *head*

Given a non-empty sequence σ, *head* σ is the first element of σ. For example,

$$head\langle jan, feb, mar \rangle = jan.$$

Note that *head* is undefined for the empty sequence. (Lisp programmers will recognize this as *car*.)

The Function *last*

Given a non-empty sequence σ, *last* σ is the last element of σ. For example,

$$last\langle jan, feb, mar \rangle = mar.$$

The selector *last* is not defined for the empty sequence.

The Function *front*

Given a non-empty sequence σ, *front* σ is the initial segment of σ which contains all members of σ except the last. For example,

$$front\langle jan, feb, mar, apr \rangle = \langle jan, feb, mar \rangle.$$

Again *front* is undefined for the empty sequence.

The Function *tail*

Given a non-empty sequence σ, *tail* σ is the sequence which consists of all elements of σ except the first. For example,

$$tail\langle jan, feb, mar, apr\rangle = \langle feb, mar, apr\rangle.$$

Again *tail* is undefined for the empty sequence. (Lisp programmers will recognize this as *cdr*.)

Filtering

Let *winter* be the set of all the winter months. In Britain we have:

$$winter = \{sep, oct, nov, dec, jan, feb, mar, apr\}.$$

The filtering operator $\upharpoonright$ has the following effect:

$$\langle jun, nov, feb, jul\rangle \upharpoonright winter = \langle jun, jul\rangle.$$

The Functions *after* and *drop*

Given a sequence σ and a natural number n, then σ after n is the sequence obtained by dropping the first n elements of σ, for example,

$$\langle jan, feb, mar, apr, may\rangle \text{ after } 3 = \langle apr, may\rangle.$$

It is sometimes useful to have a curried version of after; this is known as drop:

$$\text{drop} == \lambda n : \mathbf{N} \bullet (\lambda \sigma : \text{seq } X \bullet \sigma \text{ after } n).$$

The Functions *for* and *take*

Given a sequence σ and a natural number n, σ for n is the sequence made up out of the first n elements of σ, for example,

$$\langle may, jun, jul, aug\rangle \text{ for } 2 = \langle may, jun\rangle.$$

It is sometimes useful to have a curried version of for; this is known as take:

$$\text{take} == \lambda n : \mathbf{N} \bullet (\lambda \sigma : \text{seq } X \bullet \sigma \text{ for } n).$$

Reversing a Sequence

Given an arbitrary sequence σ, *rev* σ is the sequence which contains just the same elements as σ, but in reverse order, for example,

$$rev\langle aug, sep, oct, dec\rangle = \langle dec, oct, sep, aug\rangle.$$

The Function *map*

Given a function, $f: X \to Y$, and a sequence, $\sigma: \text{seq } X$, the function map applies f to each element of σ, thus:

$$\text{map } f\langle x_1, x_2, \ldots, x_n \rangle = \langle f x_1, f x_2, \ldots, f x_n \rangle.$$

In chapter 6 on functions I introduced the function *normal* which maps a month onto the number of days it contains in a non-leap year. Using this function we can illustrate the behaviour of map like this:

$$\text{map } normal\langle jan, jul, oct \rangle = \langle 31, 31, 31 \rangle.$$

Note that map $f \ \sigma$ is equivalent to $\sigma \, \mathbin{\raise1pt\hbox{$\circ$}}_9 f$.

Distributed Concatenation

In the first section of this chapter I had the following example of a sequence:

$$\langle\langle \ \rangle, \langle feb, mar \rangle, \langle apr \rangle\rangle \in \text{seq(seq } Month).$$

Applying the distributed concatenation operator $\frown/$ to this yields a sequence of months:

$$\frown/\langle\langle \ \rangle, \langle feb, mar \rangle, \langle apr \rangle\rangle = \langle feb, mar, apr \rangle.$$

Disjointness and Partitioning

In discussing the specification of the small telephone number database I said—on p. 48 above—that the sets *staff* and *proles* partition the set *known*. This was captured by means of the two predicates:

$$staff \cup proles = known,$$
$$staff \cap proles = \{ \ \}.$$

The two sets *staff* and *proles* are said to be *disjoint* and together they *partition* the set *known*. Because the idea of disjointness and partitioning crop up very frequently in specification, there is a concise way of expressing this in **Z**. We can write:

$$\text{disjoint } \langle staff, proles \rangle,$$
$$\langle staff, proles \rangle \text{ partition } known.$$

These relations also work for sequences of any length. In fact, the definition of these operators in Spivey (1989b), p. 125, is even more general, since it does not just apply to sequences of sets but to any indexed family of sets.

7.5   Infinite Sequences

I shall denote the set of all finite and infinite sequences of elements drawn from X as $\text{seq}_\infty X$ and this can be straightforwardly defined in $\mathbf{Z}$ as follows:

$$\text{seq}_\infty X == \{f : \mathbf{N}_1 \nrightarrow X \mid (\forall i : \mathbf{N}_1 \mid i \in \text{dom } f \bullet (\forall j : \mathbf{N}_1 \mid j < i \bullet j \in \text{dom } f))\}.$$

Not all of the functions defined on finite sequences have analogues on $\text{seq}_\infty X$. For example, there are no analogues of *last*, *front* and *rev*. The concatenation operator cannot be applied to two infinite sequences, but we can define an analogue of type $\text{seq } X \times \text{seq}_\infty X \to \text{seq}_\infty X$ as follows:

$$
\begin{array}{|l}
\hline
\underline{\quad}^\frown\underline{\quad} : (\text{seq } X) \times (\text{seq}_\infty X) \to (\text{seq}_\infty X) \\
\hline
\forall \sigma : \text{seq } X ; \tau : \text{seq}_\infty X \bullet \\
\quad \sigma^\frown \tau = \sigma \cup \{i : \text{dom } \tau \bullet i + \#\sigma \mapsto (\tau i)\} \\
\hline
\end{array}
$$

$$=[X]=$$

This is, in fact, almost identical to the sequence concatenation operator for finite sequences.

7.6   Exercises

7.1) Let $\sigma, \tau, \upsilon : \text{seq } Char$ be sequences of characters defined like this:

$$\sigma == \langle A, C, K \rangle,$$
$$\tau == \langle B, L \rangle,$$
$$\upsilon == \langle J \rangle.$$

What are the following sequences?

a) $(\tau^\frown \sigma)^\frown (\upsilon^\frown \sigma)$.

b) $head(front(\tau^\frown \sigma))$.

c) $last(front(\tau^\frown \sigma))$.

d) $tail(front(\tau^\frown \sigma))$.

e) $\sigma^\frown \tau$.

f) $rev(\sigma^\frown \tau)$.

g) $\text{dom}(\sigma^\frown \tau)$.

h) $\text{ran}(\sigma^\frown \tau)$.

i) $(\sigma^\frown \tau)^{-1}$.

j) $(\sigma^\frown \tau)^{-1} \, {}_9^\circ \, pred \, {}_9^\circ (\sigma^\frown \tau)$.

k) $(\{E \mapsto 4, R \mapsto 5\} \cup \sigma^{-1})^{-1}$.

l) $(\sigma \frown \tau) \triangleright \{A, E, I, O, U\}$.

m) $(\tau \frown \sigma) \oplus \{3 \mapsto O\}$.

n) $\{1 \mapsto 2, 2 \mapsto 1, 3 \mapsto 4, 4 \mapsto 5, 5 \mapsto 3\} \, ̊_9 \, ((\sigma \frown \tau) \oplus \{3 \mapsto E\})$.

The function *pred* is the predecessor function which is defined like this:

$$
\begin{array}{|l}
pred: \mathbf{N}_1 \to \mathbf{N} \\
\hline
pred\ i = i - 1
\end{array}
$$

(Note that *pred* is not part of standard **Z**. The successor function *succ* is, however.)

Chapter 8

Bags

8.1 Introduction

In this chapter I look at how bags—sometimes also known as *families* or *multi-sets*—are treated in **Z**. A bag of things is similar to a set in that the order of the elements is not significant, but—unlike a set—the number of occurrences of each object in the bag is significant.

After presenting the **Z** notation for a bag—and its formal definition—in the next section, I go on in section 8.3 to describe the various bag manipulating functions that are to be found in standard **Z**. The formal definitions of these operators can be found in chapter 25.

Section 8.4 contains a specification of sorting which illustrates the use of bags and sequences and then in section 8.5 I develop a specification of a simple vending machine in order to further illustrate how bags can be used in a specification. In order to make the specification more readable I introduce two operators not found in standard **Z**, namely the function *sum* and the sub-bag relation ⊈.

8.2 Fundamental Properties

In a bag multiple occurrences of the same thing are significant. Bags are written with *square* brackets ⟦ ⟧ enclosing the members of the bag, for example,

$$\llbracket john, john, fred, tom, tom, tom \rrbracket.$$

In this bag *john* occurs twice, *fred* once and *tom* three times. Bags are like sets in that the elements of a bag are not ordered in any way. Thus, the bag just mentioned can be written:

$$\llbracket tom, john, tom, john, tom, fred \rrbracket.$$

This is a bag of people. Let *Person* denote the type of all people. Then bag *Person* is the type of all bags of people. In **Z** a bag is a partial function from the type of the elements of the bag to the positive whole numbers, so:

$$\text{bag } Person == Person \nrightarrow \mathbf{N}_1.$$

85

(In general we have that bag $X == X \nrightarrow \mathbf{N_1}$.) The bag considered above is thus the following function:

$$\{john \mapsto 2, fred \mapsto 1, tom \mapsto 3\}.$$

8.3 Bag Manipulating Functions

The function *count* tells you how many times an object occurs in a bag. Let

$$L == [\![john, john, fred, tom, tom, tom]\!].$$

Then we have:

$$count\ L\ john = 2,$$
$$count\ L\ tom = 3,$$
$$count\ L\ karen = 0,$$
$$count\ L\ janet = 0.$$

Note that if a person x is not a member of the bag L, then *count* L x is zero.

The relation $\_$ in $\_$ holds between an object and a bag just in case that object is a member of the bag. It is analogous to the set membership relation $\in$. Using the previous example once again, we have that both *john* in L and $\neg(karen$ in $L)$.

The analogue in bag theory of set union is bag union, symbolized as $\uplus$. Here is an example of its use:

$$\{john \mapsto 2,\ fred \mapsto 1,\ tom \mapsto 3\} \uplus \{john \mapsto 3, karen \mapsto 1\}$$
$$= \{john \mapsto 5, fred \mapsto 1, tom \mapsto 3, karen \mapsto 1\}.$$

Given a sequence, the function *items* returns the bag of elements of the sequence, for example,

$$items\langle john, karen, john, john\rangle = \{john \mapsto 3, karen \mapsto 1\}.$$

8.4 A Specification of Sorting

The first example of a specification that I am going to give in this chapter is that of sorting a sequence of things into non-decreasing order. This will make use of both sequences and bags.

The problem that I am going to specify requires that we are given a sequence *in?* of objects of type X and that the output of the operation must be a sequence *out!* in which all the elements occur in non-decreasing order. (I say 'non-decreasing' rather than 'increasing' in order to allow for the possibility of duplicates.)

We can only sort things of type X if there is available a total order defined on elements of type X. A *total order* $\sqsubseteq$ is a relation over X which is reflexive, that is to say:

$$\forall x: X \bullet x \sqsubseteq x,$$

anti-symmetric, that is to say:

$$\forall x, y : X \bullet x \sqsubseteq y \land y \sqsubseteq x \Rightarrow x = y,$$

and transitive, that is to say:

$$\forall x, y, z : X \bullet x \sqsubseteq y \land y \sqsubseteq z \Rightarrow x \sqsubseteq z.$$

Furthermore, it must also have the additional property that every pair of elements of X are related, that is to say:

$$\forall x, y : X \bullet x \sqsubseteq y \lor y \sqsubseteq x.$$

An example of a total order is $\leq$ on the natural numbers.

The set of all total orders defined on a set X is *totord*[X] defined as follows:

$$
\boxed{
\begin{array}{l}
\llbracket X \rrbracket \\
\hline
totord : \mathbf{P}(X \leftrightarrow X) \\
\hline
\forall F : X \leftrightarrow X \bullet \\
\quad F \in totord \iff \\
\qquad ((\forall x : X \bullet x \mapsto x \in F) \land \\
\qquad (\forall x, y : X \bullet \{x \mapsto y, y \mapsto x\} \subseteq F \Rightarrow x = y) \land \\
\qquad (\forall x, y, z : X \bullet \{x \mapsto y, y \mapsto z\} \subseteq F \Rightarrow x \mapsto z \in F) \land \\
\qquad (\forall x, y : X \bullet x \mapsto y \in F \lor y \mapsto x \in F))
\end{array}
}
$$

In order to specify the operation of sorting using $\mathbf{Z}$ we need to define a generic function *nondecreasing*: $(X \leftrightarrow X) \rightarrow \mathbf{P}(\mathrm{seq}\, X)$, which, given a total order as its argument, yields the set of all sequences that are in non-decreasing order according to that total order.

$$
\boxed{
\begin{array}{l}
\llbracket X \rrbracket \\
\hline
nondecreasing : (X \leftrightarrow X) \rightarrow \mathbf{P}(\mathrm{seq}\, X) \\
\hline
\forall F : X \leftrightarrow X; \sigma : \mathrm{seq}\, X \bullet \\
\quad \sigma \in nondecreasing\, F \iff \\
\qquad (\forall i, j : \mathrm{dom}\, \sigma \mid i < j \bullet \sigma i \mapsto \sigma j \in F)
\end{array}
}
$$

Clearly, *nondecreasing F* is a set of sequences in non-decreasing order iff F is a total order. The specification of sorting can now be given as:

$$
\boxed{
\begin{array}{l}
Sort[X] \\
\hline
in?, out! : \mathrm{seq}\, X \\
F? : X \leftrightarrow X \\
\hline
F? \in totord[X] \\
out! \in nondecreasing\, F? \\
items(out!) = items(in?)
\end{array}
}
$$

We have to input the relation $F?$ because many different total orders can be defined on the same set. The output of the sort is non-decreasing. The output sequence must contain the same items as the input with the same frequency and this is captured by means of the predicate:

$$items(out!) = items(in?).$$

Note that this specification makes use of a generic schema. This is analogous to a subroutine with formal parameters.

8.5 The Specification of a Vending Machine

8.5.1 Introduction

In order to specify a vending machine we need a set *Good* of all the items that can be bought from the machine. At any given time only a subset of *Good* will actually be available from the machine. The state of the machine is specified by means of the schema *VendingMachine*:

$$
\begin{array}{l}
\rule{0.6cm}{0pt}\textit{VendingMachine} \rule{6cm}{0.4pt} \\
\text{coin}: \mathbf{P}\,\mathbf{N} \\
\text{cost}: \textit{Good} \rightarrow\!\!\!\!\rightarrow \mathbf{N} \\
\text{stock}: \text{bag } \textit{Good} \\
\text{float}: \text{bag } \mathbf{N} \\
\rule{6.5cm}{0.4pt} \\
\text{dom } stock \subseteq \text{dom } cost \\
\text{dom } float \subseteq coin \\
\end{array}
$$

The set *coin* is the set of all acceptable coins. A coin is identified with its value in pence. The function *cost* returns the value of a good in pence. For example,

$$cost(wispa) = 17,$$
$$cost(crisps) = 19,$$
$$cost(kitkat) = 19.$$

The bag *stock* records how many items of each type of good is currently stored in the machine. For example,

$$stock = \{wispa \mapsto 3, crisps \mapsto 11, kitkat \mapsto 1\}.$$

The bag *float* records how many coins of each type are currently in the machine. For example,

$$float = \{100 \mapsto 2, 20 \mapsto 3, 10 \mapsto 1, 2 \mapsto 57, 1 \mapsto 13\}.$$

This states that *float* contains two pound coins, three 20 pence coins, one 10 pence coin, 57 two-penny coins and 13 one-penny coins. The predicate dom $stock \subseteq$ dom $cost$ says that everything in the machine must have a price associated with it. The predicate dom $float \subseteq coin$ says that the money contained in this machine must be made up out of acceptable coins.

$\Delta VendingMachine$ and $\Xi VendingMachine$ are defined in the standard way:

$$\Delta VendingMachine \triangleq VendingMachine \wedge VendingMachine'$$

$$\Xi VendingMachine \triangleq \Delta VendingMachine \mid$$
$$coin' = coin \wedge$$
$$cost' = cost \wedge$$
$$stock' = stock \wedge$$
$$float' = float$$

Initially, the vending machine is empty:

```
┌─ Init VendingMachine' ─────────────────────────────────
│ VendingMachine'
├────────────────────────────────────────────────────────
│ coin' = { }
│ cost' = { }
│ stock' = [[ ]]
│ float' = [[ ]]
└────────────────────────────────────────────────────────
```

Note that initially the function $cost'$ is empty. This means that the machine to begin with contains no record of how much any item costs. Similarly, $coin'$ is empty. To get the machine working both of these sets have to be updated.

8.5.2 Pricing Goods

The first operation that I am going to specify is that of giving a good a particular price. It can also be used to reprice an item that already has a price associated with it. This is straightforward:

```
┌─ Price ─────────────────────────────────────────────────
│ Δ VendingMachine
│ item?: Good
│ price?: N
├────────────────────────────────────────────────────────
│ cost' = cost ⊕ {item? ↦ price?}
│ coin' = coin
│ stock' = stock
│ float' = float
└────────────────────────────────────────────────────────
```

The operation $Price$ always succeeds. We can give a price to an item which the machine does not currently stock. Therefore, the total specification is given by:

$$DoPrice \triangleq Price \wedge Success$$

where the schema *Success* is defined as follows:

```
┌─ Success ────────────────────────────────────────────
│ rep!: Report
├──────────────────────────────────────────────────────
│ rep! = 'Okay'
└──────────────────────────────────────────────────────
```

8.5.3 Acceptable Coins

The next operation involves telling the machine that a particular coin is now acceptable.

```
┌─ Accept ─────────────────────────────────────────────
│ Δ VendingMachine
│ c?: N
├──────────────────────────────────────────────────────
│ c? ∉ coin
│ coin' = coin ∪ {c?}
│ cost' = cost
│ stock' = stock
│ float' = float
└──────────────────────────────────────────────────────
```

The schema *Accept* has only a single precondition, namely the predicate $c? \notin coin$; hence we need to cope with the situation in which this is false.

```
┌─ AlreadyAcceptable ──────────────────────────────────
│ Ξ VendingMachine
│ c?: N
│ rep!: Report
├──────────────────────────────────────────────────────
│ c? ∈ coin
│ rep! = 'Coin already acceptable'
└──────────────────────────────────────────────────────
```

$$DoAccept \;\hat{=}\; Accept \wedge Success$$
$$\vee$$
$$AlreadyAcceptable$$

90

8.5.4 Restocking

The next operation that I am going to specify is that of restocking the machine with more goods.

```
┌─ ReStock ─────────────────────────────────
│ Δ VendingMachine
│ new?: bag Good
├───────────────────────────────────────────
│ dom new? ⊆ dom cost
│ stock' = stock ⊎ new?
│ coin' = coin
│ cost' = cost
│ float' = float
└───────────────────────────────────────────
```

ReStock fails if you try to add some goods to the machine which do not have prices associated with them.

```
┌─ GoodsNotPriced ──────────────────────────
│ Ξ VendingMachine
│ new?: bag Good
│ rep!: Report
├───────────────────────────────────────────
│ ¬(dom new? ⊆ dom cost)
│ rep! = 'Some goods are unpriced'
└───────────────────────────────────────────
```

$$DoReStock \stackrel{\wedge}{=} ReStock \wedge Success$$
$$\vee$$
$$GoodsNotPriced$$

8.5.5 Buying

The next thing that I am going to specify is the operation of somebody buying an item from the vending machine. At this stage it is not necessary to indicate how the buyer informs the machine which particular item he wants. In the schema *Buy* the variable *in?* represents the coins that the buyer inserts into the machine, the variable *out!* represents the coins that the machine outputs as change and *item!* is the actual thing that the buyer buys. In order to specify this operation I need to use the function *sum* and the relation ⋢.

The function *sum* calculates the total value of a bag of numbers. For example,

$$sum\{2 \mapsto 7, 5 \mapsto 3\} = 14 + 15 = 29.$$

It is defined like this:

```
┌───────────────────────────────────────────
│ sum: bag N → N
├───────────────────────────────────────────
│ ∀i, j: N; L: bag N •
│     sum⟦ ⟧ = 0 ∧
│     sum({i ↦ j} ⊎ L) = i * j + sum L
└───────────────────────────────────────────
```

91

Note that I have used set union in the definition of *sum*. This has the consequence that $\#L < \#(\{i \mapsto j\} \cup L)$.

The relation $\nsubseteq$ is the analogue of the subset relation in the realm of bags. For example,

$$\{wispa \mapsto 2, crisps \mapsto 4\} \nsubseteq \{wispa \mapsto 3, crisps \mapsto 11, kitkat \mapsto 1\}.$$

It is defined in this way:

$$
\begin{array}{|l}
\hline
[X] \\
\hline
\_ \nsubseteq \_ : \mathrm{bag}\, X \leftrightarrow \mathrm{bag}\, X \\
\hline
\forall L, M : \mathrm{bag}\, X \bullet \\
\quad L \nsubseteq M \iff (\forall x : X \bullet count\, L\ x \le count\, M\ x) \\
\hline
\end{array}
$$

The relation $L \nsubseteq M$ can be pronounced 'L is a sub-bag of M'.

$$
\begin{array}{|l}
\hline
Buy \\
\hline
\Delta\, VendingMachine \\
in?, out! : \mathrm{bag}\, \mathbf{N} \\
item! : Good \\
\hline
item! \in \mathrm{dom}\, stock \\
sum(in?) \ge cost(item!) \\
out! \nsubseteq float \\
\mathrm{dom}\, in? \subseteq coin \\
sum(in?) = sum(out!) + cost(item!) \\
stock' \uplus \{item! \mapsto 1\} = stock \\
float' \uplus out! = float \uplus in? \\
coin' = coin \\
cost' = cost \\
\hline
\end{array}
$$

The predicate $item! \in \mathrm{dom}\, stock$ is one of the preconditions of the operation *Buy*. You can only buy something from the vending machine if it is in the machine. The predicate $out! \nsubseteq float$ is another precondition of *Buy*. You cannot buy something from this machine if the machine does not have the correct amount of change to give you. The precondition $\mathrm{dom}\, in? \subseteq coin$ says that only acceptable coins can be used to buy goods. The predicate:

$$sum(in?) = sum(out!) + cost(item!)$$

says that the amount of money you put into the machine must have exactly the same value as the price of the thing you are buying added to your change. The predicate:

$$stock' \uplus \{item! \mapsto 1\} = stock$$

says that the item you buy from the machine is taken out of the machine and the predicate:

$$float' \uplus out! = float \uplus in?$$

92

says that the total value of the money in the machine is increased by the cost of the item you buy. This is because:

$$cost(item!) = sum(in?) - sum(out!).$$

The operation specified by *Buy* can go wrong in four ways, namely if the item requested is not currently in stock, if the customer inserts too little money into the machine, if the machine does not have the exact change needed and if the customer tries to insert a coin which is not acceptable.

```
┌─ NotInStock ─────────────────────────────────────────
│ Ξ VendingMachine
│ item!: Good
│ rep!: Report
├──────────────────────────────────────────────────────
│ item! ∉ dom stock
│ rep! = 'Item not in stock'
└──────────────────────────────────────────────────────
```

```
┌─ TooLittleMoney ─────────────────────────────────────
│ Ξ VendingMachine
│ in?: bag N
│ item!: Good
│ rep!: Report
├──────────────────────────────────────────────────────
│ sum(in?) < cost(item!)
│ rep! = 'Insert more money'
└──────────────────────────────────────────────────────
```

```
┌─ ExactChangeUnavailable ─────────────────────────────
│ Ξ VendingMachine
│ in?, out!: bag N
│ item!: Good
│ rep!: Report
├──────────────────────────────────────────────────────
│ ¬∃ L: bag N •
│        (L ⊈ float ∧ sum(in?) = sum(L) + cost(item!))
│ rep! = 'Correct change unavailable'
└──────────────────────────────────────────────────────
```

```
┌─ ForeignCoin ────────────────────────────────────────
│ Ξ VendingMachine
│ in?: bag N
│ rep!: Report
├──────────────────────────────────────────────────────
│ ¬(dom in? ⊆ coin)
│ rep! = 'Unacceptable coin'
└──────────────────────────────────────────────────────
```

$$DoBuy \mathrel{\hat{=}} Buy \wedge Success$$
$$\vee$$
$$NotInStock$$
$$\vee$$
$$TooLittleMoney$$
$$\vee$$
$$ExactChangeUnavailable$$
$$\vee$$
$$ForeignCoin$$

8.5.6 Profit Taking

The final operation that I am going to specify here is that of money being removed from the machine:

```
┌─ RemoveMoney ──────────────────────────────────────
│ Δ VendingMachine
│ profit!: bag N
├────────────────────────────────────────────────────
│ float′ ⊎ profit! = float
│ coin′ = coin
│ cost′ = cost
│ stock′ = stock
└────────────────────────────────────────────────────
```

The operation *RemoveMoney* goes wrong if you try removing money which is not present in the machine.

```
┌─ Profiteering ─────────────────────────────────────
│ Ξ VendingMachine
│ profit!: bag N
│ rep!: Report
├────────────────────────────────────────────────────
│ ¬∃ L: bag N •
│     (float′ ⊎ L = float ∧
│     profit! = L)
│ rep! = 'Such profit non-existent'
└────────────────────────────────────────────────────
```

$$DoRemoveMoney \mathrel{\hat{=}} RemoveMoney \wedge Success$$
$$\vee$$
$$Profiteering$$

Chapter 9

Free Types

9.1 Introduction

Recursive structures, like lists and trees, are used very frequently in software engineering and in this chapter I show how they can be defined as *free types* in **Z**. I do this in the context of developing a specification of a simple proof-checker and theorem-prover for a Hilbert-style formalization of the propositional calculus. To conclude the chapter I show how free types are formally defined in **Z**. This is done to emphasize the point that **Z**'s free type notation is merely syntactic sugar. It adds nothing to the power of the language. A specification involving free types can be mechanically transformed into one in which they do not appear.

9.2 Specifying Sequence Proofs

9.2.1 Introduction

In chapter 10 I shall discuss the proof-theory of the propositional calculus using a Gentzen N-type sequent calculus which is built on the idea that a proof is a particular kind of tree of sequents. There are many notions of a formal proof in mathematical logic and here I am going to look at the concept of a *sequence proof*. A logical system built on this notion of what constitutes a proof is known as a *Hilbert-style system* and in such a system the propositional calculus can be axiomatized as shown in Fig. 9.1. The logical system PS actually has an infinite number of axioms. For example, every substitution instance of the axiom PS1 is an axiom. Thus, all the following are axioms:

$$P \Rightarrow (P \Rightarrow P),$$
$$Q \Rightarrow (Q \Rightarrow Q),$$
$$(P \Rightarrow Q) \Rightarrow (R \Rightarrow (P \Rightarrow Q)),$$

A proof starts from axioms and succeeding formulas follow from earlier ones by means of *modus ponendo ponens*. The notion of a sequence proof can be defined as follows:

> A *sequence proof* of the formula A in the logical system PS is a finite sequence of formulas σ, such that each element of σ is either an axiom or it

follows from earlier elements of σ by means of *modus ponendo ponens* and the last element of σ is the formula A.

A sample proof is shown in Fig. 9.2.[1]

Representing Formulas

In translating a Hilbert-style logical system into **Z** the first thing we have to do is to somehow represent the well-formed formulas that the system uses. This is done using **Z**'s free type notation. Let *Ident* be the set of all the identifiers used in the object language of our logical system. Then the complete object language can be specified as the **Z** free type *Wff* in the following way:

$$Wff ::= at \langle\!\langle Ident \rangle\!\rangle$$
$$| \quad neg \langle\!\langle Wff \rangle\!\rangle$$
$$| \quad conj \langle\!\langle Wff \times Wff \rangle\!\rangle$$
$$| \quad disj \langle\!\langle Wff \times Wff \rangle\!\rangle$$
$$| \quad imp \langle\!\langle Wff \times Wff \rangle\!\rangle$$
$$| \quad equiv \langle\!\langle Wff \times Wff \rangle\!\rangle$$

This says that a well-formed formula is either an atomic formula consisting of an identifier or the negation of a formula or the conjunction of two formulas or the disjunction of two formulas or the implication formed from two formulas or the bi-implication formed from two formulas. (The phrase 'well-formed formula' is often abbreviated to 'wff'.) The functions *at*, *neg*, *conj*, *disj*, *imp* and *equiv* are known as *constructors*. To illustrate the use of this free type definition the formula $P \wedge \neg Q \Rightarrow R$ is depicted by the term:

$$imp(conj(at\,P, neg(at\,Q)), at\,R),$$

and the formula $(P \Rightarrow Q) \vee (Q \Rightarrow P)$ is represented by:

$$disj(imp(at\,P, at\,Q), imp(at\,Q, at\,P)).$$

The resulting notation is, I hope you will agree, only marginally more difficult to read than Lisp.

---

[1] This example is taken from Hunter (1971), pp. 73–74, and the system PS is also from there, p. 72.

Axioms

PS1 $A \Rightarrow (B \Rightarrow A)$

PS2 $(A \Rightarrow (B \Rightarrow C)) \Rightarrow ((A \Rightarrow B) \Rightarrow (A \Rightarrow C))$

PS3 $(\neg A \Rightarrow \neg B) \Rightarrow (B \Rightarrow A)$

Rule of inference

Modus ponendo ponens :   from A and $A \Rightarrow B$ infer B

Figure 9.1: The Hilbert-style system PS.

$\langle$ $(\neg Q \Rightarrow \neg P) \Rightarrow (P \Rightarrow Q),$

   $((\neg Q \Rightarrow \neg P) \Rightarrow (P \Rightarrow Q)) \Rightarrow$

      $(\neg P \Rightarrow ((\neg Q \Rightarrow \neg P) \Rightarrow (P \Rightarrow Q))),$

   $\neg P \Rightarrow ((\neg Q \Rightarrow \neg P) \Rightarrow (P \Rightarrow Q)),$

   $(\neg P \Rightarrow ((\neg Q \Rightarrow \neg P) \Rightarrow (P \Rightarrow Q))) \Rightarrow$

      $((\neg P \Rightarrow (\neg Q \Rightarrow \neg P)) \Rightarrow (\neg P \Rightarrow (P \Rightarrow Q))),$

   $(\neg P \Rightarrow (\neg Q \Rightarrow \neg P)) \Rightarrow (\neg P \Rightarrow (P \Rightarrow Q)),$

   $\neg P \Rightarrow (\neg Q \Rightarrow \neg P),$

   $\neg P \Rightarrow (P \Rightarrow Q)$

$\rangle$

Figure 9.2: An example proof in PS.

logical system PS does not have a rule of substitution, the axioms PS1,
53 are really axiom *schemas.*[2] In other words, they are *sets* of formulas.
are represented in **Z** as follows:

$ax1, ax2, ax3 : \mathbb{P} \ Wff$

$ax1 = \{A, B: Wff \bullet imp(A, imp(B, A))\}$
$ax2 = \{A, B, C: Wff \bullet$
$\qquad imp(imp(A, imp(B, C)), imp(imp(A, B), imp(A, C)))\}$
$ax3 = \{A, B: Wff \bullet imp(imp(neg\, A, neg\, B), imp(B, A))\}$

Here, $ax1$, $ax2$ and $ax3$ are the axiom schemas. The following are examples of axioms
corresponding to the schema $ax1$:

$$imp(at\, P, imp(at\, P, at\, P)),$$
$$imp(neg(at\, Q), imp(disj(at\, P, at\, R), neg(at\, Q))).$$

Representing Rules of Inference

A rule of inference is just a relation between a finite set of formulas and a formula.
The single rule of inference of PS, namely *modus ponendo ponens*, is thus defined like
this:

$mpp : \mathbb{F} \ Wff \leftrightarrow Wff$

$mpp = \{A, B: Wff \bullet \{A, imp(A, B)\} \mapsto B\}$

Representing Proofs

The predicate $isprf(\sigma, A)$ is true iff σ is a sequence proof of A in the logical system
PS. It is defined like this in **Z**:

$isprf : \mathrm{seq}\ Wff \leftrightarrow Wff$

$\forall \sigma: \mathrm{seq}\ Wff; \ A: Wff \bullet \sigma \mapsto A \in isprf \Longleftrightarrow$
$\qquad ((\forall i: \mathrm{dom}\ \sigma \bullet (\sigma i \in ax1 \cup ax2 \cup ax3 \ \vee$
$\qquad\qquad (\exists j, k: \mathrm{dom}\ \sigma \mid j < i \wedge k < i \wedge j \neq k \bullet$
$\qquad\qquad\qquad \{\sigma j, \sigma k\} \mapsto \sigma i \in mpp))) \wedge \sigma(\#\sigma) = A)$

Note that $isprf$ is not a function. The predicate $isthm(A)$ is true iff A is a theorem of
the logical system PS. It is defined in the following way:

$$isthm(A) == \exists \sigma: \mathrm{seq}\ Wff \bullet isprf(\sigma, A).$$

---

[2]This use of the word 'schema' has nothing to do with **Z**'s two-dimensional schema notation.

9.2.2 The Specifications

A Proof-checker

A proof-checker is a program that accepts as input a sequence of formulas σ? and a formula A? and tests to see whether or not σ? is indeed a proof of A? A proof-checker for the system PS can be specified as follows:

```
┌─ ProofChecker ──────────────────────────────────
│  σ?: seq Wff
│  A?: Wff
│  rep!: {'yes', 'no'}
├──────────────────────────────────────────────────
│  (σ? ↦ A? ∈ isprf ∧ rep! = 'yes')
│             ∨
│  (σ? ↦ A? ∉ isprf ∧ rep! = 'no')
└──────────────────────────────────────────────────
```

A Theorem-prover

A theorem-prover for PS is a program which accepts a formula A? as input and tells you whether or not A? is a theorem of PS. It can be specified as follows:

```
┌─ TheoremProver ─────────────────────────────────
│  A?: Wff
│  rep!: {'yes', 'no'}
├──────────────────────────────────────────────────
│  (isthm(A?) ∧ rep! = 'yes')
│             ∨
│  (¬ isthm(A?) ∧ rep! = 'no')
└──────────────────────────────────────────────────
```

A Proof-generator

A proof-generator for PS is a program which accepts a formula A? as input and outputs a proof of A? if it is a theorem, otherwise it outputs the empty sequence. It can be specified as follows:

```
┌─ ProofGenerator ────────────────────────────────
│  A?: Wff
│  σ!: seq Wff
│  rep!: {'yes', 'no'}
├──────────────────────────────────────────────────
│  (σ! ↦ A? ∈ isprf ∧ rep! = 'yes')
│             ∨
│  (¬ isthm(A?) ∧ σ! = ⟨ ⟩ ∧ rep! = 'no')
└──────────────────────────────────────────────────
```

Discussion

The specifications of a theorem-prover and a proof-generator for PS contained in the schemas *TheoremProver* and *ProofGenerator* once again illustrate the technique of procedural abstraction, since they do not contain any information about how a a theorem-prover or a proof-generator for PS could actually be implemented in a suitable programming language. They precisely state, however, a criterion for deciding whether or not any implementation is a theorem-prover or a proof-generator for PS.

9.3   The Formal Treatment of Free Types

As explained in Spivey (1989b), pp. 81–85, the notation for free types is purely syntactic. Although it adds nothing to the power of **Z**, the use of the free type notation for recursive data types makes their treatment more perspicuous. In this section I just want to show how we could have avoided the definition of the free type *Wff* given above. That definition is identical with the following one, which does not make use of free types at all:

$$
\begin{array}{|l}
at\colon Ident \rightarrowtail\!\!\!\!\rightarrow Wff \\
neg\colon Wff \rightarrowtail\!\!\!\!\rightarrow Wff \\
conj, disj, imp, equiv\colon (Wff \times Wff) \rightarrowtail\!\!\!\!\rightarrow Wff \\
\hline
\text{disjoint } \langle \operatorname{ran} at, \operatorname{ran} neg, \operatorname{ran} conj, \operatorname{ran} disj, \operatorname{ran} imp, \operatorname{ran} equiv \rangle \\
\forall U\colon \mathbf{P} \; Wff \; \bullet \\
\qquad (at(\!| Indent |\!) \cup \\
\qquad neg(\!| Wff |\!) \cup \\
\qquad conj(\!| Wff \times Wff |\!) \cup \\
\qquad disj(\!| Wff \times Wff |\!) \cup \\
\qquad imp(\!| Wff \times Wff |\!) \cup \\
\qquad equiv(\!| Wff \times Wff |\!) \subseteq U) \Rightarrow Wff \subseteq U
\end{array}
$$

The notation $\rightarrowtail\!\!\!\!\rightarrow$ is **Z**'s way of denoting the type of all *bijective* functions between X and Y. Let $f\colon X \rightarrowtail\!\!\!\!\rightarrow Y$ be a bijection. Then, f is also known as a *one-one and onto correspondence*. To say that a function is *onto* or a *surjection* just means that its range is the whole of Y and to say that a function is *one-one* or an *injection* just means that each element in the range of the function is the value of only one argument. An important property of bijections is that their inverses are also functions. The type of all bijections between X and Y can be defined as follows:

$$X \rightarrowtail\!\!\!\!\rightarrow Y == \{f\colon X \to Y \mid (\operatorname{ran} f = Y \wedge \forall x, y\colon X \bullet fx = fy \Rightarrow x = y)\}.$$

A different definition is given in chapter 23, but this only shows that there are several ways of defining many of **Z**'s symbols. There is nothing sacrosanct about a particular definition.

The reader is referred to Spivey (1989b) for a more thorough treatment of free types. The only further thing that I want to do here is to substantiate the claim I made in chapter 3, namely that a free type definition of the form:

$$W ::= a \mid b \mid c,$$

is equivalent to the set enumeration:

$$W == \{a, b, c\}.$$

This follows from the fact that the free type definition just amounts to this:

$$
\begin{array}{l}
\hline
a, b, c \colon W \\
\hline
\text{disjoint } \langle \{a\}, \{b\}, \{c\} \rangle \\
\forall U \colon \mathbf{P}\, W \bullet \{a, b, c\} \subseteq U \Rightarrow W \subseteq U
\end{array}
$$

Part III

Methods of Reasoning

Chapter 10

Formal Proof

10.1 Propositional Calculus

10.1.1 Introduction

As already mentioned there are two main ways of studying the nature of inference, namely the *proof-theoretic* and the *model-theoretic*. In chapter 2 I considered the model-theory of the propositional calculus and in this chapter I am going to look at the proof-theory of both the propositional and predicate calculuses. There are several ways in which proofs can be studied and the proof-architecture that I present is known as a *Gentzen N-type Sequent Calculus*. In this kind of system each propositional connective is associated with one or more *introduction* rules and one or more *elimination* rules.[1]

10.1.2 Notational Conventions

A *syntactic sequent* is something of the form $\Gamma \vdash A$, where Γ is a set of formulas of the propositional calculus, $\vdash$ is the *syntactic turnstile* which can be read as 'therefore' and A is a single proposition. Thus, the above sequent can be read as 'Γ therefore A' or 'from (the set of formulas) Γ we can infer A' or 'A follows from (the set of propositions) Γ'. The set Γ is known as the set of *premises* of the sequent and the formula A is called its *conclusion*.

The capital Greek letters Γ, Δ and Σ, sometimes with subscripts, will be used for arbitrary—possibly empty—sets of formulas and the letters A, B, C, P, Q and R, sometimes with subscripts, will be used for arbitrary propositions.[2] The set consisting of the propositions A, B and C will be written:

$$A, B, C$$

Furthermore, Γ, Δ means the union of Γ and Δ and Γ, A means the set formed from adding A to the set Γ. The comma here is, therefore, an *overloaded* operator.

---

[1]The term *proof-architecture* is due to John Derrick. Sundholm (1983) is an excellent introduction to several kinds of proof-architecture. Parts of Shoesmith and Smiley (1978) are also useful.

[2]The letters A, B and C will mainly be used in stating the rules of inference for the propositional and predicate calculuses.

10.1.3 The Inference Rules

Introduction An inference rule in the sequent calculus is a relation between one or more *input sequents* and an *output sequent*. Inference rules are written in the following way:

$$\overbrace{\Gamma_1 \vdash A_1}^{\text{first input sequent}} \quad \cdots \quad \overbrace{\Gamma_n \vdash A_n}^{n\text{th input sequent}}$$
$$\underbrace{\Delta \vdash B}_{\text{output sequent}} \quad name$$

Think of this as a mini-tree with n leaves and a root. Each leaf is an input sequent and the root is the output sequent. In this book the name of the rule is written to the right of the horizontal line which separates the input sequents from the output sequent.

Let $\heartsuit$ be an arbitrary two-place connective; then an *elimination* rule for $\heartsuit$ is one in which $\heartsuit$ appears in the conclusion of at least one of the input sequents to the rule and $\heartsuit$ does not occur in the conclusion of the output sequent of the rule. An *introduction* rule for $\heartsuit$ is one in which $\heartsuit$ does not appear in the conclusion of any of the input sequents to the rule, but $\heartsuit$ does occur in the conclusion of the output sequent of the rule.

Conjunction There are two elimination rules associated with conjunction. The first is *and* elimination on the right or $\wedge\text{-}elim_1$:

$$\frac{\Gamma \vdash A \wedge B}{\Gamma \vdash A} \quad \wedge\text{-}elim_1$$

Intuitively, this rule can be understood as follows. Assume that we have established in some way that the proposition $A \wedge B$ follows from the set of propositions Γ, then the proposition A by itself follows from the set of propositions Γ.

The second elimination rule for conjunction is *and* elimination on the left or $\wedge\text{-}elim_2$:

$$\frac{\Gamma \vdash A \wedge B}{\Gamma \vdash B} \quad \wedge\text{-}elim_2$$

Conjunction has a single introduction rule:

$$\frac{\Gamma \vdash A \qquad \Delta \vdash B}{\Gamma, \Delta \vdash A \wedge B} \quad \wedge\text{-}int$$

If A follows from Γ and B follows from Δ, then clearly $A \wedge B$ follows from the union of Γ and Δ.

Disjunction There is one elimination rule associated with disjunction. It is called $\lor$-*elim*:

$$\frac{\Gamma \vdash A \lor B \qquad \Delta, A \vdash C \qquad \Sigma, B \vdash C}{\Gamma, \Delta, \Sigma \vdash C} \quad \lor\text{-}elim$$

This is the most complicated rule of inference in the sequent calculus and for that reason I will give several examples of its use later in this chapter, namely on pp. 114 and 115.

There are two introduction rules associated with disjunction, namely $\lor$-*int*$_1$ and $\lor$-*int*$_2$:

$$\frac{\Gamma \vdash A}{\Gamma \vdash A \lor B} \quad \lor\text{-}int_1 \qquad\qquad \frac{\Gamma \vdash B}{\Gamma \vdash A \lor B} \quad \lor\text{-}int_2$$

Implication There is one elimination rule associated with implication. It is called $\Rightarrow$-*elim*. Some people refer to this rule as *modus ponendo ponens*. (This is often abbreviated to *modus ponens*.) It works like this:

$$\frac{\Gamma \vdash A \qquad \Delta \vdash A \Rightarrow B}{\Gamma, \Delta \vdash B} \quad \Rightarrow\text{-}elim$$

Do not confuse the rule *modus ponens* with the formula $(A \land (A \Rightarrow B)) \Rightarrow B$ as Polimeni and Straight (1985), p. 19, do. Dodgson (1895) pointed out the error in this many years ago.

There is one introduction rule associated with implication. It is $\Rightarrow$-*int*:

$$\frac{\Gamma \vdash B}{\Gamma \setminus \{A\} \vdash A \Rightarrow B} \quad \Rightarrow\text{-}int$$

The formula A can occur in the set of premises Γ, but it does not have to.

Bi-implication The elimination rules for bi-implication allow us to change them into implications:

$$\frac{\Gamma \vdash A \Longleftrightarrow B}{\Gamma \vdash A \Rightarrow B} \quad \Longleftrightarrow\text{-}elim_1 \qquad\qquad \frac{\Gamma \vdash A \Longleftrightarrow B}{\Gamma \vdash B \Rightarrow A} \quad \Longleftrightarrow\text{-}elim_2$$

There is a single introduction rule for bi-implication:

$$\frac{\Gamma \vdash A \Rightarrow B \qquad \Delta \vdash B \Rightarrow A}{\Gamma, \Delta \vdash A \Longleftrightarrow B} \quad \Longleftrightarrow\text{-}int$$

Negation and the Always False Proposition   Negation has a single elimination rule:

$$\frac{\Gamma \vdash A \qquad\qquad \Delta \vdash \neg A}{\Gamma, \Delta \vdash \textit{false}} \quad \neg\text{-}\textit{elim}$$

Negation has a single introduction rule:

$$\frac{\Gamma, A \vdash \textit{false}}{\Gamma \vdash \neg A} \quad \neg\text{-}\textit{int}$$

The introduction and elimination rules for negation are easy to remember if you make use of the fact that $\neg A$ is logically equivalent to $A \Rightarrow \textit{false}$. Thus, they can be seen as special cases of the introduction and elimination rules for implication.

Associated with negation there is also a double negation elimination rule:[3]

$$\frac{\Gamma \vdash \neg\neg A}{\Gamma \vdash A} \quad \neg\neg\text{-}\textit{elim}$$

The final rule that I am going to introduce here only involves the always false proposition *false*. It is known as *false* elimination:

$$\frac{\Gamma \vdash \textit{false}}{\Gamma \vdash A} \quad \textit{false-elim}$$

Structural Rules   Sometimes in presentations of the sequent calculus you will see mention of a structural rule known variously as *thinning* or *weakening* which allows you to add irrelevant premises to a sequent. It looks like this:

$$\frac{\Gamma \vdash A}{\Gamma, \Delta \vdash A} \quad \textit{weak}$$

With the non-structural rules as defined above it is never necessary, however, to use weakening in a proof.

Another structural rule that is often mentioned is known as *cut*:

$$\frac{\Gamma \vdash A \qquad\qquad \Delta, A \vdash B}{\Gamma, \Delta \vdash B} \quad \textit{cut}$$

There is, however, a very important meta-theoretical result about the sequent calculus which says that any proof involving *cut* can be transformed to one which does not make use of it. Not surprisingly, it is known as *cut*-elimination.[4]

---

[3] For those of you with some knowledge of other logical systems, if the rule for double negation elimination is left out of our formal system, then the resulting system is known as *intuitionistic* logic.

[4] See Sundholm (1983) for more information.

$$\frac{P \wedge Q \vdash P \wedge Q}{P \wedge Q \vdash Q} \wedge\text{-}elim_2 \qquad \frac{P \wedge Q \vdash P \wedge Q}{P \wedge Q \vdash P} \wedge\text{-}elim_1$$
$$\frac{}{P \wedge Q \vdash Q \wedge P} \wedge\text{-}int$$

Figure 10.1: A tree-proof of the commutativity of $\wedge$.

10.1.4 Proofs

A *proof* in the sequent calculus is written as a tree with the root at the bottom. Such trees are known as *proof-trees* or *tree-proofs*. Each leaf must be of the form $\Gamma \vdash A$, where $A \in \Gamma$. An example of a proof is shown in Fig. 10.1. More rigorously, a *proof-tree* is a tree—at each node of which there is located a sequent—which satisfies the following properties:

1. Every sequent located at a leaf node must be of the form $\Gamma \vdash A$, where $A \in \Gamma$.

2. Each mini-tree must be a (substitution) instance of one of the rules of inference mentioned above. (A *mini-tree* is any tree obtained from the original tree which just consists of a node and all of that node's children.)

Some Examples of Proofs Some examples of tree-proofs should make the above ideas clearer. First, I show a proof of the sequent $\neg P \wedge Q \vdash P \Rightarrow Q$.

$$\frac{\neg P \wedge Q \vdash \neg P \wedge Q}{\neg P \wedge Q \vdash Q} \wedge\text{-}elim_2$$
$$\frac{}{\neg P \wedge Q \vdash P \Rightarrow Q} \Rightarrow\text{-}int$$

The next example is a proof of the sequent $P \wedge Q \vdash P \Longleftrightarrow Q$.

$$\frac{P \wedge Q \vdash P \wedge Q}{P \wedge Q \vdash Q} \wedge\text{-}elim_2 \qquad \frac{P \wedge Q \vdash P \wedge Q}{P \wedge Q \vdash P} \wedge\text{-}elim_1$$
$$\frac{}{P \wedge Q \vdash P \Rightarrow Q} \Rightarrow\text{-}int \qquad \frac{}{P \wedge Q \vdash Q \Rightarrow P} \Rightarrow\text{-}int$$
$$\frac{}{P \wedge Q \vdash P \Longleftrightarrow Q} \Longleftrightarrow\text{-}int$$

The next example is a proof of the sequent $P \wedge \neg Q \vdash \neg (P \wedge Q)$.

$$\frac{P \wedge \neg Q \vdash P \wedge \neg Q}{P \wedge \neg Q \vdash \neg Q} \wedge\text{-}elim_2 \qquad \frac{P \wedge Q \vdash P \wedge Q}{P \wedge Q \vdash Q} \wedge\text{-}elim_1$$
$$\frac{P \wedge \neg Q, P \wedge Q \vdash \mathit{false}}{} \neg\text{-}elim$$
$$\frac{}{P \wedge \neg Q \vdash \neg (P \wedge Q)} \neg\text{-}int$$

The next example is a proof of the sequent $Q \vdash P \wedge Q \Longleftrightarrow P$.

$$
\cfrac{
\cfrac{
\cfrac{
\cfrac{P \wedge Q \vdash P \wedge Q}{P \wedge Q \vdash P} \wedge\text{-}elim_1
}{P \wedge Q \vdash Q \Rightarrow P} \Rightarrow\text{-}int \quad Q \vdash Q
}{
\cfrac{Q, P \wedge Q \vdash P}{Q \vdash P \wedge Q \Rightarrow P} \Rightarrow\text{-}int
} \Rightarrow\text{-}elim
\qquad
\cfrac{
\cfrac{Q \vdash Q \quad P \vdash P}{Q, P \vdash P \wedge Q} \wedge\text{-}int
}{Q \vdash P \Rightarrow P \wedge Q} \Rightarrow\text{-}int
}{Q \vdash P \wedge Q \Longleftrightarrow P} \Longleftrightarrow\text{-}int
$$

Hints for Constructing Proofs   Say you are given the following problem to solve: 'Prove that the sequent $P \Rightarrow Q, Q \Rightarrow R \vdash P \Rightarrow R$ follows from the axioms and rules given above'. The first thing to do is to make the sequent you are trying to prove into the root of a proof-tree. (In trying to construct proof-trees it is best to work from the bottom upwards to the leaves.) Then look at all the available rules and pick one of those that could have been used to derive the sequent that you are trying to prove. Work out what the premises and conclusions of the chosen rule must be in order for it to have had a correct application at that point in the proof. Then repeat this process with the input sequents you have generated. If ever you get to an instance of an axiom sequent $\Gamma \vdash A$, where $A \in \Gamma$, then that branch of the proof-tree needs no further proof. (Sometimes backtracking might be necessary.)

   For the propositional calculus these hints can be turned into an algorithm. For stronger logical systems, like the predicate calculus, it can be proved that no algorithm can be devised to construct the proof of every formula submitted to it.

An Example   Consider the problem of trying to prove the sequent:

$$
P \Rightarrow Q, Q \Rightarrow R \vdash P \Rightarrow R.
$$

The first thing we do is to make this sequent into the root of a proof-tree. Then, we need to try and work out which rule was used in order to derive it. Because the conclusion of the sequent we are trying to prove is $P \Rightarrow R$, it is likely that the rule used to derive this sequent was $\Rightarrow\text{-}int$. So, we draw the following partial tree:

$$
\cfrac{P \Rightarrow Q, Q \Rightarrow R, P \vdash R}{P \Rightarrow Q, Q \Rightarrow R \vdash P \Rightarrow R} \Rightarrow\text{-}int
$$

In this case it is easy to work out what Γ, A and B are in the rule $\Rightarrow\text{-}int$. Sometimes it is not so straightforward.

Now we have to decide what rule was used to derive $P \Rightarrow Q, Q \Rightarrow R, P \vdash R$. It could have been one of several rules, but because the only connective in this sequent is implication, it is likely to have been a rule dealing with implication. It cannot have been $\Rightarrow$-*int*, so let us try $\Rightarrow$-*elim*:

$$\frac{\dfrac{\Gamma \vdash A \qquad\qquad\qquad\qquad\qquad\qquad \Delta \vdash A \Rightarrow R}{P \Rightarrow Q, Q \Rightarrow R, P \vdash R} \;{\Rightarrow}\text{-}elim}{P \Rightarrow Q, Q \Rightarrow R \vdash P \Rightarrow R} \;{\Rightarrow}\text{-}int$$

We know that B must be R in $\Rightarrow$-*elim*, but what are Γ, Δ and A? Let us try $A \equiv Q$, $\Delta \equiv Q \Rightarrow R$ and $\Gamma \equiv P, P \Rightarrow Q$. This gives us:

$$\frac{\dfrac{P, P \Rightarrow Q \vdash Q \qquad\qquad\qquad\qquad\qquad Q \Rightarrow R \vdash Q \Rightarrow R}{P \Rightarrow Q, Q \Rightarrow R, P \vdash R} \;{\Rightarrow}\text{-}elim}{P \Rightarrow Q, Q \Rightarrow R \vdash P \Rightarrow R} \;{\Rightarrow}\text{-}int$$

The sequent $Q \Rightarrow R \vdash Q \Rightarrow R$ is of the form $\Gamma \vdash A$ with $A \in \Gamma$, so it requires no further proof. It is easy to see that $P, P \Rightarrow Q \vdash Q$ is the output sequent of $\Rightarrow$-*elim* with $A \equiv P$, $B \equiv Q$, $\Gamma \equiv A$ and $\Delta \equiv P \Rightarrow Q$. Putting all this together results in the following complete proof-tree:

$$\frac{\dfrac{\dfrac{P \vdash P \qquad P \Rightarrow Q \vdash P \Rightarrow Q}{P, P \Rightarrow Q \vdash Q}\;{\Rightarrow}\text{-}elim \qquad\qquad Q \Rightarrow R \vdash Q \Rightarrow R}{P \Rightarrow Q, Q \Rightarrow R, P \vdash R}\;{\Rightarrow}\text{-}elim}{P \Rightarrow Q, Q \Rightarrow R \vdash P \Rightarrow R}\;{\Rightarrow}\text{-}int$$

Translating into a Linear Form Because tree-proofs tend to become very large many people who advocate this kind of sequent calculus actually use a linear style of presentation. For example, Suppes (1957), Lemmon (1965), Mates (1972) and Newton–Smith (1985) do this. In this section I will show you how to translate a tree-proof into an equivalent linear one.

Using the proof of the sequent $P \Rightarrow Q, Q \Rightarrow R \vdash P \Rightarrow R$ as an example, the first thing we have to do is to label each sequent. This results in the following proof:

$$\frac{\dfrac{\dfrac{1{:}\,P \vdash P \qquad 2{:}\,P \Rightarrow Q \vdash P \Rightarrow Q}{3{:}\,P, P \Rightarrow Q \vdash Q}\;{\Rightarrow}\text{-}elim \qquad\qquad 4{:}\,Q \Rightarrow R \vdash Q \Rightarrow R}{5{:}\,P \Rightarrow Q, Q \Rightarrow R, P \vdash R}\;{\Rightarrow}\text{-}elim}{6{:}\,P \Rightarrow Q, Q \Rightarrow R \vdash P \Rightarrow R}\;{\Rightarrow}\text{-}int$$

When labelling a tree-proof we can only label an internal or root node when we have labelled every node—except that node—in the subtree which has that node as its root. Leaf nodes can be labelled at any time. We then linearize the proof to a sequence of 4-tuples:

$$
\begin{array}{llll}
1 & (1) & P & ass \\
2 & (2) & P \Rightarrow Q & ass \\
1,2 & (3) & Q & 1,2 \Rightarrow\text{-}elim \\
4 & (4) & Q \Rightarrow R & ass \\
1,2,4 & (5) & R & 3,4 \Rightarrow\text{-}elim \\
2,4 & (6) & P \Rightarrow R & 5 \Rightarrow\text{-}int
\end{array}
$$

Each line of such a sequence contains four elements. The leftmost is a set of numbers which represents the set of premises of a sequent. A number i in this set stands for the formula—the third element—in line i. Moving right, the number in parentheses (j) is the line number and to the right of this we have a formula. The rightmost item on every line is an annotation. The annotation ass stands for $assumption$.

10.1.5 Derived Rules of Inference

An example of a $derived$ rule of inference is $modus\ tollendo\ tollens$:

$$
\frac{\Gamma \vdash A \Rightarrow B \qquad \Delta \vdash \neg B}{\Gamma, \Delta \vdash \neg A} \ mtt
$$

Intuitively, this rule states that if we have established that the proposition $\neg B$ follows from the set of propositions Δ and also that the proposition $A \Rightarrow B$ follows from the set of propositions Γ, then the proposition $\neg A$ follows from the union of Δ and Γ. The derived rule mtt can be proved as follows:

$$
\frac{\dfrac{A \vdash A \qquad \Gamma \vdash A \Rightarrow B}{\Gamma, A \vdash B} \Rightarrow\text{-}elim \qquad \Delta \vdash \neg B}{\dfrac{\Gamma, \Delta, A \vdash false}{\Gamma, \Delta \vdash \neg A} \neg\text{-}int} \neg\text{-}elim
$$

So, whenever we have managed to prove the sequents $\Delta \vdash \neg B$ and $\Gamma \vdash A \Rightarrow B$, then we can use the derived rule mtt to prove $\Delta, \Gamma \vdash \neg A$. Think of mtt as a $macro$ which is replaced by its partial proof.

Another useful derived rule of inference is $modus\ tollendo\ ponens$:

$$
\frac{\Gamma \vdash P \vee Q \qquad \Delta \vdash \neg P}{\Gamma, \Delta \vdash Q} \ mtp
$$

This can be derived by means of the following proof:

$$\cfrac{\Gamma \vdash P \vee Q \qquad \cfrac{\cfrac{\Delta \vdash \neg P \qquad P \vdash P}{\Delta, P \vdash false} \; \neg\text{-}elim}{\cfrac{\Delta, P \vdash false}{\Delta, P \vdash Q} \; false\text{-}elim} \qquad Q \vdash Q}{\Gamma, \Delta \vdash Q} \; \vee\text{-}elim$$

Schematically, in linear form the proof looks like this:

$$
\begin{array}{lll}
\Gamma & (i) \quad P \vee Q & \\
\Delta & (j) \quad \neg P & \\
j+1 & (j+1) \quad P & ass \\
\Delta, j+1 & (j+2) \quad false & j, j+1 \; \neg\text{-}elim \\
\Delta, j+1 & (j+3) \quad Q & j+2 \; false\text{-}elim \\
j+4 & (j+4) \quad Q & ass \\
\Gamma, \Delta & (j+5) \quad Q & i, j+3, j+4 \; \vee\text{-}elim \\
\end{array}
$$

10.1.6 Some Examples of Proofs

Here I am going to prove that conjunction distributes backwards through disjunction. This is expressed in the sequent:

$$(P \vee Q) \wedge R \dashv\vdash (P \wedge R) \vee (Q \wedge R).$$

(This distributive property will be required on pp. 127ff. of the next chapter where I prove that set intersection distributes backwards through set union.) The notation $A \dashv\vdash B$ means that both $A \vdash B$ and $B \vdash A$ obtain. Hence the proof of the sequent just mentioned is done in two stages. First, I prove $(P \vee Q) \wedge R \vdash (P \wedge R) \vee (Q \wedge R)$. This is done by means of the following proof:

$$
\begin{array}{lll}
1 & (1) \quad (P \vee Q) \wedge R & ass \\
1 & (2) \quad R & 1 \; \wedge\text{-}elim_2 \\
1 & (3) \quad P \vee Q & 1 \; \wedge\text{-}elim_1 \\
4 & (4) \quad P & ass \\
1,4 & (5) \quad P \wedge R & 4, 2 \; \wedge\text{-}int \\
1,4 & (6) \quad (P \wedge R) \vee (Q \wedge R) & 5 \; \vee\text{-}int_1 \\
7 & (7) \quad Q & ass \\
1,7 & (8) \quad Q \wedge R & 7, 2 \; \wedge\text{-}int \\
1,7 & (9) \quad (P \wedge R) \vee (Q \wedge R) & 8 \; \vee\text{-}int_2 \\
1 & (10) \quad (P \wedge R) \vee (Q \wedge R) & 3, 6, 9 \; \vee\text{-}elim \\
\end{array}
$$

The operation of the rule $\vee$-*elim* is a bit tricky to get used to, so I will explain its operation here in more detail. Recall the tree representation of the rule $\vee$-*elim*:

$$\frac{\Gamma \vdash A \vee B \qquad \Delta, A \vdash C \qquad \Sigma, B \vdash C}{\Gamma, \Delta, \Sigma \vdash C} \ \vee\text{-}elim$$

Line (3) of the above proof is:

$$\overbrace{(P \vee Q) \wedge R}^{\Gamma} \vdash \overbrace{P \vee Q}^{A \vee B}$$

Line (6) is:

$$\overbrace{(P \vee Q) \wedge R,}^{\Delta} \ \overbrace{P}^{A} \ \vdash \overbrace{(P \wedge R) \vee (Q \wedge R)}^{C}$$

And line (9) is:

$$\overbrace{(P \vee Q) \wedge R,}^{\Sigma} \ \overbrace{Q}^{B} \ \vdash \overbrace{(P \wedge R) \vee (Q \wedge R)}^{C}$$

In this case Γ, Δ and Σ happen to be the same. So, applying the graphical version of the rule $\vee$-*elim* we get:

$$(P \vee Q) \wedge R \vdash (P \wedge R) \vee (Q \wedge R),$$

which is represented in the above proof as line (10).

Second, we have to prove $(P \wedge R) \vee (Q \wedge R) \vdash (P \vee Q) \wedge R$. The following proof achieves this:

1	(1)	$(P \wedge R) \vee (Q \wedge R)$	*ass*
2	(2)	$P \wedge R$	*ass*
2	(3)	P	2 $\wedge$-*elim*$_1$
2	(4)	$P \vee Q$	3 $\vee$-*int*$_1$
2	(5)	R	2 $\wedge$-*elim*$_2$
2	(6)	$(P \vee Q) \wedge R$	4, 5 $\wedge$-*int*
7	(7)	$Q \wedge R$	*ass*
7	(8)	Q	7 $\wedge$-*elim*$_1$
7	(9)	$P \vee Q$	8 $\vee$-*int*$_2$
7	(10)	R	7 $\wedge$-*elim*$_2$
7	(11)	$(P \vee Q) \wedge R$	9, 10 $\wedge$-*int*
1	(12)	$(P \vee Q) \wedge R$	1, 6, 11 $\vee$-*elim*

I will again explain the last line of this proof in a bit more detail. Line (1) is:

$$\overbrace{(P \wedge R) \vee (Q \wedge R)}^{\Gamma} \vdash \overbrace{(P \wedge R)}^{A} \vee \overbrace{(Q \wedge R)}^{B}$$

Line (6) is:

$$\overbrace{P \wedge R}^{A} \vdash \overbrace{(P \vee Q) \wedge R}^{C}$$

Here Δ is the empty set. Line (11) is:

$$\overbrace{Q \wedge R}^{B} \vdash \overbrace{(P \vee Q) \wedge R}^{C}$$

Here, Σ is empty as well. So, the conclusion is:

$$(P \wedge R) \vee (Q \wedge R) \vdash (P \vee Q) \wedge R.$$

This explains the meaning of line (12) in the above proof.

The next thing that I am going to prove is the following de Morgan's law:

$$\neg(P \vee Q) \dashv\vdash \neg P \wedge \neg Q.$$

First, I prove $\neg P \wedge \neg Q \vdash \neg(P \vee Q)$. The proof is as follows:

1	(1)	$\neg P \wedge \neg Q$	ass
2	(2)	$P \vee Q$	ass
1	(3)	$\neg P$	1 $\wedge$-$elim_1$
1,2	(4)	Q	2,3 mtp
1	(5)	$\neg Q$	1 $\wedge$-$elim_2$
1,2	(6)	$false$	4,5 $\neg$-$elim$
1	(7)	$\neg(P \vee Q)$	6 $\neg$-int

This illustrates the use of the derived rule *mtp*. We could have proved the same result without the use of the rule, thus:

1	(1)	$\neg P \wedge \neg Q$	ass
2	(2)	$P \vee Q$	ass
1	(3)	$\neg P$	1 $\wedge$-$elim_1$
4	(4)	P	ass
1,4	(5)	$false$	3,4 $\neg$-$elim$
1,4	(6)	Q	5 $false$-$elim$
7	(7)	Q	ass
1,2	(8)	Q	2,6,7 $\vee$-$elim$
1	(9)	$\neg Q$	1 $\wedge$-$elim_2$
1,2	(10)	$false$	8,9 $\neg$-$elim$
1	(11)	$\neg(P \vee Q)$	10 $\neg$-int

This shows why derived rules of inference, like *mtp*, can be thought of as macros, since their use can always be eliminated and replaced by applications of the primitive rules of inference.

Second, I prove the sequent $\neg(P \vee Q) \vdash \neg P \wedge \neg Q$, as follows:

1	(1)	$\neg(P \vee Q)$	ass
2	(2)	P	ass
2	(3)	$P \vee Q$	2 $\vee$-int_1
1,2	(4)	$false$	1,3 $\neg$-$elim$
1	(5)	$\neg P$	4 $\neg$-int
6	(6)	Q	ass
6	(7)	$P \vee Q$	6 $\vee$-int_2
1,6	(8)	$false$	1,7 $\neg$-$elim$
1	(9)	$\neg Q$	8 $\neg$-int
1	(10)	$\neg P \wedge \neg Q$	5,9 $\wedge$-int

The next example is a proof of the law of the excluded middle. The proof of $\vdash P \vee \neg P$ is as follows:

1	(1)	$\neg(P \vee \neg P)$	ass
1	(2)	$\neg P \wedge \neg\neg P$	1 de Morgan
1	(3)	$\neg\neg P$	2 $\wedge$-$elim_2$
1	(4)	P	3 $\neg\neg$-$elim$
1	(5)	$\neg P$	2 $\wedge$-$elim_1$
1	(6)	$false$	4,5 $\neg$-$elim$
	(7)	$\neg\neg(P \vee \neg P)$	6 $\neg$-int
	(8)	$P \vee \neg P$	7 $\neg\neg$-$elim$

This proof contains the annotation 1 *de Morgan* in line (2). This illustrates how we can use previously derived sequents as rules of inference in succeeding proofs.

10.1.7 Soundness and Completeness

In this chapter I have presented the proof-theory of the propositional calculus and in chapter 2 I presented its model-theory. This calculus is both complete and sound. To say that a logical system is *sound* means that if $\Gamma \vdash P$ is a derivable sequent, then $\Gamma \models P$ is valid and to say that a logical system is *complete* or *adequate* means that if $\Gamma \models P$ is valid, then $\Gamma \vdash P$ is a derivable sequent.

Although the two notions of syntactic and semantic consequence are extensionally equivalent in the case of the propositional calculus, this is not true of all logical systems. What is true of all logical systems, however, is that the semantic concept of logical consequence is always prior to the syntactic concept.[5] What this means in practice is that if we construct a logical system and devise a proof-theory and a model-theory for it and then discover that either soundness or completeness fails, then—if it is possible to remedy the situation—it is the proof-theory that we must alter rather than the model-theory.

---

[5]This has been forcefully argued by Dummett (1975) and I have found by talking to several mathematical logicians that it is generally accepted by them.

10.2 Predicate Calculus

10.2.1 Quantifier Rules

Free, Binding and Bound Variable Occurrences

A *primitive* predicate is one which does not contain either any truth-functional connectives or any quantifiers. For example, *x borders albania* is a primitive predicate. Every occurrence of a variable x is free in a primitive predicate. So, the only occurrence of x in *x borders albania* is free, both occurrences of x in *x borders x* are free and both the occurrence of x and that of y in *x borders y* are free.

In order to work out if a particular occurrence of x is free in an arbitrary formula A we use a recursive definition. An occurrence of the variable x is *free* in the formula A iff its being so follows from one or more of the following seven clauses:

1. An occurrence of x is free in $\neg A$ iff the corresponding occurrence of x is free in A.

2. An occurrence of x is free in $A \wedge B$ iff the corresponding occurrence of x is free in A or B (depending on which conjunct it occurs in).

3. An occurrence of x is free in $A \vee B$ iff the corresponding occurrence of x is free in A or B.

4. An occurrence of x is free in $A \Rightarrow B$ iff the corresponding occurrence of x is free in A or B.

5. An occurrence of x is free in $A \Longleftrightarrow B$ iff the corresponding occurrence of x is free in A or B.

6. An occurrence of x is free in $\forall y: Y \bullet A$ iff x is different from y and that occurrence of x is free in A.

7. An occurrence of x is free in $\exists y: Y \bullet A$ iff x is different from y and that occurrence of x is free in A.

The occurrence of a variable x in a quantified formula $\forall x: X \bullet A$ or $\exists x: X \bullet A$ following either the universal or the existential quantifier is called the *binding* occurrence of that variable and the formula A is called the *scope* of that binding occurrence.

An occurrence of a variable x is *bound* in a formula $\forall x: X \bullet A$ or $\exists x: X \bullet A$ iff x is not a binding occurrence and the corresponding occurrence of x is free in A.

Note that it is *occurrences* of variables that are either free, binding or bound and not variables. This is because the same variable can occur both free and bound in the same formula. For example, consider the formula:

$$x \text{ borders } y \wedge \forall x: Europe \bullet (y \text{ borders } x \vee \exists x: Europe: x \text{ borders } y).$$

All occurrences of y are free in this formula as is the first occurrence of x. The second and fourth occurrences of x are binding occurrences and the third and fifth

117

occurrences of x are bound occurrences. The third occurrence of x is bound by the second occurrence and lies in its scope. The fifth occurrence of x is bound by the fourth occurrence and it lies within the scope of that occurrence.

The Universal Quantifier

There is one elimination rule associated with the universal quantifier, namely $\forall$-*elim*:

$$\frac{\Gamma \vdash \forall x\colon X \bullet A}{\Gamma \vdash A[t/x]} \quad \forall\text{-}elim$$

Here, t is any term of the same type as x. The notation $A[t/x]$ stands for that formula which is obtained by substituting t for all free occurrences of x in A.

There is a single introduction rule for the universal quantifier, namely $\forall$-*int*:

$$\frac{\Gamma \vdash A}{\Gamma \vdash \forall x\colon X \bullet A[x/a]} \quad \forall\text{-}int$$

Here, x must be a variable of type X and a a constant of the same type which must not occur in Γ.

The Existential Quantifier

There is one elimination rule associated with the existential quantifier, namely $\exists$-*elim*:

$$\frac{\Gamma \vdash \exists x\colon X \bullet A \qquad \Delta, A[a/x] \vdash C}{\Gamma, \Delta \vdash C} \quad \exists\text{-}elim$$

Here, a is a constant of type X which must not occur in Γ, Δ, $\exists x\colon X \bullet A$ or C. The reason for using the letter C in the statement of this rule—rather than B—is to bring out the connection between this rule and the rule of or-elimination.

There is one introduction rule associated with the existential quantifier, namely $\exists$-*int*:

$$\frac{\Gamma \vdash A[t/x]}{\Gamma \vdash \exists x\colon X \bullet A} \quad \exists\text{-}int$$

Here, t must be a term of type X and x is a variable of the same type.

Rules for Identity

The elimination rule for identity is:

$$\frac{\Gamma \vdash A \qquad \qquad \Delta \vdash t = u}{\Gamma, \Delta \vdash B} \quad \text{=-}elim$$

Here, t and u are any terms of the same type and B is like A except that u has been substituted for t one or more times. There is *no* need to substitute u for *all* occurrences of t.

The introduction rule for identity is slightly different from those we have encountered so far. It allows us to start proofs from leaf nodes of the form $\vdash t = t$, where t is any term. It will be referred to as =-*int*.

10.2.2   Some Predicate Calculus Proofs

In order to illustrate the rules of inference just introduced I will now give some sample proofs. These will be written in the linear style introduced at the end of the previous section. The sequent that I am going to prove first is:

$$\forall x \colon X \bullet (Px \Rightarrow Qx), \forall x \colon X \bullet (Qx \Rightarrow Rx) \vdash \forall x \colon X \bullet (Px \Rightarrow Rx),$$

where I write Px, Qx and Rx in order to indicate that x can occur free in each of those predicates.

1	(1)	$\forall x \colon X \bullet (Px \Rightarrow Qx)$	*ass*
1	(2)	$Pa \Rightarrow Qa$	1 $\forall$-*elim*
3	(3)	$\forall x \colon X \bullet (Qx \Rightarrow Rx)$	*ass*
3	(4)	$Qa \Rightarrow Ra$	3 $\forall$-*elim*
5	(5)	Pa	*ass*
1,5	(6)	Qa	2,5 $\Rightarrow$-*elim*
1,3,5	(7)	Ra	4,6 $\Rightarrow$-*elim*
1,3	(8)	$Pa \Rightarrow Ra$	7 $\Rightarrow$-*int*
1,3	(9)	$\forall x \colon X \bullet (Px \Rightarrow Rx)$	8 $\forall$-*int*

To illustrate the existential quantifier rules I am going to prove the sequent:

$$\forall x \colon X \bullet (Px \Rightarrow Qx), \exists x \colon X \bullet \neg Qx \vdash \exists x \colon X \bullet \neg Px. \tag{10.1}$$

$$
\begin{array}{llll}
1 & (1) & \forall x\colon X \bullet (Px \Rightarrow Qx) & ass \\
2 & (2) & \exists x\colon X \bullet \neg Qx & ass \\
3 & (3) & \neg Qa & ass \\
1 & (4) & Pa \Rightarrow Qa & 1\ \forall\text{-}elim \\
5 & (5) & Pa & ass \\
1,5 & (6) & Qa & 4,5\ \Rightarrow\text{-}elim \\
1,3,5 & (7) & false & 3,6\ \neg\text{-}elim \\
1,3 & (8) & \neg Pa & 7\ \neg\text{-}int \\
1,3 & (9) & \exists x\colon X \bullet \neg Px & 8\ \exists\text{-}int \\
1,2 & (10) & \exists x\colon X \bullet \neg Px & 2,9\ \exists\text{-}elim
\end{array}
$$

Because the rule $\exists$-*elim* is a bit complicated I will explain its operation in this proof in some detail. Recall the rule $\exists$-*elim*:

$$
\frac{\Gamma \vdash \exists x\colon X \bullet A \qquad\qquad \Delta, A[a/x] \vdash C}{\Gamma, \Delta \vdash C} \;\; \exists\text{-}elim
$$

Here, a is a constant of type X which must not occur in Γ, Δ, $\exists x\colon X \bullet A$ or C. Line (2) of the above proof is:

$$
\overbrace{\exists x\colon X \bullet \neg Qx}^{\Gamma} \vdash \overbrace{\exists x\colon X \bullet \neg Qx}^{\exists x\colon X \bullet A}
$$

And line (9) is:

$$
\overbrace{\forall x\colon X \bullet (Px \Rightarrow Qx)}^{\Delta}, \overbrace{\neg Qa}^{A[a/x]} \vdash \overbrace{\exists x\colon X \bullet \neg Px}^{C}
$$

The side conditions are easy to verify, so the conclusion is:

$$
\overbrace{\exists x\colon X \bullet \neg Qx}^{\Gamma}, \overbrace{\forall x\colon X \bullet (Px \Rightarrow Qx)}^{\Delta} \vdash \overbrace{\exists x\colon X \bullet \neg Px}^{C}
$$

and this is what line (10) of the proof states.

The connection between $\exists$-*elim* and $\vee$-*elim* can be brought out clearly by considering the sequent (10.1) in a situation where the type X contains just two elements, say b and c.

$$
\begin{array}{llll}
1 & (1) & \forall x\colon X \bullet (Px \Rightarrow Qx) & ass \\
2 & (2) & \neg Qb \vee \neg Qc & ass
\end{array}
$$

$$
\begin{array}{llll|llll}
3 & (3) & \neg Qb & ass & 10 & (10) & \neg Qc & ass \\
1 & (4) & Pb \Rightarrow Qb & 1\ \forall\text{-}elim & 1 & (11) & Pc \Rightarrow Qc & 1\ \forall\text{-}elim \\
5 & (5) & Pb & ass & 12 & (12) & Pc & ass \\
1,5 & (6) & Qb & 4,5\ \Rightarrow\text{-}elim & 1,12 & (13) & Qc & 11,12\ \Rightarrow\text{-}elim \\
1,3,5 & (7) & false & 3,6\ \neg\text{-}elim & 1,10,12 & (14) & false & 10,13\ \neg\text{-}elim \\
1,3 & (8) & \neg Pb & 7\ \neg\text{-}int & 1,10 & (15) & \neg Pc & 14\ \neg\text{-}int \\
1,3 & (9) & \neg Pb \vee \neg Pc & 8\ \vee\text{-}int_i & 1,10 & (16) & \neg Pb \vee \neg Pc & 15\ \vee\text{-}int_i
\end{array}
$$

$$
\begin{array}{llll}
1,2 & (17) & \neg Pb \vee \neg Pc & 2,9,16\ \vee\text{-}elim
\end{array}
$$

120

Recall the rule ∨-*elim*:

$$\frac{\Gamma \vdash A \vee B \qquad \Delta, A \vdash C \qquad \Sigma, B \vdash C}{\Gamma, \Delta, \Sigma \vdash C} \quad \vee\text{-}elim$$

Line (2) of the above proof is:

$$\overbrace{\neg Qb \vee \neg Qc}^{\Gamma} \vdash \overbrace{\neg Qb}^{A} \vee \overbrace{\neg Qc}^{B}$$

Line (9) is:

$$\overbrace{\forall x\colon X \bullet (Px \Rightarrow Qx), \overbrace{\neg Qb}^{A}}^{\Delta} \vdash \overbrace{\neg Pb \vee \neg Pc}^{C}$$

And line (16) is:

$$\overbrace{\forall x\colon X \bullet (Px \Rightarrow Qx), \overbrace{\neg Qc}^{B}}^{\Sigma} \vdash \overbrace{\neg Pb \vee \neg Pc}^{C}$$

Thus, by ∨-*elim* we have:

$$\overbrace{\neg Qb \vee \neg Qc}^{\Gamma}, \overbrace{\forall x\colon X \bullet (Px \Rightarrow Qx)}^{\Delta, \Sigma} \vdash \overbrace{\neg Pb \vee \neg Pc}^{C}.$$

Because of the analogy between ∨-*elim* and ∃-*elim*, Lemmon (1965), p. 112, calls the predicate $A[a/x]$ in the rule ∃-*elim* the *typical disjunct*.

The next formula of the predicate calculus that I am going to prove is:

$$\exists x\colon X \bullet \forall y\colon Y \bullet Pxy \vdash \forall y\colon Y \bullet \exists x\colon X \bullet Pxy, \qquad (10.2)$$

where x and y can both occur free in Pxy.

1	(1)	$\exists x\colon X \bullet \forall y\colon Y \bullet Pxy$	ass
2	(2)	$\forall y\colon Y \bullet Pay$	ass
3	(3)	Pab	2 ∀-*elim*
2	(4)	$\exists x\colon X \bullet Pxb$	3 ∃-*int*
2	(5)	$\forall y\colon Y \bullet \exists x\colon X \bullet Pxy$	4 ∀-*int*
1	(6)	$\forall y\colon Y \bullet \exists x\colon X \bullet Pxy$	1,5 ∃-*elim*

Because the rule ∃-*elim* takes a bit of getting used to, I will again explain its application in line (6) in a bit more detail. Recall the graphical form of ∃-*elim*:

$$\frac{\Gamma \vdash \exists x\colon X \bullet A \qquad \Delta, A[a/x] \vdash C}{\Gamma, \Delta \vdash C} \quad \exists\text{-}elim$$

Here, a is a constant of type X which must not occur in Γ, Δ, $\exists x \colon X \bullet A$ or C. Line (1) in our proof is:

$$\overbrace{\exists x \colon X \bullet \forall y \colon Y \bullet Pxy}^{\Gamma} \vdash \overbrace{\exists x \colon X \bullet \forall y \colon Y \bullet Pxy}^{\exists x \colon X \bullet A}$$

Line (5) is:

$$\overbrace{\forall y \colon Y \bullet Pay}^{A[a/x]} \vdash \overbrace{\forall y \colon Y \bullet \exists x \colon X \bullet Pxy}^{C}$$

and Δ here is empty.

The side conditions in the rule $\exists$-*elim* are easy to verify, therefore we can infer:

$$\overbrace{\exists x \colon X \bullet \forall y \colon Y \bullet Pxy}^{\Gamma} \vdash \overbrace{\forall y \colon Y \bullet \exists x \colon X \bullet Pxy}^{C}$$

and this is line (6) in the proof.

It should be noted that the converse of (10.2) is not a valid sequent. It is easy to construct a counterexample. Let Pxy be the relation 'x is a parent of y'. Then, although it is true that everybody has a parent, that is to say, $\forall y \colon Y \bullet \exists x \colon X \bullet Pxy$, it is false to say that there exists a single[6] person who is a parent of everyone, that is to say, $\exists x \colon X \bullet \forall y \colon Y \bullet Pxy$.

The next sequent that I prove is very useful in simplifying many kinds of schemas and I use it several times in later chapters of this book (for example, in section 12.5):

$$Pa \dashv\vdash \exists x \colon X \bullet Pa.$$

This is proved in two parts. First, I prove $Pa \vdash \exists x \colon X \bullet Pa$.

$$
\begin{array}{llll}
1 & (1) & Pa & ass \\
1 & (2) & \exists x \colon X \bullet Pa & 1\ \exists\text{-}int
\end{array}
$$

Let $A \equiv Pa$ in $\exists$-*int* and let t be any constant other than a, so $A[t/x] \equiv Pa$.
Second, I prove $\exists x \colon X \bullet Pa \vdash Pa$.

$$
\begin{array}{llll}
1 & (1) & \exists x \colon X \bullet Pa & ass \\
2 & (2) & Pa & ass \\
1 & (3) & Pa & 1,2\ \exists\text{-}elim
\end{array}
$$

Let $A \equiv Pa$, $A[b/x] \equiv Pa$, $C \equiv Pa$ in $\exists$-*elim* to get the final line. Note that $\Delta \equiv \{\ \}$.

The next sequent using the inference rules governing identity that I am going to prove is:

$$Py \dashv\vdash \exists z \colon X \bullet z = y \wedge Pz.$$

This again will prove very useful in simplifying schemas. (For example, I use it on p. 138 to simplify the schema *PreEnter1*.) First, I show $Py \vdash \exists z \colon X \bullet z = y \wedge Pz$.

---

[6]'Single' in the sense of there being the only one, not in the sense of being unmarried.

$$
\begin{array}{lll}
1 & (1) \quad Py & ass \\
  & (2) \quad y = y & =\text{-}int \\
1 & (3) \quad y = y \wedge Py & 1,2 \ \wedge\text{-}int \\
1 & (4) \quad \exists z\colon X \bullet z = y \wedge Pz & 3 \ \exists\text{-}int
\end{array}
$$

Let $A \equiv z = y \wedge Pz$ and $A[y/z] \equiv y = y \wedge Py$ in $\exists$-*elim* to get the final line. Second, I show $\exists z\colon X \bullet z = y \wedge Pz \vdash Py$.

$$
\begin{array}{lll}
1 & (1) \quad \exists z\colon X \bullet z = y \wedge Pz & ass \\
2 & (2) \quad a = y \wedge Pa & ass \\
2 & (3) \quad a = y & 2 \ \wedge\text{-}elim_i \\
2 & (4) \quad Pa & 2 \ \wedge\text{-}elim_i \\
2 & (5) \quad Py & 3,4 \ =\text{-}elim \\
1 & (6) \quad Py & 1,5 \ \exists\text{-}elim
\end{array}
$$

Let $A \equiv z = y \wedge Pz$ and $A[a/z] \equiv a = y \wedge Pa$ in $\exists$-*elim* to get the final line. Again, $\Delta = \{\ \}$.

10.3   Exercises

10.1) Construct proofs of each of the following:

    a) $P \wedge (Q \wedge R) \dashv\vdash (P \wedge Q) \wedge R$.

    b) $P \vee (Q \vee R) \dashv\vdash (P \vee Q) \vee R$.

    c) $P \wedge Q \dashv\vdash (P \vee \neg Q) \wedge Q$.

    d) $P \Rightarrow Q \dashv\vdash \neg P \vee Q$.

    e) $Q \Rightarrow R \vdash (P \vee Q) \Rightarrow (P \vee R)$.

    f) $P_1 \Rightarrow P_2, P_3 \Rightarrow P_4 \vdash (P_1 \vee P_3) \Rightarrow (P_2 \vee P_4)$.

10.2) Prove the following sequents:

    a) $\forall x\colon X \bullet (Px \wedge Qx) \dashv\vdash (\forall x\colon X \bullet Px) \wedge (\forall x\colon X \bullet Qx)$.

    b) $\exists x\colon X \bullet (Px \vee Qx) \dashv\vdash (\exists x\colon X \bullet Px) \vee (\exists x\colon X \bullet Qx)$.

    c) $\forall x\colon X \bullet Px \dashv\vdash \neg \exists x\colon X \bullet \neg Px$.

    d) $\forall x\colon X \bullet (Px \Rightarrow Qx), \forall x\colon X \bullet Px \vdash \forall x\colon X \bullet Qx$.

    e) $\exists x\colon X \bullet (Px \wedge Qx) \vdash (\exists x\colon X \bullet Px) \wedge (\exists x\colon X \bullet Qx)$.

Chapter 11

Rigorous Proof

11.1 Introduction

In the previous chapter I developed a proof-theory for first-order logic. Mathematicians rarely, however, construct fully formal proofs of the theorems that interest them. Almost all of the time they make use of *rigorous* proofs. There is, however, a fairly widespread belief among mathematicians that every correct rigorous proof could be transformed into a fully formal one. First-order logic can be thought of as the machine language of mathematics and then rigorous proofs can be compared to programs written in a high-level programming language.[1] In this chapter, therefore, I give several examples of rigorous proofs and I also introduce the topic of proof by induction, both for natural numbers and also for sequences.

11.2 Reasoning about Sets

In this section I give a few examples of how we can reason about sets. The proofs are presented less formally than in the previous chapter, but they are still rigorous. They are presented in the way that a mathematician might carry them out. They could be transformed into proofs in the sequent calculus and I give an example of how this can be done. The first thing that I am going to prove is the following identity:

$$U \cap U = U. \tag{11.1}$$

One way of proving an identity between sets, say $X = Y$, is to prove both of the predicates $X \subseteq Y$ and $Y \subseteq X$. Thus, in order to prove (11.1) we have to prove both that $U \cap U \subseteq U$ and that $U \subseteq U \cap U$. The proofs are very similar, so I shall only do the first one here.

---

[1] Several books have been published recently which introduce the idea of a rigorous, but not fully formal, mathematical proof. See, for example, Morash (1987), Franklin and Daoud (1988) and Cupillari (1989). It is also a good idea to read Lakatos (1976) to get an idea of the real role of proofs in mathematics. If you think Lakatos is too reactionary, then read Feyerabend (1982,1987,1988).

The predicate $U \cap U \subseteq U$ makes use of set intersection and the subset relation. The definition of set intersection is:

$$
\begin{array}{|l}
\hline
\underline{[X]} \\
\_ \cap \_ : \mathbf{P}\,X \times \mathbf{P}\,X \to \mathbf{P}\,X \\
\hline
\forall U, V : \mathbf{P}\,X \; \bullet \\
\quad U \cap V = \{x : X \mid x \in U \wedge x \in V\} \\
\hline
\end{array}
$$

In order to be able to use the definition of set intersection in proofs we have to "derive" from it the predicate:

$$x \in U \cap V \Longleftrightarrow (x \in U \wedge x \in V). \tag{11.2}$$

(Note that I have left out the universal quantifiers from this predicate. It is usual to do that in mathematics. The convention there is that free variables, like the x, U and V in (11.2), are universally quantified over.) The predicate (11.2) is obtained as follows. From the definition of set intersection we clearly have that:

$$U \cap V = \{x : X \mid x \in U \wedge x \in V\}.$$

From this it follows that:

$$y \in U \cap V \Longleftrightarrow y \in \{x : X \mid x \in U \wedge x \in V\}.$$

On p. 29 of chapter 3 I discussed the law:

$$x \in \{J \mid P \bullet t\} \Longleftrightarrow \exists J \mid P \bullet t = x,$$

where J is a signature, P a predicate, t a term and x a variable that is not declared in J. Combining the previous two results gives us:

$$y \in U \cap V \Longleftrightarrow (\exists x : X \mid x \in U \wedge x \in V \bullet x = y),$$

which is equivalent to:

$$y \in U \cap V \Longleftrightarrow (y \in U \wedge y \in V).$$

This is what I had above, except that the variable there was x and not y.

The definition of the subset relation is:

$$
\begin{array}{|l}
\hline
\underline{[X]} \\
\_ \subseteq \_ : \mathbf{P}\,X \leftrightarrow \mathbf{P}\,X \\
\hline
\forall U, V : \mathbf{P}\,X \; \bullet \\
\quad U \subseteq V \Longleftrightarrow (\forall x : X \bullet x \in U \Rightarrow x \in V) \\
\hline
\end{array}
$$

The predicate $U \subseteq V \Longleftrightarrow (\forall x : X \bullet x \in U \Rightarrow x \in V)$ can be used in proofs just as it is.

So, in order to prove that $U \cap U \subseteq U$ all we have to prove is that, for all $x : X$, the following holds: $x \in U \cap U \Rightarrow x \in U$. In order to prove this assume that $x \in U \cap U$. From the definition of set intersection we have:

$$x \in U \cap U \iff (x \in U \wedge x \in U).$$

As we have assumed that $x \in U \cap U$, we can infer that $x \in U \wedge x \in U$ and from this it follows that $x \in U$. Thus, we have proved the implication $x \in U \cap U \Rightarrow x \in U$, for all $x : X$, and this is identical to $U \cap U \subseteq U$, by the definition of the subset relation.

This proof can be formalized as follows:

1	(1)	$a \in W \cap W$	ass
	(2)	$\forall U, V : \mathbf{P}\, X; x : X \bullet (x \in U \cap V \iff x \in U \wedge x \in V)$	definition of $\cap$
	(3)	$\forall V : \mathbf{P}\, X; x : X \bullet (x \in W \cap V \iff x \in W \wedge x \in V)$	2 $\forall$-*elim*
	(4)	$\forall x : X \bullet (x \in W \cap W \iff x \in W \wedge x \in W)$	3 $\forall$-*elim*
	(5)	$a \in W \cap W \iff a \in W \wedge a \in W$	4 $\forall$-*elim*
	(6)	$a \in W \cap W \Rightarrow a \in W \wedge a \in W$	5 $\iff$-*elim₁*
1	(7)	$a \in W \wedge a \in W$	1,6 $\Rightarrow$-*elim*
1	(8)	$a \in W$	7 $\wedge$-*elim₁*
	(9)	$a \in W \cap W \Rightarrow a \in W$	1,8 $\Rightarrow$-*int*
	(10)	$\forall x : X \bullet (x \in W \cap W \Rightarrow x \in W)$	9 $\forall$-*int*
	(11)	$\forall U, V : \mathbf{P}\, X \bullet (U \subseteq V \iff (\forall x : X \bullet x \in U \Rightarrow x \in V))$	definition of $\subseteq$
	(12)	$\forall V : \mathbf{P}\, X \bullet (W \cap W \subseteq V \iff (\forall x : X \bullet x \in W \cap W \Rightarrow x \in V))$	11 $\forall$-*elim*
	(13)	$W \cap W \subseteq W \iff (\forall x : X \bullet x \in W \cap W \Rightarrow x \in W)$	12 $\forall$-*elim*
	(14)	$(\forall x : X \bullet x \in W \cap W \Rightarrow x \in W) \Rightarrow W \cap W \subseteq W$	13 $\iff$-*elim₂*
	(15)	$W \cap W \subseteq W$	10,14 $\Rightarrow$-*elim*

People generally find rigorous proofs easier to follow than fully formal proofs, though it would not be a difficult problem to write a program to check the correctness of this formal proof.

To further illustrate the method of rigorous proof I shall prove that set intersection distributes backwards through set union:[2]

$$(U \cup V) \cap W = (U \cap W) \cup (V \cap W). \tag{11.3}$$

This proof will illustrate a different proof strategy from the one used in the proof that $W \cap W = W$. The formula (11.3) makes use of set union, whose definition is:

$$\begin{array}{|l}
\overline{[X]} \\
\quad \_ \cup \_ : \mathbf{P}\, X \times \mathbf{P}\, X \to \mathbf{P}\, X \\
\hline
\quad \forall U, V : \mathbf{P}\, X \bullet \\
\qquad U \cup V = \{x : X \mid x \in U \vee x \in V\} \\
\hline
\end{array}$$

---

[2]This property of set union and intersection will be needed on pp. 150ff. of chapter 13 where I explain the notion of a retrieve function.

In order to be able to use the definition of set union in proofs we have to "derive" from it the predicate:

$$x \in U \cup V \iff (x \in U \lor x \in V). \tag{11.4}$$

The proof of (11.3) goes as follows, where each step follows from the previous one because it is an application of (11.4) or (11.2), unless otherwise indicated:

$$x \in (U \cup V) \cap W \iff (x \in U \cup V) \land x \in W,$$
$$\iff (x \in U \lor x \in V) \land x \in W,$$
$$\iff (x \in U \land x \in W) \lor (x \in V \land x \in W),$$

by using the tautology $(P \lor Q) \land R \iff (P \land R) \lor (Q \land R)$,

$$\iff (x \in U \cap W) \lor (x \in V \cap W),$$
$$\iff x \in (U \cap W) \cup (V \cap W).$$

This proof makes use of the fact that in the propositional calculus $\land$ distributes backwards through $\lor$. This was proved formally on pp. 113ff. of the previous chapter.

The next thing that I am going to prove in order to illustrate the notion of a rigorous proof is that set difference distributes backwards through set union:[3]

$$(U \cup V) \setminus W = (U \setminus W) \cup (V \setminus W). \tag{11.5}$$

The definition of $\setminus$ is:

$$
\begin{array}{l}
\rule{3cm}{0.4pt} [X] \rule{6cm}{0.4pt} \\
\quad \_ \setminus \_ : \mathbf{P}\,X \times \mathbf{P}\,X \to \mathbf{P}\,X \\
\rule{5cm}{0.4pt} \\
\quad \forall U, V : \mathbf{P}\,X \bullet U \setminus V = \{x : X \mid x \in U \land x \notin V\}
\end{array}
$$

From this we obtain the equivalence:

$$x \in U \setminus V \iff x \in U \land x \notin V. \tag{11.6}$$

The prove of (11.5) goes as follows, where each step follows from the previous one because it is an application of (11.4) or (11.6), unless otherwise indicated:

$$x \in (U \cup V) \setminus W \iff (x \in U \cup V) \land x \notin W,$$
$$\iff (x \in U \land x \in V) \land x \notin W,$$
$$\iff (x \in U \land x \notin W) \land (x \in V \land x \notin W),$$

by using the tautology $(P \land Q) \land R \iff (P \land R) \land (Q \land R)$,

$$\iff (x \in U \setminus W) \land (x \in V \setminus W),$$
$$\iff x \in (U \setminus W) \cup (V \setminus W).$$

---

[3]This property of set difference and union will be needed on p. 137 of chapter 12, where it is used to help simplify a schema, and on p. 152 of chapter 13 where I explain the notion of a retrieve function.

11.3 Mathematical Induction

The principle of mathematical induction is a rule of inference that allows us to prove that certain things are true of all the non-negative numbers. It says that in order to show that $P(n)$ holds for all natural numbers, all we have to show is:

1. $P(0)$ holds.

2. $\forall i: \mathbf{N} \bullet P(i) \Rightarrow P(i+1)$.

Here, part 1 is known as the *base case* and part 2 is known as the *inductive step*.

For example, say we want to prove the following property:

$$\sum_{i=0}^{i=n} i^2 = \frac{n(n+1)(2n+1)}{6}, \tag{11.7}$$

which I shall abbreviate to $P(n)$, thus:

$$P(n) == \sum_{i=0}^{i=n} i^2 = \frac{n(n+1)(2n+1)}{6}.$$

Base Case First, I have to show that $P(0)$ holds. When $n = 0$, we have that:

$$LHS \text{ of } (11.7) = \sum_{i=0}^{i=0} i^2 = 0.$$

Also when $n = 0$,

$$RHS \text{ of } (11.7) = \frac{0(0+1)(0+1)}{6} = 0.$$

Thus, the base case has been established, since the *LHS* and *RHS* of (11.7) are both equal to 0.

Inductive Step I need to show that the formula:

$$\sum_{i=0}^{i=n+1} i^2 = \frac{(n+1)(n+2)(2(n+1)+1)}{6}, \tag{11.8}$$

is true on the assumption that the inductive hypothesis (11.7) holds.

$$LHS \text{ of } (11.8) = \sum_{i=0}^{i=n} i^2 + (n+1)^2,$$

$$= \frac{n(n+1)(2n+1)}{6} + (n+1)^2,$$

by the inductive hypothesis,

$$= \frac{(n+1)(n(2n+1) + 6(n+1))}{6},$$

$$= \frac{(n+1)(2n^2 + 7n + 6)}{6},$$

$$= \frac{(n+1)(n+2)(2n+3)}{6},$$

$$= \textit{RHS of (11.8)}.$$

Thus, the inductive step has been established. Since both the base case and the inductive step have been established, the property that (11.7) is true for all natural numbers follows by mathematical induction.

11.4   Induction for Sequences

Sequence induction is similar to mathematical induction. It says that in order to show that some property $P(\sigma)$ holds for all sequences σ all we have to show is that:[4]

1. $P(\langle\,\rangle)$ holds.

2. If $P(\sigma)$ holds for any sequence σ, then so does $P(\langle x \rangle \frown \sigma)$. In symbols:

$$\forall x \colon X; \sigma \colon \operatorname{seq} X \bullet P(\sigma) \Rightarrow P(\langle x \rangle \frown \sigma).$$

Here, part 1 is known as the *base case* and part 2 is known as the *inductive step*.

To illustrate sequence induction I shall prove that concatenation is associative, that is to say, that the property:

$$\sigma \frown (\tau \frown v) = (\sigma \frown \tau) \frown v,$$

holds for all sequences σ, τ and v. The proof makes use of the fact that $\langle\,\rangle \frown \sigma = \sigma$ and also of the following property:

$$(\langle x \rangle \frown \sigma) \frown \tau = \langle x \rangle \frown (\sigma \frown \tau). \tag{11.9}$$

Both of these results are straightforwardly derived from the formal definition of the concatenation operator.

Base Case   We have to prove that:

$$\langle\,\rangle \frown (\tau \frown v) = (\langle\,\rangle \frown \tau) \frown v.$$

Since $\langle\,\rangle \frown \sigma = \sigma$ for all sequences σ, we have:

$$\langle\,\rangle \frown (\tau \frown v) = \tau \frown v,$$

$$= (\langle\,\rangle \frown \tau) \frown v.$$

This establishes the base case.

---

[4] Just as there are several variants of mathematical induction for numbers—see, for example, Spivey (1989b), p. 117—there are also several variants of sequence induction; see section 26.3 below for more information.

Inductive Step   We have to prove that:

$$((\langle x \rangle \frown \sigma) \frown (\tau \frown v) = (((\langle x \rangle \frown \sigma) \frown \tau) \frown v, \tag{11.10}$$

on the assumption that:

$$\sigma \frown (\tau \frown v) = (\sigma \frown \tau) \frown v, \tag{11.11}$$

holds, for all sequences σ, τ and v. This is proved in the following way:

$$\textit{LHS of } (11.10) = (\langle x \rangle \frown \sigma) \frown (\tau \frown v),$$
$$= \langle x \rangle \frown (\sigma \frown (\tau \frown v)),$$

by the property (11.9),

$$= \langle x \rangle \frown ((\sigma \frown \tau) \frown v),$$

by the inductive hypothesis (11.11),

$$= (\langle x \rangle \frown (\sigma \frown \tau)) \frown v,$$

by the property (11.9),

$$= (((\langle x \rangle \frown \sigma) \frown \tau) \frown v,$$

again by the property (11.9),

$$= \textit{RHS of } (11.10).$$

This established the inductive step. Thus, by sequence induction it follows that concatenation is associative.

11.5   Exercises

11.1) Let $U, V, W : \mathbf{P}\, X$. Prove the following properties:

   a) $U = X \setminus (X \setminus U)$.
   b) $X \setminus (U \cap V) = (X \setminus U) \cup (X \setminus V)$.

11.2) Prove the following results using mathematical induction:

   a) $\sum\limits_{i=0}^{i=n} i = \frac{n(n+1)}{2}$.

   b) $\sum\limits_{i=0}^{i=n} i^3 = \left(\frac{n(n+1)}{2}\right)^2$.

Chapter 12

Immanent Reasoning

12.1　Introduction

One of the major advantages of using a formal language like **Z** is that it is very easy to reason about the specifications written in it. In part II of this book I gave a tutorial introduction to the topic of how to use **Z** *descriptively* to specify various kinds of systems and in chapters 10 and 11 I explained how to carry out formal and rigorous proofs, respectively. In this chapter I am going to combine these two topics and give examples of proofs explicitly concerned with specifications. The title of this chapter, namely 'Immanent Reasoning', refers to the fact that the things I am going to prove relate to a single specification.[1] In the next chapter I look at proofs which relate two specifications. It is also possible to conduct proofs which seek to relate specifications and programs, but that topic is beyond the scope of this book.[2]

12.2　Specifying a Classroom

In order to illustrate the sort of thing that you can prove about a specification I will use a simple example of a classroom.[3] The specification uses the type *Person* of all people and the constant *Max*, which is the maximum number of people that can fit into the classroom that we are modelling. The state of the classroom system is given by the following schema:

$$\begin{array}{|l}
\hline
\_\,Class1 \underline{\hspace{4cm}} \\
d\colon \mathbf{P}\ Person \\
\hline
\#d \le Max \\
\hline
\end{array}$$

---

[1] The notion of *immanent reasoning* is derived, ultimately, from Vollenhoven, though he uses it in a very different context. He contrasts it with both *transcendent* and *transcendental reasoning*.

[2] Hoare logics are one way of relating specifications and programs. See, for example, Hoare (1969), Gries (1981), Backhouse (1986), Baber (1987), Gumb (1989) and Dromey (1989).

[3] This is a fairly common example. Jones (1980), pp. 136–138 and 142–143, uses it and Sørensen used it in lectures at Oxford University's Programming Language Group that I attended in 1984–1985.

The schemas $\Delta\,Class1$ and $\Xi\,Class1$ are defined in the standard way, as is the initial state $Init1'$:

$$\Delta\,Class1 \mathbin{\hat=} Class1 \wedge Class1'$$

$$\Xi\,Class1 \mathbin{\hat=} \Delta\,Class1 \mid d' = d$$

$$Init1' \mathbin{\hat=} Class1' \mid d' = \{\ \}$$

Only two operations will be defined on this state. The first is of someone entering the classroom:

```
┌─ Enter1 ──────────────────────────────────
│ Δ Class1
│ p?: Person
├───────────────────────────────────────────
│ #d < Max
│ p? ∉ d
│ d' = d ∪ {p?}
└───────────────────────────────────────────
```

The second is of someone leaving the classroom:

```
┌─ Leave1 ──────────────────────────────────
│ Δ Class1
│ p?: Person
├───────────────────────────────────────────
│ p? ∈ d
│ d' = d \ {p?}
└───────────────────────────────────────────
```

12.3 Schemas and Predicates

Before I can give some examples of proofs about specifications, I have to say something about the way in which schema names can occur as parts of predicates. I shall introduce this topic by means of some examples.

Consider the classroom specification given above. We might want to state various properties about the system being described. For example, we might want to express the fact that sometimes the classroom is empty. This is represented as follows:

$$\exists d: \mathbf{P}\ Person \mid \#d \leq Max \bullet d = \{\ \}. \tag{12.1}$$

Alternately, we might want to express the possibility that the classroom never contains any women. Using $male: \mathbf{P}\ Person$ to represent the set of all men, this would be represented as:

$$\forall d: \mathbf{P}\ Person \mid \#d \leq Max \bullet d \subseteq male. \tag{12.2}$$

This will, in general, be false for most classrooms.

There might be occasions on which we want to know the actual number of people in the classroom. The function:

$$\lambda d: \mathbf{P}\ Person \mid \#d \leq Max \bullet \#d, \tag{12.3}$$

returns the size of a classroom.

If you look at the predicates (12.1) and (12.2) and also at the the expression (12.3), you should notice that each of them contains the declaration and predicate combination $d: \mathbf{P}\ Person \mid \#d \leq Max$ as a part and this combination should remind you of the schema $Class1$, which is made up out of the same declaration and predicate. Because of this, it is possible to represent (12.1) as $\exists Class1 \bullet d = \{\ \}$ and to represent (12.2) as $\forall Class1 \bullet d \subseteq male$ and to represent (12.3) as $\lambda Class1 \bullet \#d$. In fact, this is how schemas came about historically.[4]

As well as occurring after the symbols $\exists$, $\forall$ and λ, schema names in **Z** can also occur where you would expect a predicate. In this case it is just as if you had written down the predicate part of the schema involved. Thus, the predicate:

$$\exists d': \mathbf{P}\ Person \mid \#d' \leq Max \bullet Init1',$$

is equivalent to:

$$\exists d': \mathbf{P}\ Person \mid \#d' \leq Max \bullet d' = \{\ \}.$$

Using both of the conventions discussed in the section it is possible to express this very concisely as $\exists Class1' \bullet Init1'$.

12.4   The Initialization Proof-obligation

One of the things that you have either to prove, or to convince yourself of in some other way, about every specification that you write is that the initial state exists. In the case of the classroom system this proof-obligation is expressed by the predicate $\exists Class1' \bullet Init1'$. As explained in the previous section, this is equivalent to:

$$\exists d': \mathbf{P}\ Person \mid \#d' \leq Max \bullet d' = \{\ \}.$$

As explained in chapter 2, this restricted existential quantification is equivalent to the unrestricted form:

$$\exists d': \mathbf{P}\ Person \bullet \#d' \leq Max \wedge d' = \{\ \}.$$

You may think that this predicate is so obviously true—because clearly the empty set of people exists—that is does not require proof, but in general this will not be the case. The way we prove this result is by means of the rule of existential quantifier introduction discussed on p. 118 above. This states that from $A[t/x]$ we can infer $\exists x: X \bullet A$, if x is a variable of type X and t is a term of type X. (The notation $A[t/x]$ refers to that predicate formed from A by substituting t for all free occurrences of x.)

---

[4]It is also possible to include a schema name as part of a set comprehension and also as part of a μ-expression, which is explained on p. 240 below.

From the definition of the cardinality operator $\#$ it follows that $\#\{\ \} = 0$. 0 is the least element of $\mathbf{N}$, so $0 \leq Max$. From the properties of identity it follows that $\{\ \} = \{\ \}$. These considerations allow us to conclude that $\#\{\ \} \leq Max \wedge \{\ \} = \{\ \}$. This is clearly equivalent to:

$$\#d' \leq Max \wedge d' = \{\ \}[\{\ \}/d'],$$

where the variable d' is of type $\mathbf{P}\ Person$. The rule of existential quantifier introduction therefore allows us to infer the following:

$$\exists d' : \mathbf{P}\ Person \bullet \#d' \leq Max \wedge d' = \{\ \}.$$

This proves that for the classroom system the initial state exists.

12.5 Constructing Theories about Specifications

Given a specification there are usually lots of things that we can prove about it and so it is possible to construct a *theory* about that specification. Such a theory increases our understanding of the specification and reinforces our faith in its correctness. In this section I want to give a simple example of the sort of thing that we can prove about the classroom specification.

The property of the classroom specification that I am going to consider is that if someone enters a classroom and then that same person leaves it, then the state of the classroom is unaltered. This can be represented in $\mathbf{Z}$ by means of the predicate:

$$(Enter1 \ {}_{9} \ Leave1) \iff (\Xi Class1 \mid p? \notin d). \tag{12.4}$$

The predicate on the right of the bi-implication sign of (12.4) is:

$$\#d < Max \wedge \#d' < Max \wedge d' = d \wedge p? \notin d,$$

thus to establish the truth of (12.4) I just have to show that the predicate on the left of that bi-implication sign is equivalent to this. Let $Alpha \mathrel{\hat{=}} Enter1 \ {}_{9} \ Leave1$. Then, $Alpha$ is the following schema:

```
┌─ Alpha ────────────────────────────────
│ d, d' : P Person
│ p? : Person
├────────────────────────────────────────
│ ∃d⁺ : Person •
│     (#d ≤ Max ∧
│     #d < Max ∧
│     p? ∉ d ∧
│     d⁺ = d ∪ {p?} ∧
│     #d⁺ ≤ Max ∧
│     p? ∈ d⁺ ∧
│     d' = d⁺ \ {p?})
└────────────────────────────────────────
```

136

We are just interested in the predicate part of this schema. If x does not occur free in P, then:

$$\exists x \colon X \bullet (P \wedge Q) \dashv\vdash P \wedge (\exists x \colon X \bullet Q) \tag{12.5}$$

is a valid sequent of the predicate calculus. Considering the predicate part of the schema *Alpha*, the sequent (12.5) allows us to move all those conjuncts that do not contain d^+ out of the scope of the existential quantifier. Doing that results in the predicate:

$$\#d \leq Max \wedge \#d < Max \wedge p? \notin d \wedge$$
$$\exists d^+ \colon Person \bullet d^+ = d \cup \{p?\} \wedge \#d^+ \leq Max \wedge p? \in d^+ \wedge d' = d^+ \setminus \{p?\}.$$

Since $\#d < Max$ implies $\#d \leq Max$ we can drop the conjunct $\#d \leq Max$ from this. On p. 122 I proved the sequent $Py \dashv\vdash \exists z \colon X \bullet z = y \wedge Pz$. Using this from right to left allows us to remove the existential quantifier from the predicate part we are simplifying. Performing those two operations results in the predicate:

$$\#d < Max \wedge p? \notin d \wedge \#(d \cup \{p?\}) \leq Max \wedge p? \in d \cup \{p?\} \wedge d' = (d \cup \{p?\}) \setminus \{p?\}. \tag{12.6}$$

Clearly, $p? \in d \cup \{p?\}$; therefore, this conjunct can be dropped. Now, consider the conjunct $d' = (d \cup \{p?\}) \setminus \{p?\}$. As set difference distributes backwards through set union—as proved on p. 128 above—this is equivalent to $d' = (d \setminus \{p?\}) \cup (\{p?\} \setminus \{p?\})$ and this simplifies to $d' = d$ because $p? \notin d$. Next, I consider the conjunct $\#(d \cup \{p?\}) \leq Max$. Since $\#d < Max$ and $p? \notin d$, it follows that $\#(d \cup \{p?\}) = \#d + 1$. This means that we can drop the conjunct $\#(d \cup \{p?\}) \leq Max$ from (12.6), since it is implied by the first two conjuncts of that predicate. Applying all these simplifications to (12.6) results in the predicate:

$$\#d < Max \wedge p? \notin d \wedge d' = d,$$

and this is equivalent to:

$$\#d < Max \wedge p? \notin d \wedge d' = d \wedge \#d' < Max,$$

and this is exactly the same as the predicate part of the schema $\Xi Class1 \mid p? \notin d$. Thus, I have established the "theorem" (12.4).

12.6 Investigating Preconditions

Throughout this book I talk about the *preconditions* of a schema specifying some state transformation. Such language is justified in this section.

Z contains a precondition operator pre which makes a schema out of a schema by hiding all the after and output variables of the given schema. Thus, since *Enter1* is a schema, so is pre *Enter1*. Z also contains the convention that $PreS \triangleq pre\ S$, for all schema names S.[5] Thus, *PreEnter1* is just another way of referring to the schema pre *Enter1*.

---

[5] See Spivey (1989b), p. 72 for more information.

Given a schema S which specifies some operation or state transformation, what *PreS* does is to indicate those states on which the operation S can be successfully carried out. In other words, if a state satisfies *PreS*, then the operation specified by S can be carried out on that state. So, *PreEnter1* tells us on which states *Enter1* can be performed. What *PreEnter1* actually amounts to is this:

```
┌─ PreEnter1 ─────────────────────────────────────────
│ d: P Person
│ p?: Person
├─────────────────────────────────────────────────────
│ ∃d': P Person •
│     (#d ≤ Max ∧
│     #d' ≤ Max ∧
│     #d < Max ∧
│     p? ∉ d ∧
│     d' = d ∪ {p?})
└─────────────────────────────────────────────────────
```

Usually the predicate part of a precondition schema can be considerably simplified and in most cases the existential quantifier can be removed. I will now show how *PreEnter1* can be simplified.

We can take all the predicates which do not contain the variable d' out of the scope of the existential quantifier. This is because $\exists x: X \bullet (P \land Q) \dashv\vdash P \land \exists x: X \bullet Q$, is a valid predicate calculus sequent if x does not occur free in P, but it can occur free in Q. Because of this *PreEnter1* is equivalent to:

```
┌─ PreEnter1 ─────────────────────────────────────────
│ d: P Person
│ p?: Person
├─────────────────────────────────────────────────────
│ #d ≤ Max
│ #d < Max
│ p? ∉ d
│ ∃d': P Person • (#d' ≤ Max ∧ d' = d ∪ {p?})
└─────────────────────────────────────────────────────
```

On p. 122 of chapter 10 I proved that the sequent $Py \dashv\vdash \exists z: X \bullet Pz \land z = y$ is valid in the predicate calculus with identity. Because of this we can replace the existentially quantified predicate in *PreEnter1* with the predicate $\#(d \cup \{p?\}) \leq Max$. Because $p? \notin d$, we have $\#(d \cup \{p?\}) = \#d + 1$. Therefore, $\#d < Max$ and as $\#d < Max$ implies $\#d \leq Max$, we can simplify *PreEnter1* to the following:

```
┌─ PreEnter1 ─────────────────────────────────────────
│ d: P Person
│ p?: Person
├─────────────────────────────────────────────────────
│ #d < Max
│ p? ∉ d
└─────────────────────────────────────────────────────
```

The predicate part of *PreEnter1* is $\#d < Max \wedge p? \notin d$ and this is referred to as the *precondition* of the schema *Enter1*. We can also say that the two predicates $\#d < Max$ and $p? \notin d$ are the two *preconditions* of *Enter1*. This is, in fact, the terminology that I use throughout this book. For example, on p. 41 I said that the preconditions of the schema *AddEntry* are the predicates:

$$name? \in members,$$
$$name? \mapsto newnumber? \notin telephones,$$

and also that the state invariant is a kind of precondition. The state invariant in this case is the predicate:

$$\text{dom } telephones \subseteq members.$$

I will briefly justify that here. The expanded version of *AddEntry* is:

AddEntry

$members, members': \mathbf{P} \; Person$
$telephones, telephones': Person \leftrightarrow Phone$
$name?: Person$
$newnumber?: Phone$

---

dom $telephones \subseteq members$
dom $telephones' \subseteq members'$
$name? \in members$
$name? \mapsto newnumber? \notin telephones$
$telephones' = telephones \cup \{name? \mapsto newnumber?\}$
$members' = members$

The schema pre *AddEntry* or *PreAddEntry* is, therefore:

PreAddEntry

$members: \mathbf{P} \; Person$
$telephones: Person \leftrightarrow Phone$
$name?: Person$
$newnumber?: Phone$

$\exists members': \mathbf{P} \; Person; \; telephones': Person \leftrightarrow Phone \; \bullet$
    (dom $telephones \subseteq members \wedge$
    dom $telephones' \subseteq members' \wedge$
    $name? \in members \wedge$
    $name? \mapsto newnumber? \notin telephones \wedge$
    $telephones' = telephones \cup \{name? \mapsto newnumber?\} \wedge$
    $members' = members)$

As already mentioned, if x does not occur free in P, then the following is a valid interderivable sequent of the predicate calculus:

$$\exists x: X \; \bullet \; (P \wedge Q) \; \dashv\vdash \; P \wedge \exists x: X \; \bullet \; Q.$$

Because of this the predicate of the schema pre *AddEntry* is equivalent to:

$$\text{dom } telephones \subseteq members \wedge$$
$$name? \in members \wedge$$
$$name? \mapsto newnumber? \notin telephones \wedge$$
$$\exists members': \mathbf{P}\, Person; telephones': Person \leftrightarrow Phone \bullet$$
$$(\text{dom } telephones' \subseteq members' \wedge$$
$$telephones' = telephones \cup \{name? \mapsto newnumber?\} \wedge$$
$$members' = members). \tag{12.7}$$

As already mentioned, on pp. 122ff. I proved the sequent $Py \dashv\vdash \exists z: X \bullet z = y \wedge Pz$. Using this twice on the existentially quantified part of (12.7) results in the predicate:

$$\text{dom } telephones \subseteq members \wedge$$
$$name? \in members \wedge$$
$$name? \mapsto newnumber? \notin telephones \wedge$$
$$\exists members': \mathbf{P}\, Person; telephones': Person \leftrightarrow Phone \bullet$$
$$\text{dom}(telephones \cup \{name? \mapsto newnumber?\}) \subseteq members. \tag{12.8}$$

On pp. 122ff. I proved the sequent $Pa \dashv\vdash \exists x: X \bullet Pa$, which allows us to drop (or insert) vacuous quantifiers. Because of this the final conjunct of (12.8) is equivalent to:

$$\text{dom}(telephones \cup \{name? \mapsto newnumber?\}) \subseteq members,$$

as neither *members'* nor *telephones'* occurs in it. By the properties of the domain operator this is equivalent to dom $telephones \cup \{name?\} \subseteq members$, and this is always true, since we have

$$\text{dom } telephones \subseteq members \wedge name? \in members.$$

Hence, the existentially quantified predicate in (12.7) is equivalent to the always true predicate. Therefore, the formula (12.7) is logically equivalent to:

$$\text{dom } telephones \subseteq members \wedge name? \in members \wedge$$
$$name? \mapsto newnumber? \notin telephones.$$

The schema pre *AddEntry*, therefore, simplifies to:

PreAddEntry
PhoneDB
name?: Person
newnumber?: Phone

$name? \in members$
$name? \mapsto newnumber? \notin telephones$

A Note on Terminology Before proceeding I just want to say something about the use of the word 'precondition'. The predicate part of the schema *PreAddEntry*—that I have just worked out—consists of the conjunction of the following three predicates:

$$\text{dom } telephones \subseteq members, \tag{12.9}$$

$$name? \in members, \tag{12.10}$$

$$name? \mapsto newnumber? \notin telephones. \tag{12.11}$$

The schema *PreAddEntry* delimits the class of states of the telephone database system to those on which the operation specified by the schema *AddEntry* can be successfully carried out. In doing this the state invariant—in my example, the predicate (12.9)— plays a different role from the other two predicates, namely (12.10) and (12.11). The state invariant is part of the predicate part of *every* schema specifying an operation on the telephone database system. Throughout the entire specification we are only considering states which satisfy the state invariant. The predicate (12.9) is part of the predicate part of every precondition schema derived from a schema specifying an operation on the telephone database system, whereas the predicates (12.10) and (12.11) are peculiar to the predicate part of *PreAddEntry*. The state invariant can be thought of as a precondition to the entire specification, whereas the other preconditions of each operation are specific to that operation. Because of the different role that the state invariant plays, it is often not thought of as forming part of the specific preconditions of an operation. Thus, people tend to talk, for example, of (12.10) and (12.11) as being *the* two joint preconditions of *AddEntry* and I have frequently used this elliptical way of talking in this book.

12.7 Totality

Another useful thing to know about a specification is which operations are *total* and which are not. The operation *Enter1* is not total, because it is not specified what happens when $\neg(\#d < Max)$, and it is not specified what happens when $p? \in d$. In order to specify a total operation corresponding to someone entering the classroom we need some additional schemas. The schema *Full1* specifies what happens when $\#d \geq Max$.

```
┌─ Full1 ─────────────────────────────
│ ΞClass1
│ p?: Person
│ rep!: Report
├─────────────────────────────────────
│ #d ≥ Max
│ rep! = 'Class full'
└─────────────────────────────────────
```

The schema *AlreadyPresent1* specifies what happens when $p? \in d$, that is to say, when the person $p?$ who is trying to enter the classroom is already in the classroom.

```
┌─ AlreadyPresent1 ────────────────────────────────
│ ΞClass1
│ p?: Person
│ rep!: Report
├──────────────────────────────────────────────────
│ p? ∈ d
│ rep! = 'Already here'
└──────────────────────────────────────────────────
```

The schema *Success* just outputs the message 'Okay'. It is used to tell us that the operation *Enter1* has been successfully carried out.

```
┌─ Success ────────────────────────────────────────
│ rep!: Report
├──────────────────────────────────────────────────
│ rep! = 'Okay'
└──────────────────────────────────────────────────
```

It is now possible to specify the total operation of someone attempting to enter the classroom:

$$DoEnter1 \triangleq (Enter1 \wedge Success) \vee Full1 \vee AlreadyPresent1$$

It is useful to know which operations are total and which are not. An operation is *total* if it is defined on every state which satisfies the state invariant.[6] This again brings out the special role of the state invariant in a specification.

12.8   Operation Refinement

The final topic that I want to deal with in this chapter is that of *operation refinement*. This takes place within a single specification in that only one kind of state space is involved. It is a way of relating operations defined on the same data.

The concrete operation *OpC* is a refinement of the abstract operation *OpA*, both defined on the same state space, iff both of the following predicates are true:

$$\text{pre } OpA \Rightarrow \text{pre } OpC,$$
$$\text{pre } OpA \wedge OpC \Rightarrow OpA.$$

The first of these specifies that the concrete operation succeeds whenever the abstract one does, although there might be situations in which the concrete state succeeds but the abstract one does not. The second predicate specifies that the abstract and concrete operations produce the same results on the same starting states.

---

[6]This means that the precondition of a total operation need not be the always true proposition.

Chapter 13

Reification and Decomposition

13.1 Introduction

The reader should, by now, understand the structure of a formal specification written in **Z**. One of the first things that has to be done is to define the state of the system being described. For example, the state of a classroom could be specified like this, where *Person* is the type of all people:

$$
\begin{array}{|l}
\hline
\_Class1 \underline{\hspace{6cm}} \\
\hline
d : \mathbf{P}\ Person \\
\hline
\#d \leq Max \\
\hline
\end{array}
$$

Here, d is the set of all the people currently in the classroom and *Max* is a number representing the capacity of the classroom. After the state has been defined, various operations are then specified. For example, the operation of someone leaving the classroom can be specified in this way:

$$
\begin{array}{|l}
\hline
\_Leave1 \underline{\hspace{6cm}} \\
\hline
\Delta\,Class1 \\
p? : Person \\
\hline
p? \in d \\
d' = d \setminus \{p?\} \\
\hline
\end{array}
$$

The purpose of a formal specification is to help us in the writing of programs and to enable us to prove that a particular program either does or does not meet its specification. Because **Z** contains many very high-level abstract mathematical data types and because operations are specified by giving their preconditions and postconditions, the "distance" between the specification and available programming language constructs may seem far too great to bridge. Thus, it is often a good idea to write another specification which uses less abstract data types and more "algorithmic" constructs in it. This second specification can then be thought of as being intermediate between the

143

original specification and the eventual program. (I shall call this second intermediate specification the *design* in this chapter.) Clearly, the specification and the design have to be related in some way. What we require is that any program which is a correct implementation of the design is also a correct implementation of the specification. When this requirement obtains we say that the state of the design is a *reification* or *refinement* of the state of the specification and that the operations in the specification have been *decomposed* into those of the design or that the operations in the design *model* those in the specification.

Even in the case of the classroom specification a design would be useful. We might decide to implement the set d of people by means of a linked list or an array, but any proofs relating specification and program would be very complicated. By writing a design involving sequences rather than sets, we divide the large distance between specification and program into two manageable parts and the resulting proofs are individually much less complicated.

So, to summarize, the process of taking an abstract mathematical data type, like a set, and representing it by a sequence, say, is called *data reification*. This is the process of transforming one data type into another one. It transforms an abstract data type into a more concrete one. It is possible to carry out data refinement in **Z** by using appropriate schemas, and I will in fact do that in the latter part of this chapter, but because the ideas involved are fairly complex I begin this chapter by explaining the important notion of a retrieve function and how to establish the correctness of a proposed retrieve function without using schemas. When the ideas involved are understood, it is then easier to see how a schema can be used instead of a retrieve function and to appreciate the proof-obligations involved.

13.2   Modelling Sets by Sequences

Although sets are available in some programming languages I am going to consider the reification of sets into sequences in order to illustrate the ideas involved. For illustrative purposes I am going to consider sets of people and, as usual, *Person* is the type of all people. Let $U: \mathbf{P}\,Person$ be a set of people. For example, $U = \{john, mary, tom\}$. We want to represent the set U by means of an appropriate sequence of people $\sigma: \text{iseq}\,Person$, where iseq X is the type of all finite injective sequences of elements drawn from X. An injective sequence is just one which does not contain any repetitions. So, for example, we might have $\sigma = \langle john, tom, mary \rangle$. In this example, $\mathbf{P}\,Person$ is the abstract type and iseq $Person$ is the concrete type.

The way we relate the abstract and concrete data types is by means of a *retrieve* function. The retrieve function maps the concrete type into the abstract one:

$$ret: \text{iseq}\,Person \rightarrow \mathbf{P}\,Person.$$

In the case of sets being modelled as injective sequences a suitable retrieve function is $ret\,\sigma = \text{ran}\,\sigma$. The retrieve function has to be from the concrete type to the abstract one because many sequences correspond to the same set. This is illustrated in Fig. 13.1.

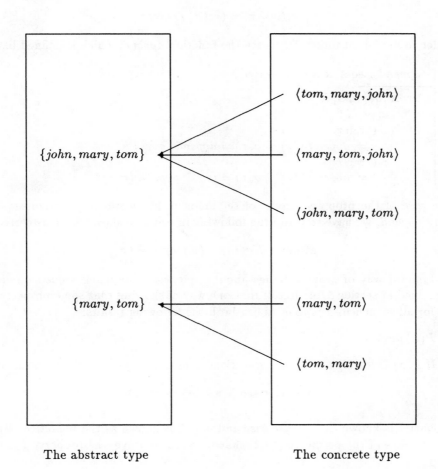

The abstract type   The concrete type

Figure 13.1: The retrieve function.

13.2.1 Correctness of Operation Modelling

In relating abstract and concrete types we have to relate operations defined on the abstract type, like set union, intersection and difference, to operations defined on the concrete type. For an operation $\heartsuit$ in the concrete world to correctly model the operation $\triangle$ in the abstract world the diagram in Fig. 13.2 must commute; that is to say, the following result must be provable:

$$ret(\sigma \heartsuit \tau) = (ret\ \sigma) \triangle (ret\ \tau). \tag{13.1}$$

In order to model set union, let us try the function *append*, which is defined like this:

$$
\begin{array}{|l}
\hline
append\colon \text{iseq}\ X \times \text{iseq}\ X \to \text{iseq}\ X \\
\hline
\forall x\colon X; \sigma, \tau\colon \text{iseq}\ X\ \bullet \\
\quad (append\ (\langle\ \rangle, \tau) = \tau)\ \wedge \\
\quad (x \in \text{ran}\ \tau \\
\qquad \Rightarrow append\ (\langle x \rangle \frown \sigma, \tau) = append\ (\sigma, \tau))\ \wedge \\
\quad (x \notin \text{ran}\ \tau \\
\qquad \Rightarrow append\ (\langle x \rangle \frown \sigma, \tau) = \langle x \rangle \frown append\ (\sigma, \tau)) \\
\end{array}
$$

In the case of the proposed model of set union in the world of injective sequences, namely *append*, we have to prove the following in order to show that it is correct:

$$ret(append(\sigma, \tau)) = (ret\ \sigma) \cup (ret\ \tau). \tag{13.2}$$

One standard way of proving things about sequences is by using *sequence induction* as explained in section 11.4. Recall that one way of showing that some property $P(\sigma)$ holds for all sequences σ is to establish both the following results:

1. $P(\langle\ \rangle)$ holds.

2. If $P(\sigma)$ holds for any sequence σ, then so does $P(\langle x \rangle \frown \sigma)$. In symbols, this is:

$$\forall x\colon X; \sigma\colon \text{seq}\ X\ \bullet\ P(\sigma) \Rightarrow P(\langle x \rangle \frown \sigma).$$

Here, part 1 is known as the *base case* and part 2 is known as the *inductive step*.

In the case of the predicate (13.2) that we want to prove, the property $P(\_)$ is:

$$ret(append\ (\_, \tau)) = (ret\ \_) \cup (ret\ \tau).$$

First, I will prove the base case and then the inductive step.

The abstract world

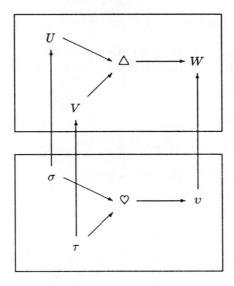

The concrete world

Figure 13.2: Correctness condition for operation modelling.

Base Case   We need to prove that the property is true for the empty sequence $\langle\ \rangle$; that is to say, we need to prove the following:

$$ret(append\ (\langle\ \rangle, \tau)) = (ret\langle\ \rangle) \cup (ret\ \tau).$$

I do this by showing that both sides are equal to the same thing.

$$LHS = ret\ \tau,$$

by the first clause of the definition of *append*.

$$RHS = \{\ \} \cup ret\ \tau,$$

since $ret\ \tau = ran\ \tau$ and $ran\langle\ \rangle = \{\ \}$,

$$= ret\ \tau,$$

by properties of set union. So, *LHS = RHS* and the base case is proved.

Inductive Step   To prove the inductive step we have to prove that:

$$ret(append\ (\langle x \rangle \frown \sigma, \tau)) = (ret(\langle x \rangle \frown \sigma)) \cup (ret\,\tau), \qquad (13.3)$$

holds on the assumption that the following is true:

$$ret(append\ (\sigma, \tau)) = (ret\,\sigma) \cup (ret\,\tau). \qquad (13.4)$$

The formula (13.4) is known as the *inductive hypothesis*.

To prove the inductive step there are two cases to consider:

1. $x \in$ ran τ.

2. $x \notin$ ran τ.

Taking the first case first.

$$LHS \text{ of } (13.3) = ret(append(\sigma, \tau)),$$

by the second clause of the definition of *append*,

$$= ret\,\sigma \cup ret\,\tau,$$

by the inductive hypothesis (13.4).

$$RHS \text{ of } (13.3) = ret\langle x \rangle \cup ret\,\sigma \cup ret\,\tau,$$

because $ret\,\sigma = $ ran σ and ran$(\sigma \frown \tau) = $ ran $\sigma \cup$ ran τ,

$$= \{x\} \cup ret\,\sigma \cup ret\,\tau,$$

$$= ret\,\sigma \cup ret\,\tau,$$

as $x \in ret\,\tau$. The result is proved as both the *LHS* and *RHS* of (13.3) are equal to the same thing.

Now we look at the second case.

$$LHS \text{ of } (13.3) = ret(\langle x \rangle \frown append(\sigma, \tau)),$$

by the third clause of the definition of *append*,

$$= ret\langle x \rangle \cup ret(append(\sigma, \tau)),$$

since $ret\,\sigma = $ ran σ and ran$(\sigma \frown \tau) = $ ran $\sigma \cup$ ran τ,

$$= ret\langle x \rangle \cup ret\,\sigma \cup ret\,\tau.$$

$$RHS \text{ of } (13.3) = ret\langle x \rangle \cup ret\,\sigma \cup ret\,\tau.$$

The result is proved as both the *LHS* and *RHS* of (13.3) are equal to the same thing.

Having proved both the base case and the inductive step, it follows by the principle of sequence induction that the formula (13.2) holds for all injective sequences σ and τ. So, I have proved that *append* correctly models the behaviour of $\cup$ in the concrete realm.

13.2.2 Modelling Set Intersection

The next thing that I am going to do is to show how set intersection and set difference can be modelled in the world of injective sequences by means of the functions *inter* and *subtract*. The function *inter* is defined as follows:

$$
\begin{array}{|l}
inter: \mathrm{iseq}\, X \times \mathrm{iseq}\, X \to \mathrm{iseq}\, X \\
\hline
\forall x: X; \sigma, \tau: \mathrm{iseq}\, X \bullet \\
\qquad (inter(\langle\ \rangle, \tau) = \langle\ \rangle) \wedge \\
\qquad (x \in \mathrm{ran}\, \tau \\
\qquad\qquad \Rightarrow inter(\langle x \rangle \frown \sigma, \tau) = \langle x \rangle \frown inter(\sigma, \tau)) \wedge \\
\qquad (x \notin \mathrm{ran}\, \tau \\
\qquad\qquad \Rightarrow inter(\langle x \rangle \frown \sigma, \tau) = inter(\sigma, \tau))
\end{array}
$$

To prove that *inter* correctly models $\cap$ we have to prove:

$$ret(inter(\sigma, \tau)) = ret\,\sigma \cap ret\,\tau. \tag{13.5}$$

This is done by using induction on the sequence σ. As usual, the proof is split into the base case and the inductive step.

Base Case For the base case we have to prove that (13.5) holds when $\sigma = \langle\ \rangle$.

$$
\begin{aligned}
\textit{LHS of } (13.5) &= ret(inter(\langle\ \rangle, \tau)), \\
&= ret\langle\ \rangle,
\end{aligned}
$$

by the first clause of the definition of *inter*,

$$= \{\ \}.$$

The next thing that I am going to show is that the *RHS* of (13.5) is also equal to the empty set.

$$
\begin{aligned}
\textit{RHS of } (13.5) &= ret\langle\ \rangle \cap ret\,\tau, \\
&= \{\ \} \cap ret\,\tau, \\
&= \{\ \}.
\end{aligned}
$$

The base case is established, since the *LHS* and *RHS* of (13.5) are both equal to the same thing, namely the empty set.

Inductive Step We need to prove:

$$ret(inter(\langle x \rangle \frown \sigma, \tau)) = ret(\langle x \rangle \frown \sigma) \cap ret\,\tau, \tag{13.6}$$

on the assumption that:

$$ret(inter(\sigma, \tau)) = ret\,\sigma \cap ret\,\tau.$$

We do this by case analysis, treating the situation in which $x \in \mathrm{ran}\,\tau$ first and then the situation in which $x \notin \mathrm{ran}\,\tau$.

Case 1 In this situation we have that $x \in \operatorname{ran} \tau$. I look at the *LHS* and *RHS* of (13.6) in turn.

$$LHS \text{ of } (13.6) = ret(\langle x \rangle \frown inter(\sigma, \tau)),$$
$$= ret\langle x \rangle \cup ret(inter(\sigma, \tau)),$$
$$= \{x\} \cup (ret\,\sigma \cap ret\,\tau),$$

by the inductive hypothesis.

$$RHS \text{ of } (13.6) = (ret\langle x \rangle \cup ret\,\sigma) \cap ret\,\tau,$$
$$= (\{x\} \cup ret\,\sigma) \cap ret\,\tau,$$
$$= (\{x\} \cap ret\,\tau) \cup (ret\,\sigma \cap ret\,\tau),$$

because $\cap$ distributes backwards through $\cup$,

$$= \{x\} \cup (ret\,\sigma \cap ret\,\tau).$$

As both the *LHS* and *RHS* of (13.6) are equal to the same thing, I have established that (13.6) is true in the case when $x \in \operatorname{ran} \tau$. (That $\cap$ distributes backwards through $\cup$ was proved on pp. 127ff. above.)

Case 2 In this case we have that $x \notin \operatorname{ran} \tau$. Again, I look at the *LHS* and *RHS* of (13.6) in turn.

$$LHS \text{ of } (13.6) = ret(inter(\sigma, \tau)),$$

by the third clause of the definition of *inter*,

$$= ret\,\sigma \cap ret\,\tau,$$

by the inductive hypothesis.

$$RHS \text{ of } (13.6) = (ret\langle x \rangle \cup ret\,\sigma) \cap ret\,\tau,$$
$$= (\{x\} \cup ret\,\sigma) \cap ret\,\tau,$$
$$= (\{x\} \cap ret\,\tau) \cup (ret\,\sigma \cap ret\,\tau),$$
$$= \{\ \} \cup (ret\,\sigma \cap ret\,\tau),$$
$$= ret\,\sigma \cap ret\,\tau.$$

As both the *LHS* and *RHS* of (13.6) are equal to the same thing, I have established that (13.6) is true in the case when $x \in \operatorname{ran} \tau$. Since $x \in \operatorname{ran} \tau \vee x \notin \operatorname{ran} \tau$ is always true in classical logic it follows that the inductive step has been established.

Since both the base case and the inductive step have been proved, the truth of the formula (13.5) follows by the principle of sequence induction.

13.2.3　Modelling Set Difference

The function *subtract* is defined in this way:

> *subtract*: iseq X × iseq X → iseq X
>
> ---
>
> $\forall x\colon X; \sigma, \tau\colon$ iseq X •
> $(subtract(\langle\ \rangle, \tau) = \langle\ \rangle) \wedge$
> $(x \in \mathrm{ran}\ \tau$
> $\Rightarrow subtract(\langle x \rangle \frown \sigma, \tau) = subtract(\sigma, \tau)) \wedge$
> $(x \notin \mathrm{ran}\ \tau$
> $\Rightarrow subtract(\langle x \rangle \frown \sigma, \tau) = \langle x \rangle \frown subtract(\sigma, \tau))$

To prove that *subtract* correctly models \ we have to prove:

$$ret(subtract(\sigma, \tau)) = ret\ \sigma \setminus ret\ \tau. \tag{13.7}$$

This is done using sequence induction. First, I prove the base case and then the inductive step.

Base Case　For the base case we have to prove that (13.7) holds when $\sigma = \langle\ \rangle$. I show that in that situation both the *RHS* and *LHS* of (13.7) are equal to the empty set. First, I look at the *LHS* of (13.7).

$$\begin{aligned} LHS \text{ of } (13.7) &= ret(subtract(\langle\ \rangle, \tau)), \\ &= ret\ \langle\ \rangle, \\ &= \{\ \}. \end{aligned}$$

Having established that the *LHS* of (13.7) is equal to the empty set, I turn my attention to the *RHS* of (13.7).

$$\begin{aligned} RHS \text{ of } (13.7) &= ret\ \langle\ \rangle \setminus ret\ \tau, \\ &= \{\ \} \setminus ret\ \tau, \\ &= \{\ \}. \end{aligned}$$

Having shown that the *LHS* and *RHS* of (13.7) are both equal to the empty set, I have established the base case.

Inductive Step　We need to prove:

$$ret(subtract(\langle x \rangle \frown \sigma, \tau)) = ret(\langle x \rangle \frown \sigma) \setminus ret\ \tau, \tag{13.8}$$

on the assumption that:

$$ret(subtract(\sigma, \tau)) = ret\ \sigma \setminus ret\ \tau.$$

We do this by case analysis, treating the situations in which $x \in \mathrm{ran}\ \tau$ and $x \notin \mathrm{ran}\ \tau$ separately. First, I look at the situation in which $x \in \mathrm{ran}\ \tau$.

Case 1   In this case we have that $x \in \text{ran}\,\tau$. First, I look at the *LHS* of (13.8).

$$\text{LHS of (13.8)} = ret(subtract(\sigma, \tau)),$$

by the definition of *subtract*,

$$= ret\,\sigma \setminus ret\,\tau,$$

by the inductive hypothesis. Now, I look at the *RHS* of (13.8).

$$\text{RHS of (13.8)} = (ret\langle x \rangle \cup ret\,\sigma) \setminus ret\,\tau,$$
$$= (\{x\} \cup ret\,\sigma) \setminus ret\,\tau,$$
$$= ret\,\sigma \setminus ret\,\tau,$$

since $x \in \text{ran}\,\tau$ and $ret\,\tau = \text{ran}\,\tau$. Thus, I have shown that (13.8) holds when $x \in \text{ran}\,\tau$, since both the *LHS* and *RHS* of it are equal to the same thing.

Case 2   In this case we have that $x \notin \text{ran}\,\tau$. First, I look at the *LHS* of (13.8).

$$\text{LHS of (13.8)} = ret(\langle x \rangle \frown subtract(\sigma, \tau)),$$
$$= ret\langle x \rangle \cup ret(subtract(\sigma, \tau)),$$
$$= ret\langle x \rangle \cup (ret\,\sigma \setminus ret\,\tau),$$

by the inductive hypothesis,

$$= \{x\} \cup (ret\,\sigma \setminus ret\,\tau).$$

Now I am going to consider the *RHS* of (13.8).

$$\text{RHS of (13.8)} = (ret\langle x \rangle \cup ret\,\sigma) \setminus ret\,\tau,$$
$$= (\{x\} \cup ret\,\sigma) \setminus ret\,\tau,$$
$$= (\{x\} \setminus ret\,\tau) \cup (ret\,\sigma \setminus ret\,\tau),$$

because $\setminus$ distributes backwards through $\cup$,

$$= \{x\} \cup (ret\,\sigma \setminus ret\,\tau).$$

as $x \notin \text{ran}\,\tau$. Thus, I have shown that (13.8) is true when $x \in \text{ran}\,\tau$. Since we must have that either $x \in \text{ran}\,\tau$ or $x \notin \text{ran}\,\tau$, it follows that the inductive step has been established. Since both the base case and the inductive step have been shown to be true, it follows by the principle of sequence induction that the property (13.7) is true for all injective sequences σ and τ. (That set difference distributes backwards through set union was proved in section 11.2.)

13.3 Reification and Decomposition using Schemas

13.3.1 Introduction

When I introduced schemas in chapter 4 I explained how they are used to define the state space of some problem domain and also how they are used to specify various operations on that state space. In the earlier part of this chapter I have explained the important notion of a retrieve function which relates objects in a concrete world to those objects in an abstract realm which they are modelling. In this section I am going to explain how a schema can be used to perform the work done by a retrieve function and also how the correctness criterion (13.1) appears when we are using a schema to relate an abstract and a more concrete specification.[1] In order to illustrate the use of a schema to relate a concrete and abstract specification I will make use of the classroom example again.

13.3.2 Example Specification and Design

To save space in this section I shall refer to the abstract specification simply as the *specification* and the more concrete specification I shall call the *design*. The example specification and design that I shall discuss are shown in Fig. 13.3.

13.3.3 Relating Specification and Design

The next thing that needs to be done is to relate the abstract and concrete states. This is done in **Z** by means of the following schema:

$$
\begin{array}{|l}
\_\; Class1\,Class2 \underline{\hspace{6cm}} \\
Class1 \\
Class2 \\
\hline
d = \mathrm{ran}\, l \\
\end{array}
$$

In full this schema is:

$$
\begin{array}{|l}
\_\; Class1\,Class2 \underline{\hspace{6cm}} \\
d\!: \mathbf{P}\; Person \\
l\!: \mathrm{seq}\; Person \\
\hline
\#d \leq Max \\
\#l \leq Max \\
d = \mathrm{ran}\, l \\
\end{array}
$$

Recall that when I was explaining the retrieve function *ret*, which allows us to model a set U by a sequence σ, I said that $U = ret\,\sigma$. (For this example $ret\,\sigma = \mathrm{ran}\,\sigma$.) That is the reason why the predicate $d = \mathrm{ran}\,l$ is included in *Class1 Class2*.

---

[1] It is possible to model an abstract specification by a concrete one even if there is no *function* from the concrete objects to the abstract ones. Sometimes a *relation* between abstract and concrete objects suffices. I will say more about this in section 13.3.5 below.

$[Person]$ $Max: \mathbf{N}$

$\begin{array}{|l} \hline \_\,Class1\,_____ \\ d: \mathbf{P}\; Person \\ \hline \#d \leq Max \\ \hline \end{array}$

$\Delta\, Class1 \;\stackrel{\wedge}{=}\; Class1 \wedge Class1'$

$\Xi\, Class1 \;\stackrel{\wedge}{=}\; \Delta\, Class1 \mid d' = d$

$Init1' \;\stackrel{\wedge}{=}\; Class1' \mid d' = \{\ \}$

$\begin{array}{|l} \hline \_\,Enter1\,_____ \\ \Delta\, Class1 \\ p?: Person \\ \hline \#d < Max \\ p? \notin d \\ d' = d \cup \{p?\} \\ \hline \end{array}$

$\begin{array}{|l} \hline \_\,Leave1\,_____ \\ \Delta\, Class1 \\ p?: Person \\ \hline p? \in d \\ d' = d \setminus \{p?\} \\ \hline \end{array}$

The specification

$[Person]$ $Max: \mathbf{N}$

$\begin{array}{|l} \hline \_\,Class2\,_____ \\ l: \text{iseq}\; Person \\ \hline \#l \leq Max \\ \hline \end{array}$

$\Delta\, Class2 \;\stackrel{\wedge}{=}\; Class2 \wedge Class2'$

$\Xi\, Class2 \;\stackrel{\wedge}{=}\; \Delta\, Class2 \mid l' = l$

$Init2' \;\stackrel{\wedge}{=}\; Class2' \mid l' = \langle\ \rangle$

$\begin{array}{|l} \hline \_\,Enter2\,_____ \\ \Delta\, Class2 \\ p?: Person \\ \hline \#l < Max \\ p? \notin \text{ran}\, l \\ l' = append(l, \langle p? \rangle) \\ \hline \end{array}$

$\begin{array}{|l} \hline \_\,Leave2\,_____ \\ \Delta\, Class2 \\ p?: Person \\ \hline p? \in \text{ran}\, l \\ l' = subtract(d, \langle p? \rangle) \\ \hline \end{array}$

The design

Figure 13.3: Classroom specification and design.

13.3.4 Correctness of Design

In order to prove that the design is a correct reification of the specification we have to prove a number of things. In the first place we have to prove that the initial states correspond to one another and then—for each operation in the design—we have to prove that it is both correct and also that it is applicable. Proving correctness and applicability for an operation defined using schemas corresponds to proving the correctness criterion (13.1) for the retrieve function.

Correspondence of Initial States

The schema $Class1Class2$ is like the retrieve function I described earlier. In order to show that initial states correspond in the abstract and concrete worlds we have to prove:

$$Init2' \land Class1Class2' \Rightarrow Init1'.$$

Expanding this predicate we get:

$$\#l' \leq Max \land l' = \langle \, \rangle \land d' = \operatorname{ran} l' \Rightarrow \#d' \leq Max \land d' = \{ \, \}. \qquad (13.9)$$

As is conventional in mathematics we assume that all the free variables in this predicate are universally quantified over. Consider the consequent of (13.9). It is equivalent to $\# \{ \, \} \leq Max$ which is equivalent to $true$ because $\# \{ \, \} = 0$. As the consequent of (13.9) is true, the entire predicate is true, by the properties of $\Rightarrow$; therefore I have proved that the initial states correspond.

Applicability of $Enter2$

In order to prove that the operation $Enter2$ is applicable we have to establish the following predicate:

$$\operatorname{pre} Enter1 \land Class1Class2 \Rightarrow \operatorname{pre} Enter2. \qquad (13.10)$$

This states that if we start from a state in the state space of the abstract world which satisfies the preconditions of $Enter1$ (that is to say, a state in which the operation $Enter1$ can be performed successfully), then any concrete state corresponding to that abstract state by means of $Class1Class2$ can also be performed successfully. Fig. 13.4 represents this graphically. Expanding (13.10) we get the predicate:

$$(\# < Max \land p? \notin d) \land (\#d \leq Max \land \#l \leq Max \land d = \operatorname{ran} l) \Rightarrow (\#l < Max \land p? \notin \operatorname{ran} l).$$

This is true, since $\#d = \#l$ (sinc l is an injective sequence, that is to say, one without repetitions) and $d = \operatorname{ran} l$.

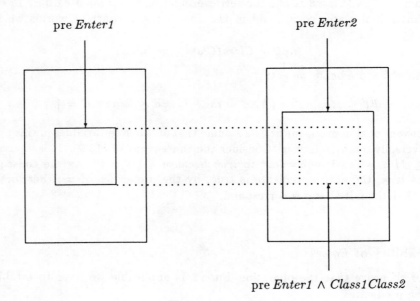

pre *Enter1*

pre *Enter2*

pre *Enter1* ∧ *Class1 Class2*

Entire abstract state space   Entire concrete state space

Figure 13.4: Applicability.

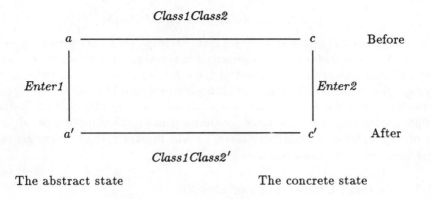

Figure 13.5: Correctness.

Correctness of *Enter2*

The correctness of *Enter2* is expressed by means of the predicate:

$$\text{pre } Enter1 \wedge \Delta\, Class1\, Class2 \wedge Enter2 \Rightarrow Enter1\,. \tag{13.11}$$

The significance of the proof requirement (13.11) is best explained with reference to Fig. 13.5. The predicate (13.11) expresses symbolically the following requirement. Let a be a state in the specification which satisfies pre *Enter1*, that is to say, it is a state which allows the operation *Enter1* to be carried out, and let c be the concrete state in the design which corresponds to a through the schema *Class1 Class2*. Since I have already proved that *Enter1* is applicable, we know that c satisfies pre *Enter2*; therefore, we know that there is an after state c' which is the result of carrying out the operation *Enter2* starting from the before state c. Furthermore, let a' be the state back in the specification which is related through *Class1 Class2'* to c'. Given all these states—which is conveyed by the antecedent of (13.11)—then what the conclusion of (13.11) says is that a' is the result of applying *Enter1* to the state a. In other words, the diagram in Fig. 13.5 commutes.

Now I am going to convince you of the truth of (13.5). Expanding it we get:

$$(\#d < Max \wedge p? \notin d \wedge d = \operatorname{ran} l \wedge d' = \operatorname{ran} l' \wedge$$
$$\#l < Max \wedge p? \notin \operatorname{ran} l \wedge l' = append(l', \langle p? \rangle))$$
$$\Rightarrow (\#d < Max \wedge p? \notin d \wedge d' = d \cup \{p?\})\,.$$

This may seem exceedingly complicated at first sight, but to prove that it is true just amounts to proving the following:

$$\operatorname{ran}(append(l, \langle p? \rangle)) = d \cup \{p?\},$$

when $p? \notin d$, and this follows straightforwardly from the definitions of *append* and ran.

157

Discussion

The proof-obligations just discussed are not as general as they could be. They are simplified because the retrieve schema has the following property:

$$\forall Class2 \bullet \exists_1 Class1 \bullet Class1\,Class2, \tag{13.12}$$

that is to say, one and only one abstract state corresponds to any given concrete state. An injective sequence of people, whose length is less than or equal to *Max*, corresponds to one and only one set made up out of those self-same people, though—of course—many sequences correspond to that set. It is possible—and at times necessary—to make use of retrieve schemas which do not have this property. In this case the initialization proof obligation and the correctness requirement are more complicated, although the proof of applicability remains the same. I will illustrate these more general proof requirements with the same classroom example.

13.3.5 General Correctness of Design

Correspondence of Initial States

Given a specification and a design linked by a schema which does not necessarily satisfy the property exemplified by (13.12) the first thing we have to prove is that the initial states of the specification and the design correspond to one another. (Remember that *Class1 Class2* is like the retrieve function I described earlier.) So, what we have to establish is the following predicate:

$$Init2' \Rightarrow \exists\, Class1' \bullet Init1' \wedge Class1\,Class2'.$$

In words this says that if we have an initial state in the design, then there exists a state in the specification which is an initial state and which is related to the initial state of the design by means of *Class1 Class2'*. Expanding this predicate we get:

$$(\#l' \leq Max \wedge l' = \langle\,\rangle) \Rightarrow$$
$$(\exists d' : \mathbf{P}\ Person \mid \#d' \leq Max \bullet \#d' \leq Max \wedge$$
$$d' = \{\,\} \wedge \#d' \leq Max \wedge \#l' \leq Max \wedge d' = \operatorname{ran} l').$$

Substituting $\{\,\}$ for d' within the existential quantifier and removing duplicate conjuncts gives us:

$$(\#l' \leq Max \wedge l' = \langle\,\rangle) \Rightarrow$$
$$(\exists d' : \mathbf{P}\ Person \mid \#\{\,\} \leq Max \bullet \#l' \leq Max \wedge \{\,\} = \operatorname{ran} l'),$$

which is equivalent to:

$$(\#l' \leq Max \wedge l' = \langle\,\rangle) \Rightarrow (\#\{\,\} \leq Max \wedge \#l' \leq Max \wedge \{\,\} = \operatorname{ran} l'),$$

because the binding variable d' does not bind anything. Substituting $\langle\,\rangle$ for l' in this gives us:

$$\#\langle\,\rangle \leq Max \Rightarrow (\#\{\,\} \leq Max \wedge \{\,\} = \operatorname{ran}\langle\,\rangle).$$

This is true because $\#\{\,\} = \#\langle\,\rangle = 0$ and $\operatorname{ran}\langle\,\rangle = \{\,\}$.

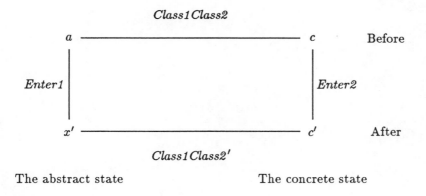

Figure 13.6: Correctness in the general case.

Correctness of *Enter2*

For each operation we have to prove *correctness* and *applicability*. The proof of applicability in the general case is proved in exactly the same way as discussed on p. 155 above. In order to prove that the operation *Enter2* is correct in the general case we have to establish the following predicate:

$$\text{pre } Enter1 \wedge Class1\,Class2 \wedge Enter2 \Rightarrow \exists\, Class1' \bullet Class1\,Class2' \wedge Enter1.$$

In order to understand this proof requirement let a be an abstract state, let c be a concrete state corresponding to a by means of *Class1 Class2* and let c' be a concrete state that results from c by the application of *Enter2*. Then, this proof requirement states that given a, c and c' as mentioned, there exists an abstract state x' which is the result of applying *Enter1* to a and it is also related to c' by means of *Class1 Class2'*. The diagram in Fig. 13.6 might help to clarify this proof requirement. The above formula states that there exists an x' which satisfies the diagram in Fig. 13.6.

159

Part IV

Case Studies

Chapter 14

Two Small Case Studies

14.1   The Bill of Materials Problem

14.1.1   Introduction

In this chapter I develop two small case studies. The first is a **Z** version of the bill of materials problem and the second is the specification of a simple route planner. Jones (1980), pp. 125–126 and 201–203, discusses the bill of materials problem. Imagine that a manufacturing company maintains a database which keeps information on the immediate constituents of the various articles that it makes. These immediate constituents may themselves be made up out of other components and so on, but clearly there must be some primitive components which are not made up out of any simpler components. All this information is kept in the database as well.

Given such a database—known as a *bill of materials*—there are various pieces of information that we are interested in extracting from it, such as (a) all the components that are used in the construction of a particular item and (b) all the items in the construction of which one particular component is used.

14.1.2   Representing the Database

An example of a bill of materials is pictured in Fig. 14.1.[1] In this diagram if a part x is joined by a line to a part y and x is to the left of y, then that is to be understood as meaning that y is an immediate constituent of x. Thus, p_7, p_3 and p_2 are immediate constituents of p_1. Lines are terminated by small filled-in circles, so p_3 is an immediate constituent of p_5, but neither p_6 nor p_7 are. The primitive non-composite parts are p_4, p_6 and p_7.

There are various ways in which a bill of materials can be represented in **Z**. We can, for example, represent a bill of materials by means of a partial function $bom: Part \nrightarrow \mathbf{F} \, Part$ from parts to finite sets of parts. Here, $Part$ is the type of all parts, both primitive and composite, and for a given part x, $bom\,x$ is the set of all

---

[1]This is exactly the same example that Jones (1980) discusses. See his Fig. 28 on p. 125. I have used his example so that it is easy for the reader to compare our discussions of this problem.

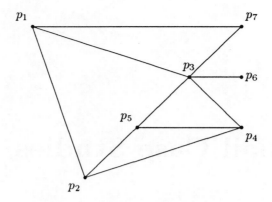

Figure 14.1: An example of a bill of materials.

$$bom = \{p_1 \mapsto \{p_2, p_3, p_7\},$$
$$p_2 \mapsto \{p_4, p_5\},$$
$$p_3 \mapsto \{p_4, p_6, p_7\},$$
$$p_4 \mapsto \{ \ \},$$
$$p_5 \mapsto \{p_3, p_4\},$$
$$p_6 \mapsto \{ \ \},$$
$$p_7 \mapsto \{ \ \}\}.$$

Figure 14.2: The function *bom*.

immediate constituents of x. If x is non-composite, then $bom\,x = \{\ \}$.[2] Using this representation, the information contained in Fig. 14.1 is expressed in the function *bom* which is shown in Fig. 14.2. It is not difficult to define a relation which holds between two things iff the first is a constituent—not necessarily immediate—of the second.[3]

$$\boxed{\begin{array}{l} =[X]\!= \\ \hline isconstit\colon (X \twoheadrightarrow \mathbf{F}\,X) \to (X \leftrightarrow X) \\ \hline \forall f\colon X \twoheadrightarrow \mathbf{F}\,X; x, y\colon X \bullet \\ \qquad x \mapsto y \in isconstit\,f \iff \\ \qquad\qquad (y \in fx \vee \exists z\colon X \mid z \in fx \bullet y \mapsto z \in isconstit\,f) \end{array}}$$

We have that $x \mapsto y \in isconstit(bom)$ iff y is a constituent of x.

We are only interested in bills of materials that are free of cycles, that is to say, no part can be a constituent of itself. The set of all cycle-free bills of materials is

---

[2]This is the representation that Jones adopts, except that he expresses it in VDM and not **Z**.
[3]See Jones (1980), p. 202.

cyclefree[*Part*], where *cyclefree* is defined as follows:

$$
\begin{array}{|l}
\hline
[X] \\
\hline
\textit{cyclefree}: \mathbf{P}(X \nrightarrow \mathbf{F}\,X) \\
\hline
\forall f: X \nrightarrow \mathbf{F}\,X \bullet \\
\quad f \in \textit{cyclefree} \iff \neg\exists x: X \bullet x \mapsto x \in \textit{isconstit}\ f \\
\hline
\end{array}
$$

14.1.3 Specifying Parts Explosion

The first thing that I am going to specify is the set of all constituents—both immediate and non-immediate—of a particular part, p, with respect to a given bill of materials, *bom*. The part itself is to figure amongst its constituents. The required set is *expl1* [*Part*](*bom, p*), where *expl1* is defined like this:[4]

$$
\begin{array}{|l}
\hline
[X] \\
\hline
\textit{expl1}: (X \nrightarrow \mathbf{F}\,X) \times X \rightarrow \mathbf{F}\,X \\
\hline
\forall f: X \nrightarrow \mathbf{F}\,X; x: X \bullet \\
\quad \textit{expl1}\,(f, x) = \{x\} \cup \bigcup\{y: X \mid y \in fx \bullet \textit{expl1}\,(f, y)\} \\
\hline
\end{array}
$$

The next thing that we want to specify is the set of all parts in the construction of which a particular part, p, figures, with respect to a bill of materials, *bom*. The part p is to appear in the set returned. The required set is *figs1* [*Part*](*bom, p*), where *figs1* is defined as follows:

$$
\begin{array}{|l}
\hline
[X] \\
\hline
\textit{figs1}: (X \nrightarrow \mathbf{F}\,X) \times X \rightarrow \mathbf{F}\,X \\
\hline
\forall f: X \nrightarrow \mathbf{F}\,X; x: X \bullet \\
\quad \textit{figs1}\,(f, x) = \{x\} \cup \{y: X; U: \mathbf{F}\,X \mid y \mapsto U \in f \wedge x \in U \bullet y\} \\
\hline
\end{array}
$$

14.1.4 Another Specification of the Problem

Given any problem to specify there are usually several ways of representing the information or data involved. In this subsection I am going to illustrate this by giving another specification of the parts explosion problem. Rather than representing a bill of materials as a function of type *Part* $\nrightarrow$ **F** *Part*, I shall represent it by means of a relation of type *Part* $\leftrightarrow$ *Part*. The information contained in Fig. 14.1 is now contained in the relation *moo*: *Part* $\leftrightarrow$ *Part*, defined as shown in Fig. 14.3. An ordered pair $x \mapsto y$ is an element of *moo* iff y is an immediate constituent of x. The part y is a constituent of x iff $x \mapsto y \in moo^{+}$, that is to say, the transitive closure[5] of *moo*, and *moo* is cycle-free iff $\neg\exists x: Part \bullet x \mapsto x \in moo^{+}$. Using this representation of

---

[4]This is just a translation into **Z** of Jones's solution. See Jones (1980), p. 126.

[5]The transitive closure of a relation—and its reflexive-transitive closure—are explained in section 5.3 and defined formally at the end of chapter 22.

$$moo = \{p_1 \mapsto p_2,$$
$$p_1 \mapsto p_3,$$
$$p_1 \mapsto p_7,$$
$$p_2 \mapsto p_4,$$
$$p_2 \mapsto p_5,$$
$$p_3 \mapsto p_4,$$
$$p_3 \mapsto p_6,$$
$$p_3 \mapsto p_7,$$
$$p_5 \mapsto p_3,$$
$$p_5 \mapsto p_4\}.$$

Figure 14.3: The relation *moo*.

the bill of materials the definition of the set of all constituents—both immediate and non-immediate—of a particular part, p, with respect to a given bill of materials, *moo*, is $moo^*(\!|\{p\}|\!)$, where F^* forms the reflexive-transitive closure of F.

The definition of the set of all parts in the construction of which a particular part, p, figures, with respect to a bill of materials *moo*, is given by $(moo^*)^{-1}(\!|\{p\}|\!)$. It is possible to introduce definitions of functions *expl2* and *figs2* like this:

$$\boxed{\begin{array}{l} [X] \\ \hline expl2 \colon (X \nrightarrow \mathbf{F}\,X) \times X \to \mathbf{F}\,X \\ \hline \forall f \colon X \nrightarrow \mathbf{F}\,X; x \colon X \bullet \\ \qquad expl2(f, x) = f^*(\!|\{p\}|\!) \end{array}}$$

$$\boxed{\begin{array}{l} [X] \\ \hline figs2 \colon (X \nrightarrow \mathbf{F}\,X) \times X \to \mathbf{F}\,X \\ \hline \forall f \colon X \nrightarrow \mathbf{F}\,X; x \colon X \bullet \\ \qquad figs2(f, x) = (f^*)^{-1}(\!|\{p\}|\!) \end{array}}$$

Doing this, the required specifications become, respectively, $expl2[Part](moo, p)$ and $figs2[Part](moo, p)$. Because the terms used in the definition of *expl2* and *figs2* are so simple, there is little point, however, in introducing these definitions.

Using this representation of the bill of materials it is easy to express the set of all primitive components. A *primitive* component is one which does not have any immediate constituents. The set of all such components is ran *moo* \ dom *moo*. It is easy to express the connection that exists between these two representations:

$$\forall p: Part \bullet bom\, p = moo(\!|\{p\}|\!).$$

State and Operations

Using the functions defined it is a fairly straightforward exercise to develop a **Z** specification of the bill of materials problem. In doing this I will use the simpler representation of such a bill. The state is represented by means of the schema *Materials*:

```
┌─ Materials ─────────────────────────────────
│  moo: Part ↔ Part
├─────────────────────────────────────────────
│  ¬∃x: Part • x ↦ x ∈ moo⁺
└─────────────────────────────────────────────
```

The single predicate here states that the relation *moo* does not contain any cycles.

The schemas $\Delta Materials$, $\Xi Materials$ and $InitMaterials'$ are defined in the usual way:

$$\Delta Materials \triangleq Materials \wedge Materials'$$

$$\Xi Materials \triangleq \Delta Materials \mid moo' = moo$$

$$InitMaterials' \triangleq Materials' \mid moo' = \{\ \}$$

Many operations could be defined on this state, such as adding new components to the database, but I will just specify two ways of interrogating the database, namely finding out the components of a particular item and finding out all the items in the manufacture of which a particular thing is used.

```
┌─ SubComponents ─────────────────────────────
│  ΞMaterials
│  in?: Part
│  out!: P Part
├─────────────────────────────────────────────
│  in? ∈ ran moo ∪ dom moo
│  out! = moo*(|{in?}|)
└─────────────────────────────────────────────
```

```
┌─ SuperComponents ───────────────────────────
│  ΞMaterials
│  in?: Part
│  out!: P Part
├─────────────────────────────────────────────
│  in? ∈ ran moo ∪ dom moo
│  out! = (moo*)⁻¹(|{in?}|)
└─────────────────────────────────────────────
```

14.2 A Simple Route Planner

14.2.1 Introduction

In this section I am going to develop the formal specification of a simple route planner. I start by discussing the problem informally. Fig. 14.4 shows a schematic map of an imaginary geographical region. The letters A, B, C, D, E, F, G, H and I represent places. The important thing about a place is that it occurs at a road junction. A place is just a location where two or more roads meet.

The symbols r_i, for $1 \leq i \leq 16$, represent roads or road-segments. r_3 and r_{12} might be the same road—the A38, for example—but for our purposes they have to be considered distinct because if you travel on r_3 you are not forced to travel on r_{12}. I will, however, call the r_i *roads* for the sake of brevity.

For this problem we have to associate every road with two attributes, namely its length and the kind of road it is. For simplicity, I will just consider three kinds of road, namely motorways, A-roads and B-roads. The length in kilometres and the kind of each road in Fig. 14.4 is given in the following table:

Road	Length	Kind
r_1	15	motorway
r_2	11	A-road
r_3	17	B-road
r_4	12	B-road
r_5	18	A-road
r_6	20	A-road
r_7	19	B-road
r_8	19	motorway
r_9	17	A-road
r_{10}	21	B-road
r_{11}	13	B-road
r_{12}	19	B-road
r_{13}	22	A-road
r_{14}	6	B-road
r_{15}	19	A-road
r_{16}	10	A-road

Note that the map in Fig. 14.4 is not drawn to scale. It has, rather, to be understood by analogy with the map of the London Underground. It only shows the "topology" of the situation it purports to depict.

The sort of operation that we want to define is one in which the user inputs the starting point and the finishing point of his journey and any constraints that he might want to put on the roads on which he travels—for example, that he does not want to travel on a motorway—and the system outputs the shortest route that satisfies those

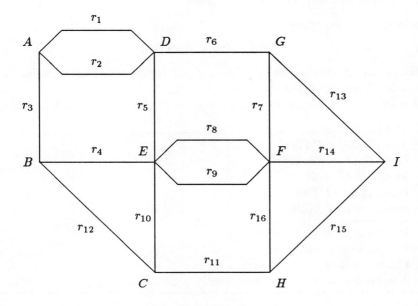

Figure 14.4: An imaginary geographical region.

constraints. (It is possible for there to be several routes of the same length which are each shorter than any other possible route. In that case the system should output all these shortest routes.)

As an example, consider a user who wants to go from A to E. There are a large number of possible routes. The best way to represent a route is as a sequence of roads. So, some of the possible routes from A to E are:

$$\sigma_1 = \langle r_3, r_4 \rangle,$$
$$\sigma_2 = \langle r_1, r_5 \rangle,$$
$$\sigma_3 = \langle r_2, r_5 \rangle,$$
$$\sigma_4 = \langle r_1, r_6, r_7, r_{14}, r_{15}, r_{11}, r_{10} \rangle,$$
$$\sigma_5 = \langle r_3, r_{12}, r_{11}, r_{15}, r_{14}, r_{16}, r_{11}, r_{10} \rangle.$$

Route σ_1 only uses B-roads, whereas σ_2 and σ_3 avoid using B-roads. Route σ_2 chooses a motorway if one is available. Routes σ_4 and σ_5 are very circuitous and σ_5 contains a cycle. In this case there are two routes shorter than all the others, namely σ_1 and σ_3, and these are both 29 kilometers long. If the user puts no constraints on the kind of road on which he wants to travel, then the system should output both of these routes. If he wants to travel only on B-roads, then the system should output σ_1, and so on.

14.2.2   Representing the State Space

This specification uses three given types:

$$[Place, Road, RoadType]$$

Place is the set of all possible locations, *Road* is the set of all possible roads and *RoadType* is the set of all possible kinds of road.

The state space of our route planner is given by means of the schema *Map*:

```
┌─ Map ──────────────────────────────────
│ joins: Road ⇸ F Place
│ kind: Road ⇸ RoadType
│ length: Road ⇸ N
│ knownplaces: F Place
│ knownroads: F Road
├─────────────────────────────────────────
│ knownplaces = ⋃ ran joins
│ knownroads ≐ dom joins
│ ∀U: ran joins • #U = 2
│ dom joins = dom kind = dom length
└─────────────────────────────────────────
```

The set of places *knownplaces* is the set of places that are actually on our map and the set of roads *knownroads* is the set of roads that are on the map. The reason for including these two sets is that we want to allow for the possibility of adding information to our database about new roads that have been constructed and new places that can be reached by road.

The function *joins* yields a set of places linked by the road given to it as an argument and the predicate $\forall U:\mathrm{ran}\ joins \bullet \#U = 2$ tells us that every road links two and only two places.

The function *kind* yields a road type as value for a road given to it as an argument and the function *length* returns the length of a road in kilometres—or miles, if you prefer. **R** could be substituted for **N**, if preferred.

The predicate:

$$\mathrm{dom}\ joins = \mathrm{dom}\ kind = \mathrm{dom}\ length, \tag{14.1}$$

informs us that every road on the map which links two places must be of a specific kind and also must have a definite length. The map shown in Fig. 14.4 is just what is known in discrete mathematics as a graph. Hence, the schema *Map* defines a graph.

Note that the predicate (14.1) is a legitimate bit of **Z** syntax. It is equivalent to:

$$\mathrm{dom}\ joins = \mathrm{dom}\ kind \wedge \mathrm{dom}\ kind = \mathrm{dom}\ length.$$

In fact, in general the chain of relationships:

$$t_1\ F_1\ t_2\ F_2\ t_3 \ldots t_{n-1}\ F_{n-1}\ t_n,$$

is equivalent to the conjunction of the individual relationships:

$$(t_1\ F_1\ t_2) \wedge (t_2\ F_2\ t_3) \wedge \ldots \wedge (t_{n-1}\ F_{n-1}\ t_n).$$

14.2.3 The Operations

In order to help me to specify operations on the state of the route planner I will first define two functions, namely *allroutes* and *shortestroutes*. First, I define *allroutes*:

$$allroutes: \mathbf{F}\ Road \rightarrow (Road \nrightarrow \mathbf{P}\ Place)$$
$$\rightarrow (Place \times Place) \rightarrow \mathbf{P}(\mathrm{seq}\ Road)$$

$\forall U: \mathbf{F}\ Road;\ f: Road \nrightarrow \mathbf{P}\ Place;\ x, y: Place;\ \sigma\ \mathrm{seq}\ Road\ \bullet$
$\sigma \in allroutes U\ f(x, y) \iff$
    $(\mathrm{ran}\ \sigma \subseteq U\ \wedge$
    $(\forall i: \mathrm{dom}\ \sigma \mid i \neq \#\sigma\ \bullet$
        $(\sigma \, \mathring{_\circ}\, f)i \cap (\sigma \, \mathring{_\circ}\, f)(i+1) \neq \{\ \}\ ) \wedge$
        $((x \in (\sigma \, \mathring{_\circ}\, f)1 \wedge y \in (\sigma \, \mathring{_\circ}\, f)(\#\sigma)) \vee (x \in (\sigma \, \mathring{_\circ}\, f)(\#\sigma) \wedge y \in (\sigma \, \mathring{_\circ}\, f)1)))$

The definition of *allroutes* works as follows. When it is used we have to supply arguments $U: \mathbf{F}\ Road$, $f: Road \nrightarrow \mathbf{P}\ Place$ and $(x, y): Place \times Place$. It has to be parameterized to a set U of roads because we only want roads that are members of *knownroads* to figure in the routes we output to the user and it has to be parameterized to a function f, since we only want the routes we output to pass through places that are on the map. The places x and y are the starting and finishing point of the journey our user is making and the set *allroutes* $U\ f(x, y)$ is the set of all routes which join x and y.

Let σ be an arbitrary route. Then the predicate ran $\sigma \subseteq U$ constrains the route to only use roads drawn from the set U. To understand the next predicate in the definition, recall that as σ is a sequence we can write it as $\langle x_1, x_2, \ldots, x_n \rangle$. When we come to use *allroutes* the actual parameters corresponding to f will be *joins*, thus $\sigma \, \mathring{_\circ}\, joins$ (which can also be written as map *joins* σ) is a sequence of sets—each of cardinality 2—of places $\langle U_1, U_2, \ldots, U_n \rangle$. For σ to be a route we want there to be at least one element in common between each two elements of map *joins* σ that are next to one another. We allow $U_i = U_{i+1}$, since there is no need to disallow cycles in our routes at this stage.

The final predicate in the definition just says that x and y are the first and last members of σ, not necessarily in that order. Clearly, someone who asks for routes from x to y will receive exactly the same response as someone who asks for all the routes from y to x. All the roads on our map are assumed to be two-way. It is now possible to define *shortestroutes* in terms of *routes*:

$$shortestroutes: \mathbf{F}\ Road \rightarrow (Road \nrightarrow \mathbf{P}\ Place)$$
$$\rightarrow (Road \nrightarrow \mathbf{N}) \rightarrow (Place \times Place) \rightarrow \mathbf{P}(\mathrm{seq}\ Road)$$

$\forall U: \mathbf{F}\ Road;\ f: Road \nrightarrow \mathbf{P}\ Place;\ g: Road \nrightarrow \mathbf{N};\ x, y: Place;\ \sigma\ \mathrm{seq}\ Road\ \bullet$
    $\sigma \in shortestroutes U\ fg(x, y) \iff$
        $(\sigma \in allroutes U\ f(x, y)\ \wedge$
        $(\forall \tau: \mathrm{seq}\ Road \mid \tau \in allroutes U\ f(x, y)\ \bullet$

$$\sum_{i=1}^{i=\#\sigma} (\sigma \, \mathring{_\circ}\, g)i \leq \sum_{i=1}^{i=\#\tau} (\tau \, \mathring{_\circ}\, g)i))$$

Although the summation operation $\sum$ is not part of standard **Z**, its meaning is so well understood that I can see no objection to using it in specifications.

Using the function *shortestroutes* it is now possible to specify the operation *Routes*. This accepts as input the starting point and the finishing point of the journey being undertaken—these are represented by *start?* and *finish?*, respectively—and produces as output the set *out!* of all routes between *start?* and *finish?*.

$$
\begin{array}{l}
\underline{\quad Routes \rule{6cm}{0pt}} \\
\Xi Map \\
start?, finish?: Place \\
out!: \mathbf{P}(\text{seq } Road) \\
\hline
\{start?, finish?\} \subseteq knownplaces \\
out! = shortestroutes\ knownroads\ joins\ length\ (start?, finish?) \\
\end{array}
$$

The schema *Routes* gives no opportunity for the user to indicate what kinds of road he wants to travel on. In order to give him that opportunity we use the schema *ChoosyRoutes*, in which the variable *k?* contains all the types of road the user does not mind travelling on.

$$
\begin{array}{l}
\underline{\quad ChoosyRoutes \rule{5cm}{0pt}} \\
\Xi Map \\
start?, finish?: Place \\
k?: \mathbf{F}\ RoadType \\
out!: \mathbf{P}(\text{seq } Road) \\
\hline
\{start?, finish?\} \subseteq knownplaces \\
out! = shortestroutes\ knownroads \\
\qquad\qquad ((kind \rhd k?) \lhd joins)\ length\ (start?, finish?) \\
\end{array}
$$

Chapter 15

Wing's Library Problem

15.1   Introduction

In this chapter I present a **Z** specification of a library system which is informally described by Wing (1988), p. 67, as follows.[1]

> Consider a small library database with the following transactions:
>
> 1. Check out a copy of a book. Return a copy of a book.
>
> 2. Add a copy of a book to the library. Remove a copy of a book from the library.
>
> 3. Get the list of books by a particular author or in a particular subject area.
>
> 4. Find out the list of books currently checked out by a particular borrower.
>
> 5. Find out what borrower last checked out a particular copy of a book.
>
> There are two types of users: staff users and ordinary borrowers. Transactions 1, 2, 4 and 5 are restricted to staff users, except that ordinary borrowers can perform transaction 4 to find out the list of books currently borrowed by themselves. The database must also satisfy the following constraints:
>
> - All copies in the library must be available for check-out or be checked out.
>
> - No copy of a book may be both available and checked out at the same time.
>
> - A borrower may not have more than a predefined number of books checked out at one time.

---

[1]This problem is based on one set by Kemmerer (1985).

15.2 Global Entities

This specification makes use of the following given types:

$$[Book, Copy, Person, Author, Subject, Report]$$

The set *Book* is the set of all possible books and *Copy* is the set of all possible copies of books. Books are considered to be abstract objects, whereas copies are physical objects. It is necessary to make this distinction in order to deal with the possibility that the library may contain several distinct copies of the same book. This happens, for example, when a book is popular and in much demand or when several editions of the same book have been produced.

The reason why I talk of 'all *possible* books' and 'all *possible* copies' is that we need to allow for the production of books and copies in the future. If I just said 'all books', someone might think that I was restricting the specification to books which actually exist at the present time.

The set *Person* is the set of all possible people. The set *Author* is the set of all possible authors and *Subject* is the set of all conceivable subjects, that is to say, the things that books can be about. The types *Author* and *Person* are distinguished because some books are considered to have been written by institutions. Some manuals and some standards fall into this category.

The final given type we need is the set *Report* which is the set of all necessary messages. It is defined by enumeration like this:

$Report ::=$ 'Okay'
    | 'Unauthorised requestor'
    | 'Not registered'
    | 'Copy checked out'
    | 'Cannot borrow any more copies'
    | 'Copy available'
    | 'This book is not new to the library'
    | 'This book is new to the library'
    | 'This copy is owned by the library'
    | 'This copy is not owned by the library'
    | 'This is the only copy in the library'
    | 'This is not the only copy in the library'
    | 'Unknown borrower'
    | 'Not authorised requestor'
    | 'Copy not previously borrowed'

We also need a constant *MaxCopiesAllowed* which is the maximum number of copies that anyone can borrow.

15.3 The State of the System

I shall describe the state of the library database in several stages. To begin with, the schema *ParaLibrary* contains information relating to the books in the library. Recall that a book is an abstract object, whereas a copy is a physical object. The library may contain several copies of the same book.

```
┌─ ParaLibrary ──────────────────────────────────────────────
│  instanceof: Copy ↠ Book
│  writtenby: Book ↠ F Author
│  about: Book ↠ F Subject
├────────────────────────────────────────────────────────────
│  dom writtenby ⊆ ran instanceof
│  dom about ⊆ ran instanceof
└────────────────────────────────────────────────────────────
```

The function *instanceof* tells us which book a copy is an instance of. There may be several copies of the same book, but a copy can only be an instance of one book. Hence, *instanceof* is a function. I am going to assume that the information component of the database does not contain any information about books which are not in the library.[2] How this assumption is captured in the specification will be explained later.[3] Because of this assumption every book in the library and known to the database must have at least one copy associated with it. The set ran *instanceof* is the set of all books in the library and dom *instanceof* is the set of all copies in the library. Given a book b the number of copies of that book in the library is $\#instanceof^{-1}(\!(\{b\}\!)\!)$.

The function *writtenby* tells us who wrote a particular book. It returns a set of authors which may be empty. Some books—like bound copies of journals—are associated with the empty set of authors.[4] Similarly, the function *about* tells us what a book is about. It returns a set of subjects, which again may be empty.[5]

The predicate dom *writtenby* ⊆ ran *instanceof*, in conjunction with (15.1) on p. 177, tells us that the database does not contain author information about books that are not in the library and the predicate dom *about* ⊆ ran *instanceof*, again in conjunction with (15.1) on page 177, tells us that the database does not contain subject information about books which are not in the library.[6]

The schema *LibraryDB* contains the rest of the information needed by the library.

---

[2] In a real-life situation it would be a good idea to check whether this is acceptable to the client for whom the software based on this specification will be produced. Needless to say, such consultation should take place as early as possible, since much of the following specification depends on it.

[3] It is captured by means of predicate (15.1) on p. 177.

[4] In a real-life situation it would be a good idea to find out whether this is acceptable to the client.

[5] Here again—in a real-life situation—it would be advisable to consult the client to see if this interpretation of the informal requirements is acceptable.

[6] Using the subset relation in these two predicates, rather than set equality, allows for the possibility that the library contains books about which it has either no author information or no subject information. I think it is desirable to allow for this. In setting up a library database, first, information relating to the borrowing of copies is input and then—possibly at a later stage—subject and author information is introduced.

```
┌─ LibraryDB ──────────────────────────────────────────────
│ borrower, staff: F Person
│ available, checkedout: F Copy
│ previouslyborrowedby, borrowedby: Copy ↦ Person
├──────────────────────────────────────────────────────────
│ borrower ∩ staff = { }
│ available ∩ checkedout = { }
│ dom borrowedby = checkedout
│ ran borrowedby ⊆ borrower
│ dom previouslyborrowedby ⊆ available ∪ checkedout
│ ran previouslyborrowedby ⊆ borrower
│ ∀p: Person | p ∈ borrower •
│     #borrowedby⁻¹(|{p}|) ≤ MaxCopiesAllowed
└──────────────────────────────────────────────────────────
```

Six identifiers are declared in this schema. The finite sets *borrower* and *staff* contain the people who can use the library and those who administer it, respectively. A member of the set *borrower* is known either as a borrower or as a registered user. The predicate *borrower* ∩ *staff* = { } tells us that the identifiers of users and staff are disjoint. This means that staff cannot borrow books from the library.[7]

The finite sets *available* and *checkedout* contain, respectively, all the copies of books that are either available for checkout or have actually been checked out. The predicate:

$$available \cap checkedout = \{\ \},$$

captures the following constraint from the statement of requirements:

- No copy of a book may be both available and checked out at the same time.

The function *borrowedby* tells us who is currently borrowing a particular copy of a book and *previouslyborrowedby* tells us who, if anyone, was the last person to borrow a copy of a book For example, let c be a particular copy of a book that is currently on loan. Then, *borrowedby* (c) is the current borrower of c and *previouslyborrowedby* (c) is the person, if any, who borrowed c immediately before the person *borrowedby* (c).

The predicate dom *borrowedby* = *checkedout* tells us that the set of copies that have been borrowed by someone or other is the same as the set of copies that are checked-out and the predicate ran *borrowedby* ⊆ *borrower* states that every checkedout copy must have been borrowed by a registered user, that is to say, a borrower.

The predicate:

$$\text{dom } previouslyborrowedby \subseteq available \cup checkedout,$$

states that previously borrowed copies are either available for checkout or have been checked out again and the predicate ran *previouslyborrowedby* ⊆ *borrower* states that the last borrower of every copy borrowed must be a registered user.

---

[7] In a real-life situation it would be a good idea to find out whether this is acceptable to the customer.

The final predicate in the schema, namely:

$$\forall p\colon Person \mid p \in borrower \bullet$$
$$\# borrowedby^{-1}(\!|\{p\}|\!) \le MaxCopiesAllowed,$$

captures the constraint:

- A borrower may not have more than a predefined number of books checked out at one time.

In some libraries borrowers are partitioned into several categories and different regulations apply to members of each category. For example, members of one category may be allowed to borrow more copies than members of another category. The constraint just quoted is consistent with that possibility, but it is also consistent with the situation I have assumed in which there is only a single ceiling on the number of copies of books that any user can borrow. In a real-life situation it would probably be a good idea to consult the client over this matter.

The complete state of the library is given by means of *LibraryState*:

```
┌─ LibraryState ─────────────────────────────────────
│ ParaLibrary
│ LibraryDB
├────────────────────────────────────────────────────
│ dom instanceof = available ∪ checkedout
└────────────────────────────────────────────────────
```

The predicate of the schema *LibraryState*, namely:

$$\text{dom } instanceof = available \cup checkedout, \tag{15.1}$$

tells us that the database does not contain information about copies of books which are not in stock.

The schemas $\Delta ParaLibrary$, $\Delta LibraryDB$ and $\Delta LibraryState$ are defined in the usual way:

$$\Delta ParaLibrary \mathrel{\hat=} ParaLibrary \wedge ParaLibrary'$$
$$\Delta LibraryDB \mathrel{\hat=} LibraryDB \wedge LibraryDB'$$
$$\Delta LibraryState \mathrel{\hat=} LibraryState \wedge LibraryState'$$

Similarly, the schemas $\Xi ParaLibrary$, $\Xi LibraryDB$ and $\Xi LibraryState$ are defined in the standard way:

$$\Xi ParaLibrary \ \hat{=} \ \Delta ParaLibrary \ |$$
$$instanceof' = instanceof \ \wedge$$
$$writtenby' = writtenby \ \wedge$$
$$about' = about$$

$$\Xi LibraryDB \ \hat{=} \ \Delta LibraryDB \ |$$
$$borrower' = borrower \ \wedge$$
$$staff' = staff \ \wedge$$
$$available' = available \ \wedge$$
$$checkedout' = checkedout \ \wedge$$
$$previouslyborrowedby' = previouslyborrowedby \ \wedge$$
$$borrowedby' = borrowedby$$

$$\Xi LibraryState \ \hat{=} \ \Xi ParaLibrary \wedge \Xi LibraryDB$$

In the initial state every variable is the empty set:

$$InitParaLibrary' \ \hat{=} \ ParaLibrary' \ |$$
$$instanceof' = \{ \ \} \ \wedge$$
$$writtenby' = \{ \ \} \ \wedge$$
$$about' = \{ \ \}$$

$$InitLibraryDB' \ \hat{=} \ LibraryDB' \ |$$
$$borrower' = \{ \ \} \ \wedge$$
$$staff' = \{ \ \} \ \wedge$$
$$available' = \{ \ \} \ \wedge$$
$$checkedout' = \{ \ \} \ \wedge$$
$$previouslyborrowedby' = \{ \ \} \ \wedge$$
$$borrowedby' = \{ \ \}$$

$$InitLibraryState' \ \hat{=} \ InitParaLibrary' \wedge InitLibraryDB'$$

15.4   The Operations

15.4.1   Checking-out and Returning Copies of Books

Checking-out Copies of Books

CheckOutCopy
Δ _LibraryState_
Ξ _ParaLibrary_
$n?: Person$
$c?: Copy$

$n? \in borrower$
$c? \in available$
$\# borrowedby^{-1}(\!|\{n?\}|\!) < MaxCopiesAllowed$

$available' = available \setminus \{c?\}$
$checkedout' = checkedout \cup \{c?\}$
$borrowedby' = borrowedby \cup \{c? \mapsto n?\}$

$previouslyborrowedby' = previouslyborrowedby$
$borrower' = borrower$
$staff' = staff$

First of all I will specify the transaction of a borrower $n?$ successfully checking out a copy $c?$ from the library. I shall ignore for the time being who is requesting the transaction to be carried out and what happens if the transaction is unsuccessful. I do mean that the two schemas Δ _LibraryState_ and Ξ _ParaLibrary_ should be included in the schema _CheckOutCopy_. This means that some variables—like _writtenby_—occur in both, but this does not cause any harm.

Note that I have introduced two blank lines into the predicate part of this schema. The purpose of these is to separate the predicates into three groups. The top group comprises the preconditions of the schema. The middle group of predicates actually records what happens when the operation being carried out is successful and the bottom group of predicates contains those variables that are left unaltered by this operation.

The preconditions of the schema _CheckOutCopy_ are the three predicates:

$$n? \in borrower,$$
$$c? \in available,$$
$$\# borrowedby^{-1}(\!|\{n?\}|\!) < MaxCopiesAllowed.$$

The first of these states that only registered users can borrow copies and the second states that only available copies can be borrowed. The third predicate says that a borrower can only borrow copies if the number of copies he currently has out on loan is strictly less than the maximum number allowed.

179

The schema *CheckOutCopy* only records the successful borrowing of a copy and the three predicates:

$$available' = available \setminus \{c?\},$$
$$checkedout' = checkedout \cup \{c?\},$$
$$borrowedby' = borrowedby \cup \{c? \mapsto n?\}.$$

record what happens when a copy has been successfully borrowed. The first two of these state that the copy $c?$ is transferred from being available for loan to actually being borrowed. The third predicate records the information that borrower $n?$ has now copy $c?$ on loan.

Every variable other than *available'*, *checkedout'* and *borrowedby'* is left unchanged by this operation. In particular the variable *previouslyborrowedby'* is unaltered. If someone borrows a copy of a book, that in no way alters the previous borrower of that copy.

Having explained what happens when a copy is successfully borrowed, I now need to take into account the status of the person who requests this transaction. This is because in the informal description of the library it is stated that only users can check out copies of books. The schema *AuthorisedRequestor* is used to record the fact that the person *requestor?* is allowed to perform those transactions that only staff members of the library can perform.

AuthorisedRequestor
$staff : \mathbf{F}\ Person$
$requestor? : Person$

$requestor? \in staff$

The successful operation of a borrower $n?$ checking out a copy $c?$ from the library—taking into account who is requesting the transaction—is specified by the schema:

$$AuthorisedRequestor \wedge CheckOutCopy$$

Now I am going to show how errors are dealt with. The conjoined schema just mentioned has four preconditions, but it can go wrong in five distinct ways. This is because there are two distinct situations in which $c? \notin available$ can be true, namely:

$$c? \notin available \cup checkedout,$$

and:

$$c? \notin available \wedge c? \in checkedout.$$

I shall specify each of these by means of its own schema.

The schema *UnauthorisedRequestor* specifies what happens when an unauthorised person tries to perform the transaction of checking out a copy of a book. The state of the database is unchanged, but an error message is displayed.

```
┌─ UnauthorisedRequestor ──────────────────────────────────────
│ ΞLibraryState
│ requestor?: Person
│ rep!: Report
├──────────────────────────────────────────────────────────────
│ requestor? ∉ staff
│ rep! = 'Unauthorised requestor'
└──────────────────────────────────────────────────────────────
```

The schema *Unregistered* specifies what happens when someone tries to borrow a copy who is not a registered borrower of the library.

```
┌─ Unregistered ───────────────────────────────────────────────
│ ΞLibraryState
│ n?: Person
│ rep!: Report
├──────────────────────────────────────────────────────────────
│ n? ∉ borrower
│ rep! = 'Not registered'
└──────────────────────────────────────────────────────────────
```

The schema *CopyNotOwned* specifies what happens when someone tries to borrow a copy which is not in the library, meaning that the library does not own a copy.

```
┌─ CopyNotOwned ───────────────────────────────────────────────
│ ΞLibraryState
│ c?: Copy
│ rep!: Report
├──────────────────────────────────────────────────────────────
│ c? ∉ available ∪ checkedout
│ rep! = 'This copy is not owned by the library'
└──────────────────────────────────────────────────────────────
```

The schema *CopyCheckedOut* specifies what happens when someone tries to borrow a copy which is owned by the library but currently has been checked out.

```
┌─ CopyCheckedOut ─────────────────────────────────────────────
│ ΞLibraryState
│ c?: Copy
│ rep!: Report
├──────────────────────────────────────────────────────────────
│ c? ∈ checkedout
│ rep! = 'Copy checked out'
└──────────────────────────────────────────────────────────────
```

The schema *TooManyCopies* specifies what happens when someone tries to borrow a copy of a book when they have already borrowed as many copies as they are allowed to.

$$\boxed{\begin{array}{l} \textit{TooManyCopies} \\ \hline \Xi\,\textit{LibraryState} \\ n?\colon \textit{Person} \\ \textit{rep!}\colon \textit{Report} \\ \hline n? \in \textit{borrower} \\ \#\,\textit{borrowedby}^{-1}(\!|\{n?\}|\!) = \textit{MaxCopiesAllowed} \\ \textit{rep!} = \text{`Cannot borrow any more copies'} \end{array}}$$

Thus, the complete specification of the transaction of borrowing a copy of a book is captured by the schema *DoCheckOutCopy*:

$$\textit{DoCheckOutCopy} \triangleq \textit{AuthorisedRequestor} \wedge \textit{CheckOutCopy} \wedge \textit{Success}$$
$$\vee$$
$$\textit{UnauthorisedRequestor}$$
$$\vee$$
$$\textit{Unregistered}$$
$$\vee$$
$$\textit{CopyNotOwned}$$
$$\vee$$
$$\textit{CopyCheckedOut}$$
$$\vee$$
$$\textit{TooManyCopies}$$

The schema *Success* just outputs a confirmatory message that the operation being performed has been successfully completed:

$$\boxed{\begin{array}{l} \textit{Success} \\ \hline \textit{rep!}\colon \textit{Report} \\ \hline \textit{rep!} = \text{`Okay'} \end{array}}$$

Returning a Copy of a Book

The specification of the transaction of returning a copy of a book is captured by means of the schema *Return*. This assumes that the transaction is successful and it ignores who is requesting the transaction.

```
┌─ Return ─────────────────────────────────────────────────
│ ΔLibraryState
│ ΞParaLibrary
│ c?: Copy
├──────────────────────────────────────────────────────────
│ c? ∈ checkedout
│
│ available' = available ∪ {c?}
│ checkedout' = checkedout \ {c?}
│ borrowedby' = {c?} ◁ borrowedby
│ previouslyborrowedby' =
│     previouslyborrowedby ⊕ {c? ↦ borrowedby(c?)}
│
│ borrower' = borrower
│ staff' = staff
└──────────────────────────────────────────────────────────
```

The inclusion of the schema $\Xi ParaLibrary$ in *Return* tells us that the information component of the library system is unaffected by someone returning a copy of a book.

The precondition of *Return* is the single predicate $c? \in checkedout$. What happens when a copy is successfully returned is captured by the middle group of four predicates in *return*. The first two of these state that the copy $c?$ is transferred from actually being borrowed to just being available for loan. The third removes the information relating to $c?$ from *borrowedby'* and the fourth predicate records the information that the last person to borrow $c?$ was *borrowedby* $(c?)$, overriding any information about who previously borrowed $c?$

The precondition of the schema *Return* can be false in two distinct situations, namely when the copy $c?$ is not owned by the library and when the copy $c?$ is owned by the library but has not been borrowed. These two cases are captured by the schemas *CopyNotOwned* and *CopyAvailable*, respectively. The definition of the first of these has already been given, in connection with the specification of the transaction of borrowing a copy, and the definition of the second follows here:

```
┌─ CopyAvailable ──────────────────────────────────────────
│ ΞLibraryState
│ c?: Copy
│ rep!: Report
├──────────────────────────────────────────────────────────
│ c? ∈ available
│ rep! = 'Copy available'
└──────────────────────────────────────────────────────────
```

Thus, the total specification of the transaction of returning a copy of a book is given by means of the schema *DoReturn*, defined as follows:

$$DoReturn \triangleq AuthorisedRequestor \wedge Return \wedge Success$$
$$\vee$$
$$UnauthorisedRequestor$$
$$\vee$$
$$CopyAvailable$$
$$\vee$$
$$CopyNotOwned$$

15.4.2 Adding and Removing Copies of Books

Adding a Copy of a Book to the Library

In adding a copy of a book to the library we need to consider two cases, namely that in which the book is new to the library and that in which the library already owns a copy of the book being added. The first of these is captured by the schema *DoAddNewBook* and the second by *DoAddAnotherCopy*.

The reason why I split the operation of adding a copy of a book into two cases is because I have made the assumption that the library database does not contain information about books which are not in the library. So, if a copy of a book not in the library is added to the library, we also have to add information about the author or authors of the book and the subjects it is about. Whereas, if the library has one or more copies of a particular book and we are just adding another copy of this book to the library, then it is not necessary to add author or subject information.

Adding a New Book to the Library   One of the reasons why the operation of adding a new book to the library is so complicated is that as well as adding the book we also have to add information about its author or authors and also about what its subject matter is. It would be possible to define an operation which just adds a book to the library and does not add any information about it. That this is possible is due to the fact that the subset relation—and not set equality—was used in the state invariant of *ParaLibrary*.

```
┌─ AddNewBook ──────────────────────────────────────────────
│ Δ LibraryState
│ c?: Copy
│ b?: Book
│ A?: F Author
│ S?: F Subject
├───────────────────────────────────────────────────────────
│ b? ∉ ran instanceof
│ c? ∉ available ∪ checkedout
│
│ available' = available ∪ {c?}
│ instanceof' = instanceof ∪ {c? ↦ b?}
│ writtenby' = writtenby ∪ {b? ↦ A?}
│ about' = about ∪ {b? ↦ S?}
│
│ checkedout' = checkedout
│ previouslyborrowedby' = previouslyborrowedby
│ borrowedby' = borrowedby
│ borrower' = borrower
│ staff' = staff
└───────────────────────────────────────────────────────────
```

One of the preconditions of *AddNewBook* is $b? \notin$ ran *instanceof*. This states that we can only add an entirely new book to the library if the library does not contain this book. The situation in which it is attempted to add a book to the library, which is not new to the library, is captured by the schema *NotNewBook*.

```
┌─ NotNewBook ──────────────────────────────────────────────
│ Ξ LibraryState
│ b?: Book
│ rep!: Report
├───────────────────────────────────────────────────────────
│ b? ∈ ran instanceof
│ rep! = 'This book is not new to the library'
└───────────────────────────────────────────────────────────
```

The other precondition is $c? \notin$ *available* ∪ *checkedout*. This states that the copy $c?$—corresponding to book $b?$—that we are adding to the library must not already be owned by the library. This situation is captured by the schema *CopyOwned* which is defined thus:

```
┌─ CopyOwned ───────────────────────────────────────────────
│ Ξ LibraryState
│ c?: Copy
│ rep!: Report
├───────────────────────────────────────────────────────────
│ c? ∈ available ∪ checkedout
│ rep! = 'This copy is owned by the library'
└───────────────────────────────────────────────────────────
```

Thus, the total specification of the transaction of adding a book entirely new to the library is given by the schema *DoAddNewBook*:

$$DoAddNewBook \,\hat{=}\, AuthorisedRequestor \wedge AddNewBook \wedge Success$$
$$\vee$$
$$UnauthorisedRequestor$$
$$\vee$$
$$NotNewBook$$
$$\vee$$
$$CopyOwned$$

Adding Another Copy of a Book   The successful transaction of adding a copy of a book to the library—in the case when the library already has at least one copy of that book—is defined by means of the schema *AddAnotherCopy*. This ignores what happens if the transaction is unsuccessful.

AddAnotherCopy
$\Delta LibraryState$
$c?: Copy$
$b?: Book$

$c? \notin available \cup checkedout$
$b? \in \text{ran } instanceof$

$available' = available \cup \{c?\}$
$instanceof' = instanceof \cup \{c? \mapsto b?\}$

$checkedout' = checkedout$
$previouslyborrowedby' = previouslyborrowedby$
$borrowedby' = borrowedby$
$borrower' = borrower$
$staff' = staff$
$writtenby' = writtenby$
$about' = about$

The schema *BookNewToLibrary* and the schema *CopyOwned* capture what happens when the preconditions of the operation *AddAnotherCopy* are violated.

BookNewToLibrary
$\Xi LibraryState$
$b?: Book$
$rep!: Report$

$b? \notin \text{ran } instanceof$
$rep! = \text{'This book is new to the library'}$

186

The total specification of adding a copy of a book to the library—in the case when that book is not new to the library—is given by the schema *DoAddAnotherCopy*:

$$DoAddAnotherCopy \triangleq AuthorisedRequestor \wedge AddAnotherCopy \wedge Success$$

$$\vee$$

$$UnauthorisedRequestor$$

$$\vee$$

$$BookNewToLibrary$$

$$\vee$$

$$CopyOwned$$

Removing a Copy of a Book from the Library

The operation of removing a copy of a book from the library is split into two cases, namely that of removing a copy of a book while leaving other copies of the same book in the library and that of removing the only copy of a book from the library. The reason for this is similar to the reason why I split the operation of adding a copy of a book to the library into two cases. If the library has two or more copies of a particular book and one of them is removed, then we want to retain author and subject information about that book. However, if the library has only a single copy of a book and we remove that copy, then we also have to remove all the author and subject information relating to that book.

Removing One of Several Copies

```
┌─ RemoveOther ─────────────────────────────────────────
│ Δ LibraryState
│ Ξ ParaLibrary
│ c?: Copy
├───────────────────────────────────────────────────────
│ c? ∈ available
│ #(instanceof⁻¹(|{instanceof(c?)}|)) > 1
│
│ available' = available \ {c?}
│ previouslyborrowedby' = {c?} ◁ previouslyborrowedby
│
│ checkedout' = checkedout
│ borrowedby' = borrowedby
│ borrower' = borrower
│ staff' = staff
```

We need the precondition $c? \in available$ because we cannot remove a copy that is currently checked out. The predicate:

$$\#(instanceof^{-1}(|\{instanceof(c?)\}|)) > 1,$$

tells us that there is more than one copy of the book one of whose instances is $c?$ This interpretation can be built up from its structure. The expression $instanceof(c?)$ is that book which has $c?$ as one of its instances, therefore, $instanceof^{-1}(\!|\{instanceof(c?)\}|\!)$ is the set of all the copies that are instances of $instanceof(c?)$.

The operation *RemoveOther* can go wrong in the following ways:

1. $c? \in checkedout$.

2. $c? \notin available \wedge c? \notin checkedout$.

3. $\#(instanceof^{-1}(\!|\{instanceof(c?)\}|\!)) = 1$.

Case 1 is captured by *CopyCheckedOut*, case 2 by the schema *CopyNotOwned* and case 3 by the schema *OnlyCopy*:

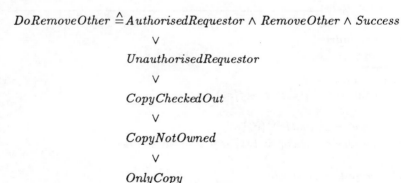

$\begin{array}{|l} \hline \textit{OnlyCopy} \\ \hline \Xi LibraryState \\ c?: Copy \\ rep!: Report \\ \hline \#(instanceof^{-1}(\!|\{instanceof(c?)\}|\!)) = 1 \\ rep! = \text{`This is the only copy in the library'} \\ \hline \end{array}$

Thus, the total specification of the operation of removing one of several copies of a book from the library is given by the schema *DoRemoveOther*:

$$DoRemoveOther \,\hat{=}\, AuthorisedRequestor \wedge RemoveOther \wedge Success$$
$$\vee$$
$$UnauthorisedRequestor$$
$$\vee$$
$$CopyCheckedOut$$
$$\vee$$
$$CopyNotOwned$$
$$\vee$$
$$OnlyCopy$$

Removing the Only Copy of a Book   When we remove the last copy of a book from the library, we also have to remove all mention of that book from the information part of the library state. The book in question does not have to be separately input, since it is $instanceof(c?)$.

$$
\begin{array}{|l}
\_\_RemoveLast_____ \\
\Delta LibraryState \\
c?: Copy \\
\hline
c? \in available \\
\#(instanceof^{-1}(\!|\{instanceof(c?)\}|\!)) = 1 \\
\\
available' = available \setminus \{c?\} \\
previouslyborrowedby' = \{c?\} \lhd previouslyborrowedby \\
instanceof' = \{c?\} \lhd instanceof \\
writtenby' = \{instanceof(c?)\} \lhd writtenby \\
about' = \{instanceof(c?)\} \lhd about \\
\\
checkedout' = checkedout \\
borrowedby' = borrowedby \\
borrower' = borrower \\
staff' = staff
\end{array}
$$

The operation *RemoveLast* can go wrong in the following ways if attempted to be carried out by a member of staff:

1. $c? \in checkedout$.

2. $c? \notin available \wedge c? \notin checkedout$.

3. $\#(instanceof^{-1}(\!|\{instanceof(c?)\}|\!)) > 1$.

Case 1 is captured by *BookCheckedOut*, case 2 by the schema *CopyNotOwned* and case 3 by the following schema:

$$
\begin{array}{|l}
\_\_NotOnlyCopy_____ \\
\Xi LibraryState \\
c?: Copy \\
rep!: Report \\
\hline
\#(instanceof^{-1}(\!|\{instanceof(c?)\}|\!)) > 1 \\
rep! = \text{`This is not the only copy in the library'}
\end{array}
$$

The total specification is captured by the following schema:

$$DoRemoveLast \;\hat{=}\; AuthorisedRequestor \land RemoveLast \land Success$$
$$\lor$$
$$UnauthorisedRequestor$$
$$\lor$$
$$CopyCheckedOut$$
$$\lor$$
$$CopyNotOwned$$
$$\lor$$
$$NotOnlyCopy$$

15.4.3 Interrogating the Library Database

The library system described so far can be interrogated in various ways. We need to describe an operation which outputs all the books written or co-authored by a particular author and we need to describe a transaction which lists all the books about a particular subject. Unlike the transactions specified so far, these operations can be performed by anyone.

Interrogation by Author

```
┌─ ByAuthor ──────────────────────────────────
│ ΞLibraryState
│ a?: Author
│ out!: 𝔽 Book
├─────────────────────────────────────────────
│ out! = {x: Book | a? ∈ writtenby x}
└─────────────────────────────────────────────
```

The schema *ByAuthor* illustrates one of the advantages of formal methods. We do not have to treat the situation in which the authoe *a?* has no books in the library as a special case. In this case *out!* has the value { }, since $a? \mapsto U \notin writtenby$ for any values of U.

It is now possible to give the total specification of the operation of interrogating the library database in order to find out what books a particular writer has co-authored or written. This is done by means of the schema *DoByAuthor*, which is defined like this:

$$DoByAuthor \;\hat{=}\; ByAuthor \land Success$$

Interrogation by Subject

Interrogating the library system by subject is analogous to interrogating it by author. In neither case do we need to take into account who is requesting the transaction, because these operations are available to all.

```
┌─ BySubject ──────────────────────────────────────
│ Ξ LibraryState
│ s?: Subject
│ out!: F Book
├──────────────────────────────────────────────────
│ out! = ⋃{x: Subject | s? ∈ about x}
└──────────────────────────────────────────────────
```

The operation *BySubject* always succeeds—just as *ByAuthor* always succeeds. If the library contains no books on the subject $s?$, then the empty set is returned.

$$DoBySubject \triangleq BySubject \land Success$$

Who has Borrowed What?

The schema *BooksBorrowedBy* defines the transaction of finding out what copies someone has borrowed.

```
┌─ BooksBorrowedBy ────────────────────────────────
│ Ξ LibraryState
│ n?: Person
│ out!: F Copy
├──────────────────────────────────────────────────
│ n? ∈ borrower
│
│ out! = borrowedby⁻¹(|{n?}|)
└──────────────────────────────────────────────────
```

This transaction can be performed by a staff user for any borrower or by a borrower for him or herself; hence we need the schema *SelfRequestor*:

```
┌─ SelfRequestor ──────────────────────────────────
│ Ξ LibraryState
│ n?, requestor?: Person
├──────────────────────────────────────────────────
│ n? = requestor?
└──────────────────────────────────────────────────
```

This transaction is unsuccessful if you try to get information about someone's borrowings if they are not registered users:

```
┌─ UnknownBorrower ────────────────────────────────
│ Ξ LibraryState
│ n?: Person
│ rep!: Report
├──────────────────────────────────────────────────
│ n? ∉ borrower
│ rep! = 'Unknown borrower'
└──────────────────────────────────────────────────
```

Another way in which this transaction can go wrong is if either it is not requested by a staff member of the library or it is not requested by a registered user:

```
┌─ NotAuthorisedRequestor ─────────────────────────────────
│ ΞLibraryState
│ n?, requestor?: Person
│ rep!: Report
├──────────────────────────────────────────────────────────
│ n? ≠ requestor?
│ requestor? ∉ staff
│ rep! = 'Not authorised requestor'
└──────────────────────────────────────────────────────────
```

The total specification is given by the following schema:

$$DoBooksBorrowedBy \,\hat{=}\, BooksBorrowedBy \land AuthorisedRequestor \land Success$$
$$\lor$$
$$BooksBorrowedBy \land SelfRequestor \land Success$$
$$\lor$$
$$UnknownBorrower$$
$$\lor$$
$$NotAuthorisedRequestor$$

Who last Borrowed a Given Copy?

The final transaction that I am going to specify is that of finding out who was the last person to borrow a particular copy of a book.

```
┌─ PreviousBorrower ───────────────────────────────────────
│ ΞLibraryState
│ n!: Person
│ c?: Copy
├──────────────────────────────────────────────────────────
│ c? ∈ available ∪ checkedout
│ {c? ↦ n!} ∈ previouslyborrowedby
└──────────────────────────────────────────────────────────
```

This transaction fails either if the copy c? is not owned by the library or if the copy c? has never been borrowed.

```
┌─ CopyNotPreviouslyBorrower ──────────────────────────────
│ ΞLibraryState
│ rep!: Report
├──────────────────────────────────────────────────────────
│ c? ∉ dom previouslyborrowedby
│ rep! = 'Copy not previously borrowed'
└──────────────────────────────────────────────────────────
```

192

Thus, the total specification of the operation of finding out who last borrowed a particular copy of a book is given like this:

$$DoPreviousBorrower \triangleq PreviousBorrower \wedge AuthorisedRequestor \wedge Success$$

$$\vee$$

$$UnauthorisedRequestor$$

$$\vee$$

$$CopyNotOwned$$

$$\vee$$

$$CopyNotPreviouslyBorrower$$

Chapter 16

The Specification of a Text-editor

16.1 Introduction

In this chapter I present part of the specification of a display-orientated text-editor. It is based on the specification of the VED and QED editors given by Sufrin (1981, 1982a), though it has also been influenced by Neilson (1988). I do not take the specification very far and the reader is very strongly urged to look up the original papers by Sufrin and Neilson.

16.2 Given Types

This specification makes use of two *given sets* or *basic types*, namely:

$$[\mathit{Char}, \mathit{Report}]$$

The type *Char* is the set of all characters that we might need, including the newline character—symbolized as \n—and *Report* is the set of all necessary messages.

$$
\begin{aligned}
\mathit{Report} ::= \;&\text{`Okay'}\\
\mid\;&\text{`At top of document'}\\
\mid\;&\text{`At bottom of document'}
\end{aligned}
$$

16.3 The State Space

The first model of an editor uses a very simple state space, namely *Doc1*, which just consists of two sequences of characters.

┌─ *Doc1* ─────────────────────────────
│ *left*, *right*: seq *Char*
│
└──────────────────────────────────────

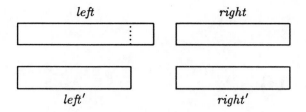

left   right

left′   right′

Figure 16.1: Deleting one character to the left of the cursor.

The sequence *left* contains all the characters in the document being edited which lie to the left of the cursor and the sequence *right* contains all the characters in the document being edited which lie to the right of the cursor.

The schemas $\Delta Doc1$, $\Xi Doc1$ and $Doc1'$ are defined in the standard way:

$$\Delta Doc1 \,\hat{=}\, Doc1 \wedge Doc1'$$

$$\Xi Doc1 \,\hat{=}\, \Delta Doc1 \mid left' = left \wedge right' = right$$

$$InitDoc1' \,\hat{=}\, Doc1' \mid left' = \langle\,\rangle \wedge right' = \langle\,\rangle$$

16.4 The Operations

In this section I am going to consider some of the basic editing operations that we demand of an editor and how they can be formally specified. I will look at the operations of deleting a character from the document, moving the cursor one character and inserting a character. To begin with I will specify these operations as they apply to the left of the cursor and then as they apply to the right of the cursor.

16.4.1 Operations to the Left of the Cursor

Deleting One Character to the Left of the Cursor

The operation of deleting a single character which is immediately to the left of the cursor—that is to say, the last character of the sequence *left*—is graphically depicted in Fig. 16.1 and it is specified like this:

```
┌─ DeleteLeftDoc1 ──────────────────────────────
│ ΔDoc1
├───────────────────────────────────────────────
│ left ≠ ⟨⟩
│ left′ = front left
│ right′ = right
└───────────────────────────────────────────────
```

The precondition of the operation *DeleteLeftDoc1* is the predicate $left \neq \langle\,\rangle$. We cannot delete the character to the left of the cursor when the sequence *left* is empty. In order

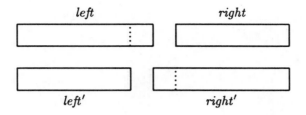

Figure 16.2: Moving one character to the left of the cursor.

to provide a total specification of this operation we need to specify what happens when the sequence *left* is empty. This is done by the schema *ErrorAtTop*:

```
┌─ ErrorAtTop ──────────────────────────────
│ ΞDoc1
│ rep!: Report
├───────────────────────────────────────────
│ left = ⟨⟩
│ rep! = 'At top of document'
└───────────────────────────────────────────
```

The total specification is given by the schema *DoDeleteLeftDoc1*, which is defined as follows:

$$DoDeleteLeftDoc1 \triangleq DeleteLeftDoc1 \wedge Success$$
$$\vee$$
$$ErrorAtTop$$

The schema *Success* used here just reports that an operation has been successfully performed.

```
┌─ Success ──────────────────────────────────
│ rep!: Report
├───────────────────────────────────────────
│ rep! = 'Okay'
└───────────────────────────────────────────
```

Moving One Character to the Left of the Cursor

The operation of moving the cursor one character to the left is graphically depicted in Fig. 16.2. It just involves taking the last character from the sequence *left* and putting it at the front of the sequence *right*.

```
┌─ MoveLeftDoc1 ─────────────────────────────
│ ΔDoc1
├───────────────────────────────────────────
│ left ≠ ⟨⟩
│ left' = front left
│ right' = ⟨last left⟩ ⌢ right
└───────────────────────────────────────────
```

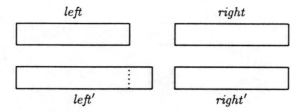

Figure 16.3: Inserting one character to the left of the cursor.

In giving the total specification of the operation *DoMoveLeftDoc1* we again need to take into account what happens when *left* is empty:

$$DoMoveLeftDoc1 \triangleq MoveLeftDoc1 \wedge Success$$

$$\vee$$

$$ErrorAtTop$$

Inserting One Character to the Left of the Cursor

The operation of inserting a single character immediately to the left of the cursor is graphically depicted in Fig. 16.3. It just involves adding the input character to the end of the sequence *left*.

```
┌─ InsertLeftDoc1 ──────────────────────────────────
│ ΔDoc1
│ ch?: Char
├───────────────────────
│ left' = left ⌢ ⟨ch?⟩
│ right' = right
└──────────────────────────────────────────────────
```

The operation of inserting a character always succeeds, so there is no need to add an error condition in its total specification:

$$DoInsertLeftDoc1 \triangleq InsertLeftDoc1 \wedge Success$$

Observation

It would be possible—and entirely straightforward—to specify operations like deleting a word to the left of the cursor or moving to the beginning of the word immediately to the left of the cursor and so on. For more details see the papers by Sufrin mentioned in the introduction to this chapter.

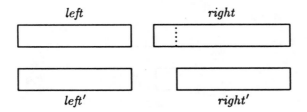

Figure 16.4: Deleting one character to the right of the cursor.

16.4.2 Operations to the Right of the Cursor

Character operations to the right of the cursor are similar to those to the left of the cursor, so they are described more succinctly.

Deleting One Character to the Right of the Cursor

The operation of deleting one character to the right of the cursor is graphically depicted in Fig. 16.4 and it is formally specified like this:

$$
\begin{array}{|l}
\hline \_DeleteRightDoc1 _____ \\
\quad \Delta Doc1 \\
\hline
\quad right \neq \langle\rangle \\
\quad right' = tail\ right \\
\quad left' = left \\
\hline
\end{array}
$$

We cannot delete a character to the right of the cursor when the sequence $right$ is empty. When that happens we want to output an appropriate error message.

$$
\begin{array}{|l}
\hline \_ErrorAtBottom _____ \\
\quad \Xi Doc1 \\
\quad rep!: Report \\
\hline
\quad right = \langle\rangle \\
\quad rep! = \text{'At bottom of document'} \\
\hline
\end{array}
$$

It is now possible to specify the total operation of deleting a single character to the right of the cursor:

$$DoDeleteRightDoc1 \stackrel{\Delta}{=} DeleteRightDoc1 \land Success$$

$$\lor$$

$$ErrorAtBottom$$

199

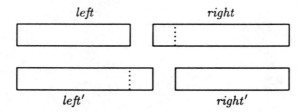

left   right

left'   right'

Figure 16.5: Moving one character to the right of the cursor.

Moving One Character to the Right of the Cursor

The operation of moving one character to the right of the cursor is graphically depicted in Fig. 16.5. It involves taking the character at the extreme left of the sequence *right* and putting it at the extreme right of the sequence *left*. The formal specification of this operation is captured by means of the schema *MoveRightDoc1*, which is defined like this:

$$
\begin{array}{l}
\underline{\quad MoveRightDoc1 \quad\rule{0pt}{0pt}} \\
\Delta Doc1 \\
\hline
right \neq \langle\rangle \\
left' = left \frown \langle head\ right\rangle \\
right' = tail\ right
\end{array}
$$

The operation of moving right one character position cannot succeed if the cursor is at the end of the document, thus this possibility has to be catered for in giving the total specification:

$$DoMoveRightDoc1 \triangleq MoveRightDoc1 \wedge Success$$

$$\vee$$

$$ErrorAtBottom$$

Inserting One Character to the Right of the Cursor

The operation of inserting a single character to the right of the cursor is graphically depicted in Fig. 16.6. It is formally specified in this way:

$$
\begin{array}{l}
\underline{\quad InsertRightDoc1 \quad\rule{0pt}{0pt}} \\
\Delta Doc1 \\
ch?: Char \\
\hline
left' = left \\
right' = \langle ch?\rangle \frown right
\end{array}
$$

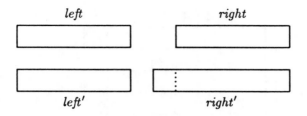

left   *right*

left'   *right'*

Figure 16.6: Inserting one character to the right of the cursor.

As in the case of inserting a character to the left of the cursor, the operation of inserting a character to the right of the cursor cannot fail. Thus, its complete specification is like this:

$$DoInsertRightDoc1 \triangleq InsertRightDoc1 \wedge Success$$

Observation

It would be possible—and entirely straightforward—to specify operations like deleting a word to the right of the cursor or moving to the beginning of the word immediately to the right of the cursor and so on.

16.5 The *Doc2* State

The *Doc1* model of an editor is very simple and it is very easy to specify operations like deleting characters, inserting them and moving through the document. It was developed for that very reason, but now it is necessary to show how the *Doc1* model can be related to the familiar editor displays that we see on our terminals. The first step in this direction is to develop a *Doc2* model in which we specify an unbounded display. This is thought of as a non-empty sequence of lines, where a line is a sequence of characters *excluding* the newline character \n. Thus, the type *Line* is defined:

$$Line == seq(Char \setminus \{\backslash n\}).$$

An *unbounded display* is a sequence of lines which we think of as displayed one below the other—with the first displayed at the top and the second immediately below it and so on—and aligned at their left edge, that is to say, they are left justified. An example of such an unbounded display is given in Fig. 16.7, where a line is represented as a rectangle. In formally specifying an unbounded display we need to take into account the cursor position.

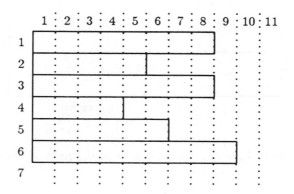

Figure 16.7: An example of an unbounded display.

```
┌─ UnboundedDisplay ────────────────────────────────────────
│  doclines: seq₁ Line
│  l, c: N₁
├───────────────────────────
│  l ≤ #doclines
│  c ≤ #(doclines l) + 1
└────────────────────────────────────────────────────────────
```

The numbers l and c refer to the cursor position. Co-ordinates are given in the form (l, c), where l is the line number—that is to say, the number on the left of the display in Fig. 16.7—and c is the column number—that is to say, the number at the top of the display in Fig. 16.7. Unlike some demented computer scientists, I start counting at 1 and not at 0.

The predicates in the schema *UnboundedDisplay*, namely:

$$l \leq \#doclines,$$

$$c \leq \#(doclines\ l) + 1,$$

ensure that the cursor lies either inside the document or just to the right of the rightmost character position on any given line. This is because if there are n characters on a line, then there are $n + 1$ cursor positions. When we come to implement the editor the cursor on a terminal will actually appear at a character position. I use the convention that the logical cursor position—that is to say, the "gap" between the two sequences *left* and *right* in *Doc1*—corresponds to the "gap" between the character position where the physical cursor appears and the character position immediately to its left.

In order to relate the *Doc1* state to the *Doc2* state we need the function *flatten*:

```
│  flatten: seq₁ Line → seq Char
├────────────────────────────────────────
│  ∀l: Line; ls: seq₁ Line •
│      flatten⟨l⟩ = l ∧
│      flatten(⟨l⟩ ⌢ ls) = l ⌢ ⟨\n⟩ ⌢ (flatten ls)
```

202

The function *flatten* takes a non-empty sequence of lines and concatenates all the members of that sequence into a single sequence of characters, while at the same time inserting newline characters between each pair of lines. An example of its use should make its operation clearer:

$$flatten\ \langle\langle a,b,c\rangle, \langle d,e,f,g\rangle, \langle h,i\rangle\rangle = \langle a,b,c,\backslash n,d,e,f,g,\backslash n,h,i\rangle.$$

The function *flatten* is, in fact, a one-one and onto function, so it has an inverse which is also a total function. This means that given an arbitrary sequence of characters, say σ, there exists one and only one non-empty sequence of lines, say *ls*, such that *flatten ls* $= \sigma$. In **Z** a one-one and onto function is known as a *bijection*. That *flatten* is a bijection is shown in this way: *flatten*: $\text{seq}_1\ Line \rightarrowtail\!\!\!\rightarrow \text{seq}\ Char$. The *Doc2* state can now be specified as follows:

Doc2 ──────────────────────
Doc1
UnboundedDisplay
──────
$left \frown right = flatten\ doclines$
$l = \#(left \rhd \{\backslash n\}) + 1$
$c = \#left - \#(flatten(doclines\ \text{for}\ (l-1)))$

The symbol $\rhd$ is range restriction and, so, the value of $\#(left \rhd \{\backslash n\})$ is the number of newline characters in the sequence *left*. The function for was described in section 7.4. Given a sequence σ and a number i, σ for i is the sequence obtained by taking the first i elements of σ in the order in which they occur in σ.

If we expand the schema *Doc2* we get the following:

Doc2 ──────────────────────
$left, right: \text{seq}\ Char$
$doclines: \text{seq}_1\ Line$
$l, c: \mathbf{N}_1$
──────
$l \le \#doclines$
$c \le \#(doclines\ l) + 1$
$left \frown right = flatten\ doclines$
$l = \#(left \rhd \{\backslash n\}) + 1$
$c = \#left - \#(flatten(doclines\ \text{for}\ (l-1)))$

To see how the final predicate, namely:

$$c = \#left - \#(flatten(doclines\ \text{for}\ (l-1))),$$

calculates the value of c given l consider the following simple example. Let *left* and *right* be the following sequences:

$$left = \langle a, b, \backslash n, c, d, e, \backslash n, f \rangle,$$
$$right = \langle g, h, \backslash n, i, j \rangle.$$

The value of $flatten^{-1}(left \frown right)$ looks like this:

$$\langle \quad \langle a, b \rangle,$$
$$\langle c, d, e \rangle,$$
$$\langle f, \underline{g}, h \rangle,$$
$$\langle i, j \rangle$$
$$\rangle$$

Here the underline _ represents the cursor position. This sequence of sequences is *doclines*, since $left \frown right = flatten\ doclines$ and *flatten*, being a bijection, has an inverse which is a total function.

The value of l is easy to determine; it is 3. Now let us consider the predicate:

$$c = \#left - \#(flatten\ (doclines\ for\ (l-1))).$$

The value of the component *doclines* for $(l-1)$ is the sequence of lines $\langle\langle a, b \rangle, \langle c, d, e \rangle\rangle$, that is to say, the sequence consisting of the first two items of the sequence *doclines*. Applying *flatten* to this results in the sequence $\langle a, b, \backslash n, c, d, e \rangle$ and the length of this is 6. The length of *left* is 8; therefore the calculated value of c is 2, as it should be.

16.5.1 Promoting *Doc1* Operations to *Doc2* Ones

It is entirely straightforward to promote *Doc1* operations to *Doc2* ones. We just conjoin each *Doc1* operation with $\Delta Doc2$, thus:

$$DoDeleteLeftDoc2 \triangleq DoDeleteLeftDoc1 \wedge \Delta Doc2$$
$$DoMoveLeftDoc2 \triangleq DoMoveLeftDoc1 \wedge \Delta Doc2$$
$$DoInsertLeftDoc2 \triangleq DoInsertLeftDoc1 \wedge \Delta Doc2$$
$$DoDeleteRightDoc2 \triangleq DoDeleteRightDoc1 \wedge \Delta Doc2$$
$$DoMoveRightDoc2 \triangleq DoMoveRightDoc1 \wedge \Delta Doc2$$
$$DoInsertRightDoc2 \triangleq DoInsertRightDoc1 \wedge \Delta Doc2$$

Each of the *Doc2* operations is quite complicated if expanded. For example, the expanded version of *DoDeleteLeftDoc2* is:

$$\begin{array}{|l}
\hline \underline{\textit{DoDeleteLeftDoc2}} \hspace{4cm} \\
\textit{left}, \textit{left}', \textit{right}, \textit{right}': \text{seq } \textit{Char} \\
\textit{doclines}, \textit{doclines}': \text{seq}_1 \textit{Line} \\
l, l', c, c': \mathbf{N}_1 \\
\textit{rep}!: \textit{Report} \\
\hline
l \leq \#\textit{doclines} \\
c \leq \#(\textit{doclines } l) + 1 \\
\textit{left} \frown \textit{right} = \textit{flatten doclines} \\
l = \#(\textit{left} \rhd \{\backslash n\}) + 1 \\
c = \#\textit{left} - \#(\textit{flatten }(\textit{doclines for } (l-1))) \\
l' \leq \#\textit{doclines}' \\
c' \leq \#(\textit{doclines}' \, l') + 1 \\
\textit{left}' \frown \textit{right}' = \textit{flatten doclines}' \\
l' = \#(\textit{left}' \rhd \{\backslash n\}) + 1 \\
c' = \#\textit{left}' - \#(\textit{flatten }(\textit{doclines}' \text{ for } (l'-1))) \\
((\textit{left} \neq \langle \rangle \wedge \\
\textit{left}' = \textit{front left} \wedge \\
\textit{right}' = \textit{right} \wedge \\
\textit{rep}! = \text{`Okay'}) \\
\hspace{1cm} \vee \\
(\textit{left} = \langle \rangle \wedge \\
\textit{left}' = \textit{left} \wedge \\
\textit{right}' = \textit{right} \wedge \\
\textit{rep}! = \text{`At top of document'})) \\
\hline
\end{array}$$

16.6 The *Doc3* Model

16.6.1 Putting a Window on the Unbounded Display

In the *Doc3* version of the editor we put a window on the unbounded display. This window will represent what we actually see on a computer terminal when the specification is implemented. An example of such a window is shown in Fig. 16.8. The portion of the unbounded display lying below line 1, above line 2, to the left of line 3 and to the right of line 4 corresponds to a particular window.

In order to model such a window I need the function *truncate*:

$$\begin{array}{|l}
\textit{truncate}: (\mathbf{N}_1 \times \mathbf{N}_1 \times \mathbf{N} \times \mathbf{N}) \rightarrow \text{seq}_1 \textit{Line} \rightarrow \text{seq } \textit{Line} \\
\hline
\forall \textit{wid}, \textit{hei}: \mathbf{N}_1; \textit{vert}, \textit{hor}: \mathbf{N}; \textit{ls}: \text{seq}_1 \textit{Line} \bullet \\
\hspace{0.5cm} \textit{truncate }(\textit{wid}, \textit{hei}, \textit{vert}, \textit{hor}) \, \textit{ls} = \\
\hspace{1.5cm} \text{map}(\text{take } \textit{wid}) \\
\hspace{2.5cm} (\text{map}(\text{drop } \textit{hor}) \\
\hspace{3.5cm} (\text{take } \textit{hei} \, (\text{drop } \textit{vert } \textit{ls})))
\end{array}$$

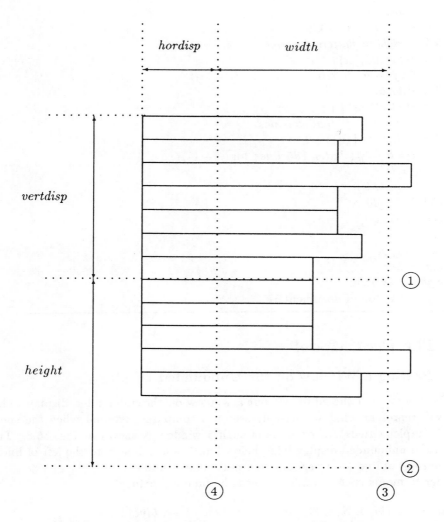

Figure 16.8: Putting a window on the unbounded display.

The effect of *truncate* is easier to understand than at first appears. The component drop *vert ls*, corresponds to the portion of the unbounded display below the horizontal line marked 1 in Fig. 16.8. The expression take *hei* (drop *vert ls*) corresponds to the portion of the unbounded display between the horizontal lines marked 1 and 2 in Fig. 16.8. I will call this expression σ for ease of reference:

$$\sigma == \text{take } hei \ (\text{drop } vert \ ls).$$

Note that σ represents a sequence. Getting the portion of the unbounded display that lies between the vertical lines marked 3 and 4 in Fig. 16.8 is a bit more complicated. The portion to the right of the vertical line 4 is map(drop *hor*) σ. This has the effect of removing the first *hor* characters from each item in σ and the portion between the vertical lines 3 and 4 is:

$$\text{map}(\text{take } wid) \ (\text{map}(\text{drop } hor) \ \sigma).$$

Recall what the function map does.[1] Given a function and a sequence, map applies that function to each element of the sequence. For example,

$$\text{map } f \ \langle a_1, a_2, \ldots, a_n \rangle = \langle fa_1, fa_2, \ldots, fa_n \rangle.$$

Because sequences are treated as functions in **Z**, map is easy to define:

$$
\begin{array}{l}
\hline
=[X,Y]\!= \\
\quad \text{map}: (X \rightarrow Y) \rightarrow \text{seq } X \rightarrow \text{seq } Y \\
\hline
\quad \forall f: X \rightarrow Y; \sigma: \text{seq } X \ \bullet \\
\qquad \text{map } f\sigma = \sigma \ \mathbin{\substack{\circ \\ \circ}} f \\
\hline
\end{array}
$$

Now it is possible to define the *Doc3* state:

$$
\begin{array}{l}
\underline{\quad Doc3 \quad\rule{6cm}{0pt}} \\
\quad Doc2 \\
\quad window: \text{seq } Line \\
\quad width, height: \mathbf{N}_1 \\
\quad hordisp, vertdisp: \mathbf{N} \\
\hline
\quad window \\
\qquad = truncate \ (width, height, hordisp, vertdisp) \ doclines \\
\quad l \leq width \\
\quad c \leq height \\
\end{array}
$$

The parameters *width* and *height* represent the width and height, respectively, of the window on the unbounded display. The final two predicates here ensure that the cursor lies inside the window. It is now possible to promote all the previously defined

---

[1] For more information about map, take and drop, see Bird and Wadler (1988), pp. 55–56 and 61ff.

operations to the *Doc3* model, but things begin to get slightly more complicated because we want to ensure that if we move either right or left then the cursor stays inside the window, so a movement of the cursor might involve a shift in the window as well. One operation that cannot cause a movement of the window—in order to ensure that the cursor lies within the window—is that of inserting a character to the right of the cursor. This is specified as follows:

$$DoInsertRightDoc3 \triangleq DoInsertRightDoc2 \wedge \Delta Doc3$$
$$| \; width' = width \wedge height' = height$$

We have to add the predicates so that the window stays the same throughout the operation. Recall that in this editor no line wrap-around takes place; thus the portion of the eleventh line of text—that is to say, the penultimate line—in Fig. 16.8 which lies to the right of the vertical line labelled 3 does not appear in the window.

Part V

Specification Animation

Chapter 17

Animation using Miranda

17.1 Introduction

In this chapter I show how a **Z** specification can be animated using Miranda. The specification that I have chosen to use as an example is that of the internal telephone number database described in chapters 4 and 5. Miranda is a functional programming language and it is chosen here because it is the best available such language. Arguably, it is the best programming language of any sort at this time. It was designed by David Turner and is described by him in Turner (1985a, 1985b, 1986). It is a pity that a more efficient implementation than Turner's does not exist.

17.2 Specifying the User-interface

The **Z** specification of the telephone number database cannot be directly implemented as an interactive program. In order to do this we need to augment it slightly. First, we add a type *Command* of all possible commands. The type *Command* contains, amongst others, the following commands: *am* (add a member), *rm* (remove a member), *ae* (add an entry), *re* (remove an entry), *fp* (interrogate by extension) and *fn* (interrogate by name). Thus, we have $\{am, rm, ae, re, fp, fn\} \subseteq Command$. We also have to add a member to the set *Report*, namely 'Unknown command'. Then we need to specify in some way that the issuing of the command *am*, for example, is to be associated with the operation specified by *DoAddMember*. The schema *AddMemberCommand* captures the fact that the command *am* has been given:

$$
\begin{array}{|l}
\hline
\_AddMemberCommand _____ \\
cmd?: Command \\
\hline
cmd? = am \\
\hline
\end{array}
$$

We can now specify an operation *ComAddMember* which captures the requirement that the operation *DoAddMember* is only to be carried out when the command *am* has been issued.

$$ComAddMember \;\hat{=}\; AddMemberCommand \wedge DoAddMember$$

211

Similarly, in order to include the circumstance in which the operation specified by means of the schema *DoRemoveMember* is attempted we need the schema:

```
┌─ RemoveMemberCommand ──────────────────────────────
│ cmd?: Command
├────────────────────────────────────────────────────
│ cmd? = rm
└────────────────────────────────────────────────────
```

The schema *ComRemoveMember* states that the operation specified by means of the schema *DoRemoveMember* is only to be carried out when the command *rm* has been issued.

$$ComRemoveMember \,\hat{=}\, RemoveMemberCommand \wedge DoRemoveMember$$

In order to include the circumstance in which the operation *DoAddEntry* is attempted we need the schema:

```
┌─ AddEntryCommand ──────────────────────────────────
│ cmd?: Command
├────────────────────────────────────────────────────
│ cmd? = ae
└────────────────────────────────────────────────────
```

The schema *ComAddEntry* states that the operation specified by means of the schema *DoAddEntry* is only to be carried out when the command *ae* has been issued.

$$ComAddEntry \,\hat{=}\, AddEntryCommand \wedge DoAddEntry$$

In order to include the circumstance in which the operation specified by means of the schema *DoRemoveEntry* is attempted we need the schema:

```
┌─ RemoveEntryCommand ───────────────────────────────
│ cmd?: Command
├────────────────────────────────────────────────────
│ cmd? = re
└────────────────────────────────────────────────────
```

$$ComRemoveEntry \,\hat{=}\, RemoveEntryCommand \wedge DoRemoveEntry$$

In order to include the circumstance in which the operation specified by means of the schema *DoFindPhones* is attempted we need the schema:

```
┌─ FindPhonesCommand ────────────────────────────────
│ cmd?: Command
├────────────────────────────────────────────────────
│ cmd? = fp
└────────────────────────────────────────────────────
```

$$ComFindPhones \,\hat{=}\, FindPhonesCommand \wedge DoFindPhones$$

In order to include the circumstance in which the operation specified by means of the schema *DoFindNames* is attempted we need the schema:

```
┌─ FindNamesCommand ─────────────────────────────────
│ cmd?: Command
├────────────────────────────────────────────────────
│ cmd? = fn
└────────────────────────────────────────────────────
```

$$ComFindNames \triangleq FindNamesCommand \wedge DoFindNames$$

The schema *UnknownCommand* records the fact that an unknown command has been given.

```
┌─ UnknownCommand ───────────────────────────────────
│ cmd?: Command
│ rep!: Report
├────────────────────────────────────────────────────
│ cmd? ≠ am
│ cmd? ≠ rm
│ cmd? ≠ ae
│ cmd? ≠ re
│ cmd? ≠ fp
│ cmd? ≠ fn
│ rep! = 'Unknown command'
└────────────────────────────────────────────────────
```

It is now possible to specify the entire internal telephone number database by means of a single schema:

$$TelephoneDatabase \triangleq ComAddMember$$

$$\vee$$

$$ComRemoveMember$$

$$\vee$$

$$ComAddEntry$$

$$\vee$$

$$ComRemoveEntry$$

$$\vee$$

$$ComFindPhones$$

$$\vee$$

$$ComFindNames$$

$$\vee$$

$$UnknownCommand$$

In order to write a Miranda animation of this specification it is first useful to transform the predicate of the schema *TelephoneDatabase* into one which consists of a conjunction of implications. If we expand the schema *TelephoneDatabase*, we find that its predicate is of the form:

$$(P_1 \wedge Q_1) \vee (P_2 \wedge Q_2) \vee \ldots \vee (P_n \wedge Q_n). \tag{17.1}$$

In fact, n will be 7 and P_7 will be the predicate:

$$cmd? \neq am \wedge cmd? \neq rm \wedge cmd? \neq ae \wedge$$
$$cmd? \neq re \wedge cmd? \neq fp \wedge cmd? \neq fn$$

and each P_i, for $1 \leq i \leq 6$, will be the unnegated version of each of the disjuncts in P_7. In general, a formula of the form (17.1) is equivalent to one of the following form:

$$(P_1 \Rightarrow Q_1) \wedge (P_2 \Rightarrow Q_2) \wedge \ldots \wedge (P_n \Rightarrow Q_n), \tag{17.2}$$

in the situation in which the formulas $P_1, \ldots, P_n$ are such that one and only one of them can be true in any conceivable state of affairs.[1] The predicates in the schema *TelephoneDatabase* are of this type, so we can transform this schema into the following form:

___ *TelephoneDatabase* _____

$members, members': \mathbf{P}\ Person$
$telephones, telephones': Person \leftrightarrow Phone$
$name?: Person$
$oldnumber?, newnumber?: Phone$
$cmd?: Command$
$names!: \mathbf{P}\ Person$
$numbers!: \mathbf{P}\ Phone$
$rep!: Report$

---

dom $telephones \subseteq members$
dom $telephones' \subseteq members'$
$cmd? = am \Rightarrow Q_1$
$cmd? = rm \Rightarrow Q_2$

. . .

$cmd? = fn \Rightarrow Q_6$
$(cmd? \neq am \vee cmd? \neq rm \vee cmd? \neq ae \vee$
$cmd? \neq re \vee cmd? \neq fp \vee cmd? \neq fn) \Rightarrow Q_7$

---

[1] An informal proof of this result goes as follows. Let P_i be the one which is true. Then—as a straightforward consequence of the classical truth-tables—we have that $(P_j \Rightarrow Q_j)$ is true and $(P_j \wedge Q_j)$ is false when $i \neq j$. So, (17.1) is true if and only if Q_i is true and false otherwise and (17.2) is true if and only if Q_i is true and false otherwise. Therefore, (17.1) and (17.2) are logically equivalent.

It should be noted that the schema *TelephoneDatabase* contains declarations of three input variables and three output variables. In certain circumstances not all of these

will be required. For example, in the operation of adding a member to the database only two inputs are needed, namely *cmd?* and *name?*, and only one output, namely *rep!*, but the presence of the other variables causes no harm. Just because they are there does not mean that any code has to be written to cope with them when we come to implement *ComAddMember*. An analogous case occurs in the predicate calculus when we have a formula that has quantifiers in it that contain variables which are not present in the body of the formula. For example, the predicate $\forall x: X \bullet Y$, is equivalent to Y if x does not occur free in Y.

The function **exp** of the animation to be described below on p. 216 will be seen to correspond very closely to the structure of the predicates in the transformed version of *TelephoneDatabase* excluding the state invariant.

17.3   The Animation

17.3.1   Overall Structure

The Miranda animation is written in the form of an interactive program. The overall structure of this program—and some of the actual functions used—are taken from the excellent book by Bird and Wadler (1988). The definitions of the functions **read1**, **read2**, **write**, **end**, **before** and **after** are to be found on pp. 200–203. The function I call **read1** Bird and Wadler call **read**.

Elements of each of the types used in the specification, namely *Person*, *Phone*, *Report* and *Command*, are represented as strings, that is to say, as lists of characters and subsets of each of these types are represented as lists. The state of the system is then represented as a tuple of two things, that is to say, as an object of type:

```
([[char]], [([char], [char])])
```

The program is invoked by calling:

```
go $-
```

This calls the function **tel** with the empty state as its first argument.

```
go :: [char] -> [char]
go = tel empty

empty :: ([*], [**])
empty = ([], [])

tel :: ([[char]], [([char], [char])]) -> [char] -> [char]
tel state
    = exp state, inv state
    = write "Invariant violated\n" (exp state), otherwise
```

The function **tel** tests to see if the invariant is satisfied. If it is, then **exp** is invoked and if it is not, then an error message is displayed and then **exp** is invoked. The actual function which tests to see if the invariant has been violated is **inv**.

```
inv :: ([*], [(*, **)]) -> bool
inv state
    = and [ member (first state) x | (x, z) <- (second state) ]
```

The function **exp** reads a command from the keyboard—after giving the prompt **Command:**—and then, depending on which command is entered, calls the relevant function to process that command. The command **end** terminates the program and if something is typed that is not a valid command, then a suitable error message is produced. The clauses defining the functions which carry out the operations associated with each command are all placed inside the **where**-clause of the definition of exp.

```
exp :: ([[char]], [([char], [char])]) -> [char] -> [char]
exp state
    = read1 "Command: " cmd
      where
      cmd "end" = write "Exit program\n" end
      cmd "am"  = read1 "Name? " tam
      cmd "rm"  = read1 "Name? " trm
      cmd "ae"  = read2 ("Name? ", "Extension? ") tae
      cmd "re"  = read2 ("Name? ", "Extension? ") tre
      cmd "fp"  = read1 "Name? " tfp
      cmd "fn"  = read1 "Extension? " tfn
      cmd other = write "Unknown command\n" donothing
```

So, the following function definition occurs inside the **where**-clause:

```
donothing = write "\n\n" (tel state)
```

17.3.2 The Operation of Adding a Member

In order to see how the schemas specifying the various operations defined on the system are implemented in Miranda, I shall go through the case of adding a member to the set *members* in some detail. Writing out the schema *DoAddMember* in full we have:

DoAddMember

members, members': **P** *Person*
telephones, telephones': *Person* ↔ *Phone*
name?: *Person*
rep!: *Report*

---

dom *telephones* ⊆ *members*
dom *telephones'* ⊆ *members'*
((*name?* ∉ *members* ∧
rep! = 'Okay' ∧
members' = *members* ∪ {*name?*} ∧
telephones' = *telephones*)
    ∨
(*name?* ∈ *members* ∧
rep! = 'Already a member' ∧
members' = *members* ∧
telephones' = *telephones*))

By the logical equivalence of the two formulas:

$$(\neg P \wedge R) \vee (P \wedge Q),\tag{17.3}$$
$$(\neg P \Rightarrow R) \wedge (P \Rightarrow Q),\tag{17.4}$$

this can be rewritten as:

DoAddMember

members, members': **P** *Person*
telephones, telephones': *Person* ↔ *Phone*
name?: *Person*
rep!: *Report*

---

dom *telephones* ⊆ *members*
dom *telephones'* ⊆ *members'*
name? ∉ *members* ⇒
    (*rep!* = 'Okay' ∧
    members' = *members* ∪ {*name?*} ∧
    telephones' = *telephones*)
name? ∈ *members* ⇒
    (*rep!* = 'Already a member' ∧
    members' = *members* ∧
    telephones' = *telephones*)

This is straightforwardly translated into Miranda as:

```
tam n = write "Okay\n" (tel (am n state)),
          ~ member (first state) n
        = write "Already member\n" (tel state), otherwise
am n state = (n : (first state), second state)
```

The variable **state** represents the before state and **am n state** the after state in the case when *name?* $\notin$ *members*, and **state** is the after state in the case when *name?* $\in$ *members*.

17.3.3 Miranda Versions of the Remaining Operations

The animation of the remaining operations is straightforward. The Miranda code follows:

```
trm n = write "Okay\n" (tel (rm n state)),
          member (first state) n
        = write "Not a member\n" (tel state),
          otherwise

rm n state = ( [ p | p <- (first state); p ~= n ],
               [ (r, s) |
                 (r, s) <- (second state); r ~= n ] )

tae (n, e) = write "Okay\n" (tel (ae n e state)),
               member (first state) n &
               ~ member (second state) (n, e)
             = write "Entry already exists\n" (tel state),
               member (second state) (n, e)
             = write "Not a member\n" (tel state),
               ~ member (first state) n
ae n e state = (first state, (n, e):(second state))

tre (n, e) = write "Okay\n" (tel (re n e state)),
               member (second state) (n, e)
             = write "Unknown entry\n" (tel state),
               otherwise
re n e state = ( first state,
                 [ (r, s) |
                   (r, s) <- (second state);
                   r ~= n; s ~= e ] )
```

```
tfp n = write (fp n state ++ "\n\n") (tel state),
            member [ x | (x, y) <- (second state) ] n
      = write "Unknown name\n" (tel state),
                otherwise
fp n state = disp [ y | (x, y) <- (second state); x = n ]

tfn e = write (fn e state ++ "\n\n") (tel state),
            member [ y | (x, y) <- (second state) ] e
      = write "Unknown extension\n" (tel state),
                otherwise
fn e state = disp [ x | (x, y) <- (second state); y = e ]
```

17.3.4 Remaining Miranda Functions

The remaining Miranda functions not found in Bird and Wadler (1988) that are needed
are included here for completeness:

```
first :: (*, **) -> *
first (x, y) = x

second :: (*, **) -> **
second (x, y) = y

disp :: [[char]] -> [char]
disp x = "Empty\n", x = []
        = hd x, # x = 1
        = hd x ++ "\n" ++ disp (tl x), otherwise
```

Chapter 18

Animation using Prolog

18.1 Introduction

In this chapter I present a Prolog animation of the internal telephone number database specification. This chapter is briefer that the previous one, because the transformations discussed in that chapter—that helped us to write a Miranda animation—are also useful in writing a Prolog animation.

18.2 The Animation

18.2.1 Global Entities

Mathematical sets are represented as Prolog lists. Both the types or sets *Person* and *Phone* are represented as lists of strings. All the messages in *Report* are included and quite a few others added. Elements of the type *Command* are represented as Prolog atoms.

18.2.2 The State of the Database

The state of the database is represented by the Prolog variables M and T, which stand for *members* and *telephones*, respectively.[1] The relation *telephones* is represented in Prolog by means of a list of 2-lists. When before and after variables are required in Z the after ones are decorated with a prime, for example *members'*. In the Prolog version I call the after variables MP and TP.

18.2.3 The Initial State

Corresponding to the schema *InitPhoneDB'* are two empty lists.

---

[1] In order to distinguish bits of Prolog from bits of Z I write the Prolog in `typewriter font` and the Z in *math italic*.

18.2.4 The Overall Structure

Corresponding to the schema *TelephoneDatabase* given in the previous chapter is the Prolog predicate `process`, which is defined like this:

```
process(am, M, T, MP, TP) :-
  write('Enter a name: '),
  readatom(Z),
  doAddMember(Z, M, T, MP, TP).

process(rm, M, T, MP, TP) :-
  write('Enter a name: '),
  readatom(Z),
  doRemoveMember(Z, M, T, MP, TP).

process(ae, M, T, MP, TP) :-
  write('Enter a name: '),
  readatom(Z),
  write('Enter a phone number: '),
  readatom(A),
  doAddEntry(Z, A, M, T, MP, TP).

process(re, M, T, MP, TP) :-
  write('Enter a name: '),
  readatom(Z),
  write('Enter a phone number: '),
  readatom(A),
  doRemoveEntry(Z, A, M, T, MP, TP).

process(fp, M, T, M, T) :-
  write('Enter a name: '),
  readatom(Z),
  doFindPhones(Z, M, T, M, T).

process(fn, M, T, M, T) :-
  write('Enter a phone number: '),
  readatom(A),
  doFindNames(A, M, T, M, T).

process(quit, M, T, MP, TP) :-
  write('Goodbye'), nl, halt.

process(_, M, T, M, T) :-
  write('Unknown command.'), nl.
```

The available commands are **am** (for 'add member'), **rm** (for 'remove member'), **ae** (for 'add entry'), **re** (for 'remove entry'), **fp** (for 'find phones') and **fn** (for 'find names'). The Prolog predicate **doAddMember** corresponds—roughly!—to the schema *DoAddMember* and similarly for other Prolog predicates beginning with **do**. The main predicate of the Prolog program is **go** which works like this:

```
go :-
   write('Hello'),
   nl,
   loop([], []).

loop(M, T) :-
   write('Enter a command: '),
   readatom(Z),
   process(Z, M, T, MP, TP),
   invariant(MP, TP),
   loop(MP, TP).
```

The clause **invariant(MP, TP)** is defined in section 18.2.8. The predicate **readatom** is the predicate of the same name defined in Covington, Nute and Vellino (1988), pp. 135–136. What it does is to read a string, that is to say, a list of ASCII values, and convert it into a Prolog atom.

18.2.5   Adding and Removing Members

Adding a Member

In the light of the discussion of the schema *DoAddMember* in the previous chapter the following Prolog animation of it should be fairly clear:

```
doAddMember(Z, M, T, M, T) :-
   member(Z, M),
   write('Already a member.'),
   nl.

doAddMember(Z, M, T, [Z|M], T) :-
   write('New member added.'),
   nl.
```

The schema *DoAddMember* is defined like this:

$$DoAddMember \triangleq AddMember \land Success$$
$$\lor$$
$$AlreadyMember$$

and the two Prolog clauses defining the predicate **doAddMember** correspond to the two schemas *AlreadyMember* and *AddMember* ∧ *Success*. (All functions like **member** are defined in section 18.2.9.)

223

Removing a Member

```
doRemoveMember(Z, M, T, MP, TP) :-
   member(Z, M),
   subtract(M,[Z],MP),
   domcores(TP, Z, T),
   write('Member removed.'),
   nl.

doRemoveMember(Z, M, T, M, T) :-
   write('Not a member.'),
   nl.
```

18.2.6   Adding and Removing Entries

Adding an Entry to the Database

```
doAddEntry(Z, A, M, T, MP, TP) :-
   member(Z, M),
   doAddEntryAux(Z, A, M, T, MP, TP).

doAddEntry(Z, A, M, T, MP, TP) :-
   write('Not a member.'),
   nl.

doAddEntryAux(Z, A, M, T, M, T) :-
   member([Z, A], T),
   write('Entry already exists.'),
   nl.

doAddEntryAux(Z, A, M, T, M, [[Z, A] | T]) :-
   write('Entry added.'),
   nl.
```

Removing an Entry from the Database

```
doRemoveEntry(Z, A, M, T, M, TP) :-
   member([Z, A], T),
   subtract(T,[[Z, A]], TP),
   write('Entry removed.'),
   nl.

doRemoveEntry(Z, A, M, T, M, T) :-
   write('Unknown entry.'),
   nl.
```

18.2.7 Interrogating the Database

Interrogating the Database by Name

```
doFindPhones(Z, M, T, M, T) :-
   domain(B, T),
   member(Z, B),
   image(C, T, Z),
   writelist(C).

doFindPhones(Z, M, T, M, T) :-
   write('Unknown name.'),
   nl.
```

Interrogating the Database by Number

```
doFindNames(A, M, T, M, T) :-
   range(B, T),
   member(A, B),
   invimage(C, T, A),
   writelist(C).

doFindNames(A, M, T, M, T) :-
   write('Unknown number.'),
   nl.
```

18.2.8 The Invariant

The predicate **invariant** checks to see whether or not the invariant has been preserved each time a command is carried out. Clearly, if the state invariant is violated, then something has gone wrong somewhere and the animation will have to be modified.

```
invariant(MP, TP) :-
   domain(Q, TP),
   subset(Q, MP),
   write('Invariant preserved.'),
   nl.

invariant(MP, TP) :-
   write('Invariant violated.'),
   nl.
```

18.2.9 Auxiliary Predicates

The animation presented here makes use of the following auxiliary predicates:

Prolog	Z
member(X, Y)	$X \in Y$
subset(X, Y)	$X \subseteq Y$
subtract(X, Y, Z)	$Z = X \setminus Y$
domain(X, Y)	$X = \operatorname{dom} Y$
range(X, Y)	$X = \operatorname{ran} Y$
image(X, Y, Z)	$X = Y (\!|\{Z\}|\!)$
invimage(X, Y, Z)	$X = Y^{-1}(\!|\{Z\}|\!)$
domcores(X, Y, Z)	$X = \{Y\} \lhd Z$

Note that the last three of these are not as general as they could be—I define, for example, $X = Y(\!|\{Z\}|\!)$ rather than $X = Y(\!|Z|\!)$—but these operators are used most frequently in the way I define them and the more general ones can be defined in terms of these.

The definitions of **member** and **subtract** that follow come from Coelho, Cotta and Pereira (1985), pp. 13 and 15. The definitions of **readstring**, **readatom** and **writestring** can be found in Covington, Nute and Vellino (1988), pp. 135–136. The predicate **readstring** displays a one-character prompt, then accepts a line of input from the keyboard and returns it as a string, that is to say, a list of ASCII values. The user can use backspace ↑h to make corrections but is prevented from backspacing past the beginning of the line. The predicate **writestring** displays a string, that is to say, a list of ASCII values.

```
member(H, [H|_]).
member(I, [_|T]) :- member(I,T).

subset([], Y).
subset([A|B], C) :- member(A, C), subset(B, C).

subtract(L,[],L) :- !.
subtract([H|T],L,U) :- member(H,L), !, subtract(T,L,U).
subtract([H|T],L,[H|U]) :- !, subtract(T,L,U).
subtract(_,_,[]).

domain([], []).
domain([H|T], [[H, _] | U]) :- domain(T, U).
```

```
range([], []).
range([H|T], [[_, H] | U]) :- range(T, U).

image([H|T], [[I, H] | U], I) :- image(T, U, I).
image(T, [[J, H] | U], I) :- J \== I, image(T, U, I).
image([], [], _).

invimage([H|T], [[H, I] | U], I) :- invimage(T, U, I).
invimage(T, [[H, J] | U], I) :- J \== I, invimage(T, U, I).
invimage([], [], _).

domcores(C, Y, [[Y, _] | D]) :- domcores(C, Y, D).
domcores([[A, B] | C], Y, [[A, B] | D]) :-
  Y \== A, domcores(C, Y, D).
domcores([], _, []).

writelist([]) :- write('That is all'), nl.
writelist([A|T]) :-
  name(A, S), writestring(S), nl, writelist(T).
```

Part VI

Reference Manual

Chapter 19

Definitions and Boxes

19.1 Introduction

There are several two-dimensional graphical constructs in **Z** and in this chapter I explain boxes used for axiomatic description, generic definition and schemas.

19.2 Axiomatic Descriptions

The general form of an axiomatic description in **Z** is as follows:

$$
\begin{array}{|l}
\hline
D \\
\hline
P
\end{array}
$$

where D is a declaration which introduces one or more global variables and P is an optional predicate that constrains the values that can be taken by the variables introduced in D. The variables declared in D cannot have been previously declared globally and their scope extends to the end of the specification.

19.3 Generic Definitions

The form of a generic definition in **Z** is:

$$
\begin{array}{|l}
\hline\hline
[X_1, \ldots, X_n] \\
D \\
\hline
P \\
\hline
\end{array}
$$

where the X_i are the formal generic parameters which can occur in the types assigned to the identifiers in the declaration D. The predicate P defines the identifiers introduced in D. A frequently used special case of **Z**'s generic definition construct is the abbreviation definition used for introducing—possibly generic—constants. Its general form is $\pi == t$ where π is a pattern and t is an expression. A pattern is either something of the form $a[X_1, \ldots, X_n]$ or something of the form a, $\alpha\, x$ or $x\, \beta\, y$, where a is a constant, x and y are variables, α is a unary prefix operator, β is an infix binary operator and the X_i are formal generic parameters. Some examples should clarify this account. All the following are legitimate abbreviation definitions:

$$\{\,\} X == \{x : X \mid \textit{false}\},$$
$$\textit{squares} == \lambda i : \mathbf{N} \bullet i * i,$$
$$\mathbf{P}_1 X == \{U : \mathbf{P}\, X \mid U \neq \{\,\}\},$$
$$X \leftrightarrow Y == \mathbf{P}(X \times Y).$$

19.4 Schemas

The form of a schema in **Z** is like this:

```
 ___S_____
|   D
|  _____
|   P
|_____
```

where S is the name of the schema, D is a declaration and P a predicate. It is possible to have generic schemas which have the following form:

```
 ___S[X_1,...,X_n]_____
|   D
|  _____
|   P
|_____
```

where the X_i can occur in the types assigned to variables declared in D. When we use a generic schema we have to give specific values to the formal generic parameters X_i, for example, $S[\mathbf{N}, \textit{Report}, \textit{Book}]$.

Chapter 20

First-order Logic

20.1 Introduction

First-order logic deals with predicates—also known as propositions—which are sentences that can be either true or false. **Z** contains the two primitive predicates *true* and *false*, which are the always true and the always false proposition, respectively.

There is a single primitive one-place propositional connective in **Z** and that is negation, symbolized as ¬ and pronounced 'not'. It has the following standard truth-table:

P	$\neg P$
t	f
f	t

Predicates can also be combined using various two-place propositional connectives. These are ∧, which is conjunction (pronounced 'and'), ∨, which is disjunction (pronounced 'or'), ⇒, which is implication (pronounced 'if—then' or 'implies') and ⟺, which is bi-implication (pronounced 'if and only if'). The meaning of these is given by the following familiar truth-tables:

P	Q	$P \wedge Q$	$P \vee Q$	$P \Rightarrow Q$	$P \Longleftrightarrow Q$
t	t	t	t	t	t
t	f	f	t	f	f
f	t	f	t	t	f
f	f	f	f	t	t

233

20.2 Useful Tautologies and Valid Sequents

The first group of useful tautologies and valid sequents that I am going to list all involve one or other of the constant propositions *true* and *false*.

$$\models \text{ true},$$
$$P \models \text{ true},$$
$$\text{false} \models P,$$
$$\text{true} \,=\!\!\models \neg\text{false},$$
$$\text{false} \,=\!\!\models \neg\text{true},$$
$$P \wedge \text{true} \,=\!\!\models P,$$
$$P \vee \text{true} \,=\!\!\models \text{true},$$
$$P \wedge \text{false} \,=\!\!\models \text{false},$$
$$P \vee \text{false} \,=\!\!\models P,$$
$$\text{true} \Rightarrow P \,=\!\!\models P,$$
$$P \Rightarrow \text{false} \,=\!\!\models \neg P.$$

The following groups of useful tautologies and valid sequents do not make use of either of the constant propositions *true* or *false*.

$$\models \neg(P \wedge \neg P), \tag{20.1}$$
$$\models P \vee \neg P, \tag{20.2}$$
$$P \,=\!\!\models P,$$
$$P \,=\!\!\models \neg\neg P,$$
$$P \wedge P \,=\!\!\models P,$$
$$P \wedge Q \models P,$$
$$P \wedge Q \models Q,$$
$$P \wedge Q \,=\!\!\models Q \wedge P, \tag{20.3}$$
$$P \wedge (Q \wedge R) \,=\!\!\models (P \wedge Q) \wedge R, \tag{20.4}$$
$$P \vee P \,=\!\!\models P,$$
$$P \models P \vee Q,$$
$$Q \models P \vee Q,$$
$$P \vee Q \,=\!\!\models Q \vee P, \tag{20.5}$$
$$P \vee (Q \vee R) \,=\!\!\models (P \vee Q) \vee R, \tag{20.6}$$
$$P \wedge (Q \vee R) \,=\!\!\models (P \wedge Q) \vee (P \wedge R), \tag{20.7}$$
$$(P \vee Q) \wedge R \,=\!\!\models (P \wedge R) \vee (Q \wedge R), \tag{20.8}$$
$$P \vee (Q \wedge R) \,=\!\!\models (P \vee Q) \wedge (P \vee R), \tag{20.9}$$
$$(P \wedge Q) \vee R \,=\!\!\models (P \vee R) \wedge (Q \vee R), \tag{20.10}$$
$$P \wedge Q \,=\!\!\models (P \vee \neg Q) \wedge Q,$$

$$P \vee Q \; =\!\!\models \; (P \wedge \neg Q) \vee Q,$$
$$P \wedge Q \; =\!\!\models \; \neg(\neg P \vee \neg Q),$$
$$P \vee Q \; =\!\!\models \; \neg(\neg P \wedge \neg Q),$$
$$\neg(P \wedge Q) \; =\!\!\models \; \neg P \vee \neg Q, \qquad (20.11)$$
$$\neg(P \vee Q) \; =\!\!\models \; \neg P \wedge \neg Q. \qquad (20.12)$$

The tautology (20.1) is known as the law of non-contradiction and (20.2) is the law of the excluded middle, which is also known as *tertium non datur*. (20.3) states that conjunction is commutative and (20.4) that it is associative. (20.5) states that disjunction is commutative and (20.6) that it is associative.

(20.7) says that conjunction distributes forwards through disjunction and (20.8) says that it distributes backwards through disjunction as well.[1] (20.9) states that disjunction distributes forwards through conjunction and (20.10) says that it also distributes backwards through conjunction. (20.11) and (20.12) are known as de Morgan's laws. Following Jones (1986a), p. 42, I call (20.11) the $\wedge$–de Morgan law and (20.12) the $\vee$–de Morgan law.

The tautology (20.13) that follows first in the following group of useful tautologies and valid sequents is known as Peirce's law.

$$\models \; ((P \Rightarrow Q) \Rightarrow P) \Rightarrow P, \qquad (20.13)$$
$$\models \; (P \Rightarrow Q) \vee (Q \Rightarrow R),$$
$$Q \; \models \; P \Rightarrow Q,$$
$$\neg P \; \models \; P \Rightarrow Q,$$
$$\neg P \Rightarrow P \; \models \; P,$$
$$P \Rightarrow \neg P \; \models \; \neg P,$$
$$P \Rightarrow Q \; =\!\!\models \; \neg(P \wedge \neg Q),$$
$$P \Rightarrow Q \; =\!\!\models \; \neg P \vee Q,$$
$$P \Rightarrow Q \; =\!\!\models \; \neg Q \Rightarrow \neg P,$$
$$(P \wedge Q) \Rightarrow R \; =\!\!\models \; (P \Rightarrow R) \vee (Q \Rightarrow R),$$
$$P \Rightarrow (Q \wedge R) \; =\!\!\models \; (P \Rightarrow Q) \wedge (P \Rightarrow R),$$
$$(P \vee Q) \Rightarrow R \; =\!\!\models \; (P \Rightarrow R) \wedge (Q \Rightarrow R),$$
$$P \Rightarrow (Q \vee R) \; =\!\!\models \; (P \Rightarrow Q) \vee (P \Rightarrow R),$$
$$(P \wedge Q) \vee (\neg P \wedge R) \; =\!\!\models \; (P \Rightarrow Q) \wedge (\neg P \Rightarrow R).$$

---

[1]People often talk of *left* and *right* distribution, but—as Woodcock and Loomes (1988), p. 128, point out in their footnote 6—such terminology is not used consistently. I urge people to use the terminology of distribution *forwards* and *backwards* for clarity.

20.3 Valid Predicate Calculus Sequents

In the following sequents x can occur free in P:

$$\forall x{:}X \bullet P \dashv\vdash \neg\exists x{:}X \bullet \neg P,$$
$$\neg\forall x{:}X \bullet P \dashv\vdash \exists x{:}X \bullet \neg P,$$
$$\exists x{:}X \bullet P \dashv\vdash \neg\forall x{:}X \bullet \neg P,$$
$$\neg\exists x{:}X \bullet P \dashv\vdash \forall x{:}X \bullet \neg P.$$

In the following group of sequents there is no restriction on which variables can cannot occur free in P and Q:

$$\forall x{:}X; y{:}Y \bullet P \dashv\vdash \forall y{:}Y; x{:}X \bullet P,$$
$$\exists x{:}X; y{:}Y \bullet P \dashv\vdash \exists y{:}Y; x{:}X \bullet P,$$
$$(\forall x{:}X \bullet P) \vee (\forall x{:}X \bullet Q) \vdash \forall x{:}X \bullet P \vee Q,$$
$$\forall x{:}X \bullet (P \wedge Q) \dashv\vdash (\forall x{:}X \bullet P) \wedge (\forall x{:}X \bullet Q),$$
$$\forall x{:}X \bullet (P \Rightarrow Q) \vdash (\forall x{:}X \bullet P) \Rightarrow (\forall x{:}X \bullet Q),$$
$$\exists x{:}X \bullet (P \vee Q) \dashv\vdash (\exists x{:}X \bullet P) \vee (\exists x{:}X \bullet Q),$$
$$\exists x{:}X \bullet (P \wedge Q) \vdash (\exists x{:}X \bullet P) \wedge (\exists x{:}X \bullet Q),$$
$$\exists x{:}X \bullet \forall y{:}Y \bullet P \vdash \forall y{:}Y \bullet \exists x{:}X \bullet P.$$

In the following sequents x cannot occur free in P, but it can occur free in Q:

$$\forall x{:}X \bullet P \dashv\vdash P,$$
$$\exists x{:}X \bullet P \dashv\vdash P,$$
$$\forall x{:}X \bullet (P \vee Q) \dashv\vdash P \vee \forall x{:}X \bullet Q,$$
$$\forall x{:}X \bullet (P \wedge Q) \dashv\vdash P \wedge \forall x{:}X \bullet Q,$$
$$\forall x{:}X \bullet (P \Rightarrow Q) \dashv\vdash P \Rightarrow \forall x{:}X \bullet Q,$$
$$(\forall x{:}X \bullet Q) \Rightarrow P \dashv\vdash \exists x{:}X \bullet (Q \Rightarrow P),$$
$$\exists x{:}X \bullet (P \vee Q) \dashv\vdash P \vee \exists x{:}X \bullet Q,$$
$$\exists x{:}X \bullet (P \wedge Q) \dashv\vdash P \wedge \exists x{:}X \bullet Q,$$
$$\exists x{:}X \bullet (P \Rightarrow Q) \dashv\vdash P \Rightarrow \exists x{:}X \bullet Q,$$
$$(\exists x{:}X \bullet Q) \Rightarrow P \dashv\vdash \forall x{:}X \bullet (Q \Rightarrow P).$$

To conclude I give some examples of sequents involving identity:

$$\vdash \forall x{:}X \bullet x = x,$$
$$\vdash \forall x, y{:}X \bullet (x = y \Rightarrow y = x),$$
$$\vdash \forall x, y, z{:}X \bullet (x = y \wedge y = z \Rightarrow x = z),$$
$$P \dashv\vdash \exists x{:}X \bullet x = y \wedge P[x/y].$$

In the last of these y can occur free in P. This sequent is similar to what Woodc (1989b), p. 67, calls the one-point rule.

Chapter 21

Set Theory

21.1 Relations Between Sets

Two things x and y are identical iff they are members of exactly the same sets:

$$\begin{array}{|l|}\hline \underline{\quad}[X]\underline{\quad} \\ \underline{\quad} = \underline{\quad}: X \leftrightarrow X \\ \hline \forall x, y \colon X \bullet \\ \qquad x = y \Longleftrightarrow (\forall U \colon \mathbf{P}\, X \bullet x \in U \Longleftrightarrow y \in U) \\ \hline \end{array}$$

This is the standard way of defining identity in a typed set theory.[1] Note that it works for individuals as well as for sets. It should be contrasted with the definition of identity in Zermelo–Fraenkel set theory:

$$x = y == (\forall z)(z \in x \Longleftrightarrow z \in y).$$

A set U is a *subset* of a set V iff every member of U is also a member of V. A set U is a *proper subset* of a set V iff every member of U is also a member of V, but $U \neq V$.

$$\begin{array}{|l|}\hline \underline{\quad}[X]\underline{\quad} \\ \underline{\quad} \subseteq \underline{\quad}, \underline{\quad} \subset \underline{\quad}: \mathbf{P}\, X \leftrightarrow \mathbf{P}\, X \\ \hline \forall U, V \colon \mathbf{P}\, X \bullet \\ \qquad U \subseteq V \Longleftrightarrow (\forall x \colon X \bullet x \in U \Rightarrow x \in V) \wedge \\ \qquad U \subset V \Longleftrightarrow (U \subseteq V \wedge U \neq V) \\ \hline \end{array}$$

---

[1]See Quine (1969), pp. 241–265 and 331. This definition is on page 260. Hatcher (1982), pp. 103–134, is also useful.

21.2 Operators on Sets

The union of two sets U and V, written $U \cup V$, denotes the set consisting of all those elements which are either in U or in V. The intersection of two sets U and V, written $U \cap V$, denotes the set consisting of all those elements which are both in U and in V. The difference between two sets U and V, written $U \setminus V$, denotes the set consisting of all those elements of U which are not also members of V. The symmetric difference between two sets U and V of the same type, written $U \triangle V$ is the set which consists of all the things that are either in U or V but not both. Symmetric difference is the only operator defined in this chapter which is not part of the standard **Z** language.

$$
\begin{array}{l}
\underline{\quad} \cup \underline{\quad},\, \underline{\quad} \cap \underline{\quad},\, \underline{\quad} \setminus \underline{\quad},\, \underline{\quad} \triangle \underline{\quad} : \mathbf{P}\,X \times \mathbf{P}\,X \to \mathbf{P}\,X \\[2mm]
\hline
\forall U, V : \mathbf{P}\,X \bullet \\
\qquad U \cup V = \{x : X \mid x \in U \lor x \in V\} \land \\
\qquad U \cap V = \{x : X \mid x \in U \land x \in V\} \land \\
\qquad U \setminus V = \{x : X \mid x \in U \land x \notin V\} \land \\
\qquad U \triangle V = (U \setminus V) \cup (V \setminus U)
\end{array}
$$

21.3 Some Laws about Sets

In what follows U, V and W are all sets of type $\mathbf{P}\,X$.

$$X \setminus X = \{\,\},$$
$$X \setminus \{\,\} = X,$$
$$X \setminus (X \setminus U) = U,$$
$$U \cup X = X,$$
$$U \cup \{\,\} = U,$$
$$U \cup U = U,$$
$$U \cup V = V \cup U,$$
$$U \cup (V \cup W) = (U \cup V) \cup W,$$
$$U \cap X = U,$$
$$U \cap \{\,\} = \{\,\},$$
$$U \cap U = U,$$
$$U \cap V = V \cap U,$$

$$U \cap (V \cap W) = (U \cap V) \cap W,$$
$$U \cap (V \cup W) = (U \cap V) \cup (U \cap W),$$
$$(U \cup V) \cap W = (U \cap W) \cup (V \cap W),$$
$$U \cup (V \cap W) = (U \cup V) \cap (U \cup W),$$
$$(U \cap V) \cup W = (U \cup W) \cap (V \cup W),$$
$$X \setminus (U \cap V) = (X \setminus U) \cup (X \setminus V),$$
$$X \setminus (U \cup V) = (X \setminus U) \cap (X \setminus V),$$
$$U \cup (V \setminus W) = (U \cup V) \setminus (W \setminus U),$$
$$U \cap (V \setminus W) = (U \cap V) \setminus W$$
$$(U \cup V) \setminus W = (U \setminus W) \cup (V \setminus W),$$
$$U \setminus (V \cap W) = (U \setminus V) \cup (U \setminus W).$$

Many of these laws should remind you of some of the valid interderivable sequents of the propositional calculus. The following table establishes one possible correspondence:

propositions	sets
true	X
false	$\{\,\}$
$\neg\_$	$X \setminus \_$
$\wedge$	$\cap$
$\vee$	$\cup$

21.4 Generalized Union and Intersection

The generalized union of a set UU of sets of type $\mathbf{P}\,X$, represented as $\bigcup UU$, is the set which contains all those members of X which are in at least one member of UU. The generalized intersection of a set UU of sets of type X, represented as $\bigcap UU$, is the set which contains all those members of X which are in all of the members of UU.

$$=[X]=$$
$$\bigcup, \bigcap: \mathbf{P}(\mathbf{P}\,X) \rightarrow (\mathbf{P}\,X): \mathbf{P}(\mathbf{P}\,X) \rightarrow (\mathbf{P}\,X)$$

$$\forall UU: \mathbf{P}(\mathbf{P}\,X) \bullet$$
$$\bigcup UU = \{x\!:\!X \mid (\exists U\!:\! UU \bullet x \in U)\} \wedge$$
$$\bigcup UU = \{x\!:\!X \mid (\forall U\!:\! UU \bullet x \in U)\}$$

21.5 Finite Sets

A *finite set* of elements of type X, symbolized as $\mathbf{F}\,X$, is a subset of X which cannot be put into a one-one and onto correspondence with a proper subset of itself.

$$\mathbf{F}\,X == \{U : \mathbf{P}\,X \mid \neg \exists V : \mathbf{P}\,U \bullet V \neq U \wedge (\exists f : V \rightarrowtail\!\!\!\rightarrow U)\}.$$

All finite sets can be put into a one-one correspondence with an initial segment of the natural numbers, whose largest element is called the *cardinality* (or *size*) of the finite set. The cardinality operator, denoted by #, is defined as follows:

$$
\begin{array}{|l}
\hline
=\!\![X]\!\!=\!\!=\!\!=\!\!=\!\!=\!\!=\!\!=\!\!=\!\!=\!\!=\!\!= \\
\;\; \#: \mathbf{F}\,X \to \mathbf{N} \\
\hline
\;\; \forall U : \mathbf{F}\,X \bullet \\
\qquad \#U = \mu n : \mathbf{N} \mid \exists f : U \rightarrowtail\!\!\!\rightarrow 1 \mathinner{\ldotp\ldotp} n \\
\hline
\end{array}
$$

The symbol μ used in this definition is $\mathbf{Z}$'s *definite description operator*. Let P be a predicate. Then $\mu x : X \mid P$ refers to the unique object x of type X which satisfies P. If such a unique object does not exist, then $\mu x : X \mid P$ is undefined.

21.6 Number Ranges

The notation $\_ \mathinner{\ldotp\ldotp} \_$ is used for number ranges:

$$
\begin{array}{|l}
\hline
\;\; \_ \mathinner{\ldotp\ldotp} \_ : \mathbf{Z} \times \mathbf{Z} \to \mathbf{Z} \\
\hline
\;\; \forall i, j : \mathbf{Z} \bullet \\
\qquad i \mathinner{\ldotp\ldotp} j = \{n : \mathbf{Z} \mid i \leq n \wedge n \leq j\}
\end{array}
$$

Chapter 22

Relations

22.1 Introduction

The type of all relations between types X and Y is symbolized as $X \leftrightarrow Y$ and is defined like this:

$$X \leftrightarrow Y == \mathbf{P}(X \times Y).$$

Let $F: X \leftrightarrow Y$ be a relation. Then, as an alternative to $(x, y) \in F$, we often write $x \mapsto y \in F$. The pair $x \mapsto y$ is often known as a *maplet*.

22.2 Domains and Ranges

$$\begin{array}{|l}
\hline
[X, Y]\rule{0pt}{0pt}\\
\hline
\mathrm{dom}: (X \leftrightarrow Y) \to \mathbf{P}\,X\\
\mathrm{ran}: (X \leftrightarrow Y) \to \mathbf{P}\,Y\\
\hline
\forall F: X \leftrightarrow Y \bullet\\
\quad \mathrm{dom}\,F = \{x: X; y: Y \mid x \mapsto y \in F \bullet x\} \wedge\\
\quad \mathrm{ran}\,F = \{x: X; y: Y \mid x \mapsto y \in F \bullet y\}\\
\hline
\end{array}$$

Let $F, G: X \leftrightarrow Y$. Then we have the following properties:

$$\begin{aligned}
\mathrm{dom}(F \cup G) &= (\mathrm{dom}\,F) \cup (\mathrm{dom}\,G),\\
\mathrm{dom}(F \cap G) &\subseteq (\mathrm{dom}\,F) \cap (\mathrm{dom}\,G),\\
\mathrm{ran}(F \cup G) &= (\mathrm{ran}\,F) \cup (\mathrm{ran}\,G),\\
\mathrm{ran}(F \cap G) &\subseteq (\mathrm{ran}\,F) \cap (\mathrm{ran}\,G).
\end{aligned}$$

22.3 Inverse

$$
\begin{array}{l}
\underline{\hspace{1em}[X,Y]\hspace{1em}} \\
\quad \_^{-1} : (X \leftrightarrow Y) \to (Y \leftrightarrow X) \\
\hline
\forall F : X \leftrightarrow Y \bullet \\
\qquad F^{-1} = \{x : X; y : Y \mid x \mapsto y \in F \bullet y \mapsto x\}
\end{array}
$$

Sometimes $F^{\sim}$ is written for F^{-1}.

22.4 Identity

$$
\begin{array}{l}
\underline{\hspace{1em}[X]\hspace{1em}} \\
\quad \mathrm{id} : \mathbf{P}\,X \to (X \leftrightarrow X) \\
\hline
\forall U : \mathbf{P}\,X \bullet \\
\qquad \mathrm{id}\,U = \{x : X \mid x \in U \bullet x \mapsto x\}
\end{array}
$$

22.5 Domain Restriction and Corestriction

Sometimes domain corestriction is called domain anti-restriction. The domain restriction ($\lhd$) and corestriction ($\llcorner$) operators are defined in the following way:

$$
\begin{array}{l}
\underline{\hspace{1em}[X,Y]\hspace{1em}} \\
\quad \_ \lhd \_,\, \_ \llcorner \_ : (\mathbf{P}\,X) \times (X \leftrightarrow Y) \to (X \leftrightarrow Y) \\
\hline
\forall U : \mathbf{P}\,X; F : X \leftrightarrow Y \bullet \\
\qquad U \lhd F = \{x : X; y : Y \mid x \mapsto y \in F \wedge x \in U \bullet x \mapsto y\} \wedge \\
\qquad U \llcorner F = \{x : X; y : Y \mid x \mapsto y \in F \wedge x \notin U \bullet x \mapsto y\}
\end{array}
$$

Let $F, G : X \leftrightarrow Y$ and $U, V : \mathbf{P}\,X$. Then we have the following properties:

$$
(U \cup V) \lhd F = (U \lhd F) \cup (V \lhd F),
$$
$$
U \lhd (F \cup G) = (U \lhd F) \cup (U \lhd G),
$$
$$
U \llcorner (F \cup G) = (U \llcorner F) \cup (U \llcorner G),
$$
$$
(U \lhd F) \cup (U \llcorner F) = F.
$$

22.6 Range Restriction and Corestriction

Sometimes range restriction is called range anti-restriction. The range restriction ($\triangleright$) and corestriction ($\blacktriangleright$) operators are defined in the following way:

$$
\begin{array}{|l|}
\hline
\text{---}[X,Y]\text{---}\!\!\!=\!\!\!=\!\!\!= \\
\quad \_\,\triangleright\,\_\,,\_\,\blacktriangleright\,\_\,:(X \leftrightarrow Y) \times (\mathbf{P}\,Y) \to (X \leftrightarrow Y) \\
\hline
\quad \forall F\colon X \leftrightarrow Y; U\colon \mathbf{P}\,Y \bullet \\
\qquad F \triangleright U = \{x\colon X; y\colon Y \mid x \mapsto y \in F \wedge y \in U \bullet x \mapsto y\} \wedge \\
\qquad F \blacktriangleright U = \{x\colon X; y\colon Y \mid x \mapsto y \in F \wedge y \notin U \bullet x \mapsto y\} \\
\hline
\end{array}
$$

Let $F, G\colon X \leftrightarrow Y$ and $U, V\colon \mathbf{P}\,Y$. Then we have the following properties:

$$F \triangleright (U \cup V) = (F \triangleright U) \cup (F \triangleright V),$$
$$(F \cup G) \triangleright U = (F \triangleright U) \cup (G \triangleright U),$$
$$(F \cup G) \blacktriangleright U = (F \blacktriangleright U) \cup (G \blacktriangleright U),$$
$$(F \triangleright U) \cup (F \blacktriangleright U) = F.$$

22.7 Forward Relational Composition

$$
\begin{array}{|l|}
\hline
\text{---}[X,Y,Z]\text{---}\!\!\!=\!\!\!=\!\!\!= \\
\quad \_\,\mathring{,}\,\_\,:(X \leftrightarrow Y) \times (Y \leftrightarrow Z) \to (X \leftrightarrow Z) \\
\hline
\quad \forall F\colon X \leftrightarrow Y; G\colon Y \leftrightarrow Z \bullet \\
\qquad \{x\colon X; z\colon Z \mid (\exists y\colon Y \bullet x \mapsto y \in F \wedge y \mapsto z \in G) \bullet x \mapsto z\} \\
\hline
\end{array}
$$

We can write $G \circ F$ for $F \,\mathring{,}\, G$. The operator $\circ$ is sometimes known as *backward relational composition*.

Forward relational composition is associative and it distributes both ways through set union. Let $F, F_1, F_2\colon X_1 \leftrightarrow X_2$, $G, G_1, G_2\colon X_2 \leftrightarrow X_3$ and $H\colon X_3 \leftrightarrow X_4$. Then we have:

$$F \,\mathring{,}\, (G \,\mathring{,}\, H) = (F \,\mathring{,}\, G) \,\mathring{,}\, H,$$
$$(F_1 \cup F_2) \,\mathring{,}\, G = (F_1 \,\mathring{,}\, G) \cup (F_2 \,\mathring{,}\, G),$$
$$F \,\mathring{,}\, (G_1 \cup G_2) = (F \,\mathring{,}\, G_1) \cup (F \,\mathring{,}\, G_2).$$

22.8 Generalized Application: Relational Image

The *relational image* of a set U through a relation F (sometimes called the F-image of U), which is written $F(\!|U|\!)$, is the set of all those elements of the range of F to which F maps elements of U. In other words, it is the set of all those objects y to which F relates some member x of U.

$$
\begin{array}{l}
\boxed{
\begin{array}{l}
=[X,Y]= \\[4pt]
\_(\!|\_|\!)\!:(X \leftrightarrow Y) \times (\mathbf{P}\,X) \to (\mathbf{P}\,Y) \\
\hline
\forall F\!:X \leftrightarrow Y;\, U\!:\mathbf{P}\,X \bullet \\
\qquad F(\!|U|\!) = \{y\!:Y \mid \exists x\!:U \bullet x \mapsto y \in F\}
\end{array}
}
\end{array}
$$

22.9 Closures

Let $F\!:X \leftrightarrow X$ be a relation. Then, F^+ is its transitive closure and F^* is its reflexive-transitive closure.

$$
\begin{array}{l}
\boxed{
\begin{array}{l}
=[X]= \\[4pt]
\_^{+},\_^{*}\!:(X \leftrightarrow X) \to (X \leftrightarrow X) \\
\hline
\forall F\!:X \leftrightarrow X \bullet \\
\qquad F^+ = \bigcap\{G\!:X \leftrightarrow X \mid F \subseteq G \wedge G \,\fatsemi\, G \subseteq G\} \wedge \\
\qquad F^* = \bigcap\{G\!:X \leftrightarrow X \mid \operatorname{id} X \subseteq G \wedge F \subseteq G \wedge G \,\fatsemi\, G \subseteq G\}
\end{array}
}
\end{array}
$$

Chapter 23

Functions

23.1   Partial Functions

A *partial function* from X to Y is a relation between X and Y which maps elements of its domain to a single element of its range. The type of all partial functions from X to Y is symbolized as $X \nrightarrow Y$ and is defined like this:

$$X \nrightarrow Y == \{F\colon X \leftrightarrow Y \mid (\forall x\colon X; y, z\colon Y \bullet x \mapsto y \in F \wedge x \mapsto z \in F \Rightarrow y = z)\}.$$

23.2   Total Functions

A *total function* from X to Y is a partial function from X to Y whose domain is the whole of X. The type of all total functions from X to Y is symbolized as $X \rightarrow Y$ and is defined like this:

$$X \rightarrow Y == \{f\colon X \nrightarrow Y \mid \operatorname{dom} f = X\}.$$

23.3   Finite Functions

A *finite partial function* from X to Y is a partial function from X to Y whose domain is a finite subset of X. The type of all finite partial functions from X to Y is symbolized as $X \nrightarrow\!\!\!\!\rightarrow Y$ and is defined like this:

$$X \nrightarrow\!\!\!\!\rightarrow Y == \{f\colon X \nrightarrow Y \mid \operatorname{dom} f \in \mathbf{F}\, X\},$$

where $\mathbf{F}\, X$ means the set of all the finite subsets of X.

23.4   Injective Functions

An *injective function* is one whose inverse is also a function. A *partial injective function* or a *partial injection* is a partial function whose inverse is also a function. It is defined as follows:

$$X \rightarrowtail\!\!\!\!\rightarrow Y == \{f\colon X \nrightarrow Y \mid f^{-1} \in Y \nrightarrow X\}.$$

A *total injective function* is a total function whose inverse is also a function. It is defined as follows:

$$X \rightarrowtail Y == \{f: X \rightarrow Y \mid f^{-1} \in Y \twoheadrightarrow X\}.$$

A *finite injective function* is a finite function whose inverse is also a function. It can be defined like this:

$$X \rightarrowtail\!\!\!\!\rightarrow Y == \{f: X \nrightarrow Y \mid f^{-1} \in Y \twoheadrightarrow X\}.$$

23.5   Surjective Functions

A *surjective function* or a *surjection* from X to Y or a function from X *onto* Y is one whose range is the whole of Y. A *partial surjective function* or *partial surjection* from X to Y is a partial function from X to Y whose range is the whole of Y. It is defined like this:

$$X \twoheadrightarrow Y == \{f: X \nrightarrow Y \mid \operatorname{ran} f = Y\}.$$

A *total surjective function* from X to Y is a total function from X to Y whose range is the whole of Y.

$$X \twoheadrightarrow Y == \{f: X \rightarrow Y \mid \operatorname{ran} f = Y\}.$$

23.6   Bijections

A function from X to Y is a *bijection* or is said to be *one-one and onto* if it is a total surjective function from X to Y which is also a total injective function.

$$X \rightarrowtail\!\!\!\twoheadrightarrow Y == (X \twoheadrightarrow Y) \cap (X \rightarrowtail Y).$$

23.7   Function Application

If f is a function from X to Y and if x is a member of the domain of f, then the term fx denotes the unique element y of Y which stands in the relation f to x, that is to say, the value of f at x. Let $f: X \nrightarrow Y$ and $x: X$. Then $x \in \operatorname{dom} f \Rightarrow (x \mapsto fx) \in f$.

23.8   Functional Overriding

$$
\begin{array}{l}
\underline{\quad[X,Y]\quad} \\
\hline
\ \_ \oplus \_ : (X \nrightarrow Y) \times (X \nrightarrow Y) \rightarrow (X \nrightarrow Y) \\
\hline
\forall f, g: X \nrightarrow Y \bullet \\
\quad f \oplus g = ((\operatorname{dom} g) \vartriangleleft f) \cup g \\
\hline
\end{array}
$$

Functional overriding is associative and { } is its identity. Let $f, g, h: X \nrightarrow Y$. Then we have:

$$f \oplus (g \oplus h) = (f \oplus g) \oplus h,$$
$$\{\ \} \oplus f = f,$$
$$f \oplus \{\ \} = f.$$

Let $U: \mathbf{P} X$ and $V: \mathbf{P} Y$. Then some further properties of $\oplus$ are:

$$U \triangleleft (f \oplus g) = (U \triangleleft f) \oplus (U \triangleleft g),$$
$$(f \oplus g) \triangleright V \subseteq (f \triangleright V) \oplus (g \triangleright V).$$

23.9 Lambda Abstraction

Do not confuse **Z**'s λ-notation with the λ-calculus. The **Z** notation is just a variant way of specifying sets of ordered n-tuples.

$$\lambda x_1: X_1; \ldots; x_n: X_n \mid P \bullet t = \{x_1: X_1; \ldots; x_n: X_n \mid P \bullet (x_1, \ldots, x_n) \mapsto t\}.$$

Chapter 24

Sequences

24.1 Basic Definitions

Given a set X, the *finite sequences* made up of elements drawn from X are the finite partial functions from $\mathbf{N}$ to X whose domains are initial segments of the non-zero natural numbers. The type iseq X of *injective* sequences consists of all those sequences that do not contain repetitions.

$$\text{seq } X == \{f : \mathbf{N} \nrightarrow X \mid \text{dom } f = 1 \mathinner{..} \#f\},$$
$$\text{seq}_1 X == \text{seq } X \setminus \{\{\ \}\},$$
$$\text{iseq } X == \text{seq } X \cap (\mathbf{N} \rightarrowtail X).$$

Usually the following notations are used for the extensional specification of sequences:

$$\langle\rangle == \{\ \},$$
$$\langle x \rangle == \{1 \mapsto x\},$$
$$\langle x_1, \ldots, x_n \rangle == \{1 \mapsto x_1, \ldots, n \mapsto x_n\}.$$

24.2 Sequence Decomposition

$$
\boxed{
\begin{array}{l}
[X] \\
\hline
head, last : \text{seq}_1 X \to X \\
front, tail : \text{seq}_1 X \to \text{seq } X \\
\hline
head = \lambda\sigma : \text{seq}_1 X \bullet (\sigma 1) \land \\
\quad last = \lambda\sigma : \text{seq}_1 X \bullet \sigma(\#\sigma) \land \\
\quad front = \lambda\sigma : \text{seq}_1 X \bullet (1 \mathinner{..} \#\sigma - 1) \lhd \sigma \land \\
\quad tail = \lambda\sigma : \text{seq}_1 X \bullet (\{0\} \lhd succ)\,\mathbin{\S}\,\sigma
\end{array}
}
$$

24.3 Sequence Operators

24.3.1 Concatenation for Sequences

$$
\begin{array}{|l|}
\hline
[X] \\
\hline
\_ \frown \_ : (\operatorname{seq} X) \times (\operatorname{seq} X) \to (\operatorname{seq} X) \\
\hline
\forall \sigma, \tau : \operatorname{seq} X \bullet \\
\quad \sigma \frown \tau = \sigma \cup \{n : \operatorname{dom} \tau \bullet n + \#\sigma \mapsto (\tau n)\} \\
\hline
\end{array}
$$

24.3.2 Reversing a Sequence

$$
\begin{array}{|l|}
\hline
[X] \\
\hline
rev \_ : (\operatorname{seq} X) \to (\operatorname{seq} X) \\
\hline
\forall \sigma : \operatorname{seq} X \bullet \\
\quad rev\, \sigma = \lambda n : \operatorname{dom} \sigma \bullet \sigma(\#\sigma - n + 1) \\
\hline
\end{array}
$$

24.3.3 Subsequence Formation

$$
\begin{array}{|l|}
\hline
[X] \\
\hline
\_ \text{ after } \_,\_ \text{ for } \_ : (\operatorname{seq} X) \times \mathbf{N} \to (\operatorname{seq} X) \\
\hline
\forall \sigma : \operatorname{seq} X; n : \mathbf{N} \bullet \\
\quad \sigma \text{ after } n = (\{0\} \lhd succ^n) \,\S\, \sigma \wedge \\
\quad \sigma \text{ for } n = 1 \mathinner{.\,.} n \lhd \sigma \\
\hline
\end{array}
$$

It is often useful to have curried versions of _ after _ and _ for _. These are known as drop and take:

$$
\begin{array}{|l|}
\hline
[X] \\
\hline
\operatorname{drop}, \operatorname{take} : \mathbf{N} \to \operatorname{seq} X \to \operatorname{seq} X \\
\hline
\operatorname{drop} = \lambda n : \mathbf{N} \bullet (\lambda \sigma : \operatorname{seq} X \bullet \sigma \text{ after } n) \wedge \\
\operatorname{take} = \lambda n : \mathbf{N} \bullet (\lambda \sigma : \operatorname{seq} X \bullet \sigma \text{ for } n) \\
\hline
\end{array}
$$

24.3.4 Filtering

$$\boxed{\begin{array}{l} [X] \\ \hline \_\upharpoonright\_: \operatorname{seq} X \times \mathbf{P} X \to \operatorname{seq} X \\ \hline \forall U : \mathbf{P} X \bullet \\ \quad \langle\rangle \upharpoonright U = \langle\rangle \wedge \\ \quad (\forall x : X \bullet \\ \qquad (x \in U \Rightarrow \langle x\rangle \upharpoonright U = \langle x\rangle) \wedge \\ \qquad (x \notin U \Rightarrow \langle x\rangle \upharpoonright U = \langle\,\rangle)) \wedge \\ \quad (\forall \sigma, \tau : \operatorname{seq} X \bullet \\ \qquad (\sigma \frown \tau) \upharpoonright U = (\sigma \upharpoonright U) \frown (\tau \upharpoonright U)) \end{array}}$$

24.4 Distributed Concatenation

$$\boxed{\begin{array}{l} [X] \\ \hline \frown/ : \operatorname{seq}(\operatorname{seq} X) \to \operatorname{seq} X \\ \hline \frown/\langle\rangle = \langle\rangle \\ \forall \sigma : \operatorname{seq} X \bullet \frown/\langle\sigma\rangle = \sigma \\ \forall \sigma, \tau : \operatorname{seq}(\operatorname{seq} X) \bullet \\ \quad \frown/(\sigma \frown \tau) = (\frown/\sigma) \frown (\frown/\tau) \end{array}}$$

24.5 Disjointness and Partition

$$\boxed{\begin{array}{l} [I, X] \\ \hline \operatorname{disjoint} \_ : \mathbf{P}(I \nrightarrow \mathbf{P} X) \\ \hline \forall f : I \nrightarrow \mathbf{P} X \bullet \\ \quad (\operatorname{disjoint} f \Longleftrightarrow \\ \qquad (\forall x, y : \operatorname{dom} f \mid x \neq y \bullet f x \cap f y = \{\,\})) \end{array}}$$

$$\boxed{\begin{array}{l} [I, X] \\ \hline \_ \operatorname{partition} \_ : (I \nrightarrow \mathbf{P} X) \leftrightarrow \mathbf{P} X \\ \hline \forall f : I \nrightarrow \mathbf{P} X; U : \mathbf{P} X \bullet \\ \quad (f \operatorname{partition} U \Longleftrightarrow \\ \qquad \operatorname{disjoint} f \wedge \bigcup\{x : \operatorname{dom} f \bullet f x\} = U) \end{array}}$$

Chapter 25

Bags

25.1 Basic Definitions

A bag is a collection of objects in which the number of times an object occurs is significant. The type of all bags of elements drawn from X is denoted by bag X. This is defined thus:

$$\text{bag } X == X \nrightarrow \mathbf{N}_1 .$$

When bags are introduced by enumeration the elements are enclosed in double square brackets, thus $[\![1, 2, 3, 4, 3, 3]\!]$. The empty bag is written $[\![\,]\!]$.

25.2 Bag Manipulating Operations

The function $count\ L\ x$ is the number of times that x occurs in L.

$[X]$
$count: \text{bag } X \rightarrowtail\!\!\!\!\rightarrow (X \rightarrow \mathbf{N})$

$\forall x: X;\ L: \text{bag } X\ \bullet$
$\quad count\ L = (\lambda x: X \bullet 0) \oplus L$

The relation x in L holds only when $count\ L\ x > 0$.

$[X]$
$\_ \text{ in } \_ : X \leftrightarrow \text{bag } X$

$\forall x: X;\ L: \text{bag } X\ \bullet$
$\quad x \text{ in } L \Longleftrightarrow x \in \text{dom } L$

Let σ be a sequence. Then *items* σ is the bag in which each element x appears exactly as often as x appears in σ.

$$
\begin{array}{|l}
\underline{[X]} \\
\hline
items \_ : \operatorname{seq} X \to \operatorname{bag} X \\
\hline
\forall \sigma : \operatorname{seq} X;\, x : X \bullet \\
\qquad count(items\, \sigma)\, x = \#\{i : \operatorname{dom} \sigma \mid \sigma i = x\}
\end{array}
$$

The union of bags is represented by the symbol $\uplus$, which is defined as follows:[1]

$$
\begin{array}{|l}
\underline{[X]} \\
\hline
\_ \uplus \_ : \operatorname{bag} X \times \operatorname{bag} X \to \operatorname{bag} X \\
\hline
\forall L, M : \operatorname{bag} X;\, x : X \bullet \\
\qquad count(L \uplus M)\, x = count\, L\, x + count\, M\, x
\end{array}
$$

Bag union is associative, commutative and has the empty bag as its identity element. Let $L, M, N : \operatorname{bag} X$. Then we have:

$$
\begin{aligned}
L \uplus (M \uplus N) &= (L \uplus M) \uplus N, \\
L \uplus M &= M \uplus L, \\
L \uplus [\![\,]\!] &= L, \\
[\![\,]\!] \uplus L &= L.
\end{aligned}
$$

The sub-bag relation is symbolized by the sign $\sqsubseteq$, which is defined like this:

$$
\begin{array}{|l}
\underline{[X]} \\
\hline
\_ \sqsubseteq \_ : \operatorname{bag} X \leftrightarrow \operatorname{bag} X \\
\hline
\forall L, M : \operatorname{bag} X \bullet L \sqsubseteq M \iff (\forall x : X \bullet count\, L\, x \le count\, M\, x)
\end{array}
$$

---

[1] Woodcock (1989b), p. 110, argues that this operation should be called *bag sum*.

Chapter 26

Rules and Obligations

26.1 First-order Logic

The Inference Rules

Introduction An inference rule in the sequent calculus is a relation between one or more *input sequents* and an *output sequent*. Inference rules are written in the following way:

$$
\underbrace{\overbrace{\Gamma_1 \vdash A_1}^{\text{first input sequent}} \quad \cdots \quad \overbrace{\Gamma_n \vdash A_n}^{n\text{th input sequent}}}{\underbrace{\Delta \vdash B}_{\text{output sequent}}} \quad name
$$

Think of this as a mini-tree with n leaves and a root. Each leaf is an input sequent and the root is the output sequent. In this book the name of the rule is written to the right of the horizontal line which separates the input sequents from the output sequent.

Let $\heartsuit$ be an arbitrary two-place connective, then an *elimination* rule for $\heartsuit$ is one in which $\heartsuit$ appears in the conclusion of at least one of the input sequents to the rule and $\heartsuit$ does not occur in the conclusion of the output sequent of the rule. An *introduction* rule for $\heartsuit$ is one in which $\heartsuit$ does not appear in the conclusion of any of the input sequents to the rule, but $\heartsuit$ does occur in the conclusion of the output sequent of the rule.

Conjunction There are two elimination rules associated with conjunction:

$$
\frac{\Gamma \vdash A \wedge B}{\Gamma \vdash A} \wedge\text{-}elim_1 \qquad\qquad \frac{\Gamma \vdash A \wedge B}{\Gamma \vdash B} \wedge\text{-}elim_2
$$

Conjunction has a single introduction rule:

$$
\frac{\Gamma \vdash A \qquad\qquad \Delta \vdash B}{\Gamma, \Delta \vdash A \wedge B} \wedge\text{-}int
$$

Disjunction   There is one elimination rule associated with disjunction:

$$\frac{\Gamma \vdash A \vee B \qquad \Delta, A \vdash C \qquad \Sigma, B \vdash C}{\Gamma, \Delta, \Sigma \vdash C} \quad \vee\text{-}elim$$

There are two introduction rules associated with disjunction:

$$\frac{\Gamma \vdash A}{\Gamma \vdash A \vee B} \quad \vee\text{-}int_1 \qquad\qquad \frac{\Gamma \vdash B}{\Gamma \vdash A \vee B} \quad \vee\text{-}int_2$$

Implication   There is one elimination rule associated with implication:

$$\frac{\Gamma \vdash A \qquad \Delta \vdash A \Rightarrow B}{\Gamma, \Delta \vdash B} \quad \Rightarrow\text{-}elim$$

There is one introduction rule associated with implication:

$$\frac{\Gamma \vdash B}{\Gamma \setminus \{A\} \vdash A \Rightarrow B} \quad \Rightarrow\text{-}int$$

The formula A can occur in the set of premises Γ, but it does not have to.

Bi-implication   The elimination rules for bi-implication allow us to change them into implications:

$$\frac{\Gamma \vdash A \Longleftrightarrow B}{\Gamma \vdash A \Rightarrow B} \quad \Longleftrightarrow\text{-}elim_1 \qquad\qquad \frac{\Gamma \vdash A \Longleftrightarrow B}{\Gamma \vdash B \Rightarrow A} \quad \Longleftrightarrow\text{-}elim_2$$

There is a single introduction rule for bi-implication:

$$\frac{\Gamma \vdash A \Rightarrow B \qquad \Delta \vdash B \Rightarrow A}{\Gamma, \Delta \vdash A \Longleftrightarrow B} \quad \Longleftrightarrow\text{-}int$$

Negation and the Always False Proposition   Negation has a single elimination rule:

$$\frac{\Gamma \vdash A \qquad \Delta \vdash \neg A}{\Gamma, \Delta \vdash false} \quad \neg\text{-}elim$$

Negation has a single introduction rule:

$$\frac{\Gamma, A \vdash false}{\Gamma \vdash \neg A} \quad \neg\text{-}int$$

The introduction and elimination rules for negation are easy to remember if you make use of the fact that $\neg A$ is logically equivalent to $A \Rightarrow false$. So, they can be seen as special cases of the introduction and elimination rules for implication.

Associated with negation there is also a double negation elimination rule:

$$\frac{\Gamma \vdash \neg\neg A}{\Gamma \vdash A} \quad \neg\neg\text{-}elim$$

The final rule that I am going to mention here involves the always false proposition $false$. It is known as $false$ elimination:

$$\frac{\Gamma \vdash false}{\Gamma \vdash A} \quad false\text{-}elim$$

Structural Rules

$$\frac{\Gamma \vdash A}{\Gamma, \Delta \vdash A} \quad weak \qquad\qquad \frac{\Gamma \vdash A \qquad \Delta, A \vdash B}{\Gamma, \Delta \vdash B} \quad cut$$

The Universal Quantifier

There is one elimination rule associated with the universal quantifier:

$$\frac{\Gamma \vdash \forall x\colon X \bullet A}{\Gamma \vdash A[t/x]} \quad \forall\text{-}elim$$

Here, t is any term of the same type as x. The notation $A[t/x]$ stands for that formula which is obtained by substituting t for all free occurrences of x in A.

There is a single introduction rule for the universal quantifier:

$$\frac{\Gamma \vdash A}{\Gamma \vdash \forall x\colon X \bullet A[x/a]} \quad \forall\text{-}int$$

Here, x must be a variable of type X and a a constant of the same type which must not occur in Γ.

The Existential Quantifier

There is one elimination rule associated with the existential quantifier:

$$\frac{\Gamma \vdash \exists x\colon X \bullet A \qquad\qquad \Delta, A[a/x] \vdash C}{\Gamma, \Delta \vdash C} \quad \exists\text{-}elim$$

Here, a is a constant of type X which must not occur in Γ, Δ, $\exists x\colon X \bullet A$ or C. The reason for using the letter C in the statement of this rule—rather than B—is to bring out the connection between this rule and the rule $\vee$-$elim$.

There is one introduction rule associated with the existential quantifier:

$$\frac{\Gamma \vdash A[t/x]}{\Gamma \vdash \exists x\colon X \bullet A} \quad \exists\text{-}int$$

Here, t must be a term of type X and x is a variable of the same type.

Rules for Identity

The elimination rule for identity is:

$$\frac{\Gamma \vdash A \qquad\qquad \Delta \vdash t = u}{\Gamma, \Delta \vdash B} \quad =\text{-}elim$$

Here, t and u are any terms of the same type and B is like A except that u has been substituted for t one or more times. There is *no* need to substitute u for *all* occurrences of t.

The introduction rule for identity is slightly different from those we have encountered so far. It allows us to start proofs from leaf nodes of the form:

$$\vdash t = t,$$

where t is any term. It will be referred to as $=$-int.

26.2 Mathematical Induction

The principle of mathematical induction is a rule of inference that allows us to prove that certain things are true of all the non-negative numbers. It says that in order to show that $P(n)$ holds for all natural numbers, all we have to show is:

1. $P(0)$ holds.

2. $\forall i\colon \mathbf{N} \bullet P(i) \Rightarrow P(i+1)$.

Here, part 1 is known as the *base case* and part 2 is known as the *inductive step*.

26.3 Induction for Sequences

Sequence induction is similar to mathematical induction. It comes in several flavours. One version says that in order to show that some property $P(\sigma)$ holds for all sequences σ all we have to show is that:

1. $P(\langle\ \rangle)$ holds.

2. If $P(\sigma)$ holds for any sequence σ, then so does $P(\langle x \rangle \frown \sigma)$. In symbols:

$$\forall x\colon X; \sigma\colon \operatorname{seq} X \bullet P(\sigma) \Rightarrow P(\langle x \rangle \frown \sigma).$$

Here, part 1 is known as the *base case* and part 2 is known as the *inductive step*.

Another version says that in order to show that some property $P(\sigma)$ holds for all sequences $\sigma\colon \operatorname{seq} X$ all you have to show is that:

1. $P(\langle\ \rangle)$ holds.

2. If $P(\sigma)$ holds for any sequence σ, then so does $P(\sigma \frown \langle x \rangle)$. In symbols:

$$\forall x\colon X; \sigma\colon \operatorname{seq} X \bullet P(\sigma) \Rightarrow P(\sigma \frown \langle x \rangle).$$

Yet another version says that in order to prove that $P(\sigma)$ holds for all sequences you just need to prove that:

1. $P(\langle\ \rangle)$ holds.

2. $P(\langle x \rangle)$ is true for all $x\colon X$.

3. If $P(\sigma)$ and $P(\tau)$ are true for all sequences σ and τ, then so is $P(\sigma \frown \tau)$. In symbols:

$$\forall \sigma, \tau\colon \operatorname{seq} X \bullet P(\sigma) \wedge P(\tau) \Rightarrow P(\sigma \frown \tau).$$

26.4 Operation Refinement

Operation refinement takes place within a single specification in that only one kind of state space is involved. It is a way of relating operations defined on the same data.

The concrete operation OpC is a refinement of the abstract operation OpA, both defined on the same state space, iff both of the following predicates are true:

$$\operatorname{pre} OpA \Rightarrow \operatorname{pre} OpC,$$
$$\operatorname{pre} OpA \wedge OpC \Rightarrow OpA.$$

The first of these states that the concrete operation succeeds whenever the abstract one does, although there might be situations in which the concrete state succeeds but the abstract one does not. The second predicate states that the abstract and concrete operations produce the same results on the same starting states.

26.5 Summary of Data Refinement

Let *Astate* be an abstract state and *Cstate* a concrete one linked by means of the schema AC. *InitA'* is the abstract initial state and *InitC'* is the concrete initial state. *OpA* and *OpC* are an abstract and a concrete operation respectively.

26.5.1 For Functions

The following proof-obligations have to be proved if the schema AC satisfies the following condition:

$$\forall Cstate \bullet \exists_1 Astate \bullet AC.$$

Initialization

$$InitC' \wedge AC' \Rightarrow InitA'.$$

Applicability

$$\text{pre } OpA \wedge AC \Rightarrow \text{pre } OpC.$$

Correctness

$$\text{pre } OpA \wedge \Delta AC \wedge OpC \Rightarrow OpA.$$

26.5.2 In General

The following proof-obligations have to be proved if the schema AC does *not* satisfy the following condition:

$$\forall Cstate \bullet \exists_1 Astate \bullet AC.$$

Initialization

$$InitC' \Rightarrow (\exists Astate' \bullet InitA' \wedge AC').$$

Applicability

$$\text{pre } OpA \wedge AC \Rightarrow \text{pre } OpC.$$

Correctness

$$\text{pre } OpA \wedge AC \wedge OpC \Rightarrow (\exists Astate' \bullet AC' \wedge OpA).$$

Part VII

Appendices

Appendix A

Variable Conventions

Each Greek and Roman letter used in this book in a mathematical formula has only a single meaning. This has led to choices that some readers may find strange, but I think the advantages gained from knowing that, for example, P always stands for a predicate and S always stands for a schema, outweigh any feeling of strangeness at using, say, J for a signature or L for a bag.

$$
\left.\begin{array}{l} A \\ B \\ C \end{array}\right\} \text{predicates} \qquad \left.\begin{array}{l} a \\ b \\ c \end{array}\right\} \text{constants}
$$

$$
\left.\begin{array}{l} D \\ E \end{array}\right\} \text{declarations} \qquad \left.\begin{array}{l} d \end{array}\right\}
$$

$$
e \;\}\; \text{unused}
$$

$$
\left.\begin{array}{l} F \\ G \\ H \end{array}\right\} \text{relations} \qquad \left.\begin{array}{l} f \\ g \\ h \end{array}\right\} \text{functions}
$$

$$
I \;\}\; \text{(index) set} \qquad \left.\begin{array}{l} i \\ j \\ k \\ l \\ m \\ n \end{array}\right\} \text{number variables}
$$

$$
\left.\begin{array}{l} J \\ K \end{array}\right\} \text{signatures}
$$

$$
\left.\begin{array}{l} L \\ M \\ N \end{array}\right\} \text{bags}
$$

$$
O \;\}\; \text{unused} \qquad o \;\}\; \text{unused}
$$

$$
\left.\begin{array}{l} P \\ Q \\ R \end{array}\right\}\text{predicates} \qquad\qquad \left.\begin{array}{l} p \\ q \\ r \end{array}\right\}\text{number variables}
$$

$$
\left.\begin{array}{l} S \\ T \end{array}\right\}\text{schemas} \qquad\qquad \begin{array}{l} s \\ t \end{array}
$$

$$
\left.\begin{array}{l} U \\ V \\ W \end{array}\right\}\text{sets} \qquad\qquad \left.\begin{array}{l} u \\ v \end{array}\right\}\text{terms or expression}
$$

$$
\left.\qquad\qquad w \right\}\text{unused}
$$

$$
\left.\begin{array}{l} X \\ Y \\ Z \end{array}\right\}\text{sets as types} \qquad\qquad \left.\begin{array}{l} x \\ y \\ z \end{array}\right\}\text{variables}
$$

$$
\left.\begin{array}{l} \Gamma \\ \Delta \\ \Sigma \end{array}\right\}\text{sets of predicates} \qquad\qquad \left.\begin{array}{l} \sigma \\ \tau \\ \upsilon \end{array}\right\}\text{sequences}
$$

The Greek letters Δ and Ξ are also used to form schema names as explained in section 4.5.3.

The only place where the above conventions may fail is inside schemas, where I have sometimes used single letter identifiers—with or without decorations—because they seemed appropriate, like $p?$ for a member of the type *Person*. With respect to schemas, the convention I have used is that schema names begin with a capital letter and embedded words also start with a capital letter, for example, *AddMember*. Similarly, types begin with a capital letter, like *Person* and *Report*, as do constants, such as *Max*. Variables and identifiers are entirely in lowercase, like *instanceof*, except that sometimes I have used a single capital letter for a set, like $A?$, because it seemed appropriate somehow.

These conventions—like all conventions—are entirely arbitrary. They do not have the status of categorical imperatives like 'Never, ever, under any circumstances, change queues at the supermarket' or 'Never, ever, under any circumstances, dedicate a book to a lover'. Although conventions are arbitrary, I would urge all specification writers to endeavour to be consistent in the conventions that they adopt. Inconsistency in variable usage is very confusing and will not help people understand the specifications that you write.

Appendix B

Answers to Exercises

Chapter 2

2.1) a) $P \wedge P$ is not a tautology. It is false when P is false as the following truth-table shows:

P	P	$\wedge$	P
t	t	t	t
f	f	f	f

b) $P \wedge \neg Q$ is not a tautology. It is false, for example, when P is false and Q is true as the following truth-table shows:

P	Q	P	$\wedge$	$\neg Q$
t	t	t	f	f
t	f	t	t	t
f	t	f	f	f
f	f	f	f	t

c) $(P \Rightarrow Q) \Rightarrow P$ is not a tautology. It is false, for example, when P and Q are both false as the following truth-table shows:

P	Q	$(P \Rightarrow Q)$	$\Rightarrow$	P
t	t	t	t	t
t	f	f	t	t
f	t	t	f	f
f	f	t	f	f

d) $P \Rightarrow (Q \Rightarrow P)$ is a tautology. This is shown by the following truth-table:

P	Q	P	$\Rightarrow$	$(Q \Rightarrow Q)$
t	t	t	t	t
t	f	t	t	t
f	t	f	t	f
f	f	f	t	t

e) $P \Rightarrow (Q \Rightarrow (P \Rightarrow P))$ is a tautology. This is shown by the following truth-table:

P	Q	P	$\Rightarrow$	$(Q \Rightarrow$	$(P \Rightarrow P))$
t	t	t	t	t	t
t	f	t	t	t	t
f	t	f	t	t	t
f	f	f	t	t	t

f) $(P \wedge Q) \Rightarrow P$ is a tautology. This is shown by the following truth-table:

P	Q	$(P \wedge Q)$	$\Rightarrow$	P
t	t	t	t	t
t	f	f	t	t
f	t	f	t	f
f	f	f	t	f

g) $P \Rightarrow (P \wedge Q)$ is not a tautology. It is false when P is true and Q is false, as the following truth-table shows:

P	Q	P	$\Rightarrow$	$(P \wedge Q)$
t	t	t	t	t
t	f	t	f	f
f	t	f	t	f
f	f	f	t	f

h) $((P \wedge Q) \Rightarrow R) \Longleftrightarrow ((P \Rightarrow R) \vee (Q \Rightarrow R))$ is a tautology. This is shown by the following truth-table:

P	Q	R	((P∧Q)	⇒	R)	⟺	((P⇒R)	∨	(Q⇒R))
t	t	t	t	t	t	t	t	t	t
t	t	f	t	f	f	t	f	f	f
t	f	t	f	t	t	t	t	t	t
t	f	f	f	t	f	t	f	t	t
f	t	t	f	t	t	t	t	t	t
f	t	f	f	t	f	t	t	t	f
f	f	t	f	t	t	t	t	t	t
f	f	f	f	t	f	t	t	t	t

2.2) a) The sequent $\neg P \Rightarrow P \models P$ is valid, as the following truth-table shows:

P	¬P	⇒	P	⊨	P
t	f	t	t		t
f	t	f	f		f

b) The sequent $P \models Q \Rightarrow (P \wedge Q)$ is valid, as the following truth-table shows:

P	Q	P	⊨	Q	⇒	(P∧Q)
t	t	t		t	t	t
t	f	t		f	t	f
f	t	f		t	f	f
f	f	f		f	t	f

c) The sequent $P \Rightarrow Q, P \Rightarrow \neg Q \models \neg P$ is valid, as the following truth-table shows:

P	Q	P⇒Q	P⇒¬Q	⊨	¬P
t	t	t	f		f
t	f	f	t		f
f	t	t	t		t
f	f	t	t		t

d) The sequent $(P \wedge Q) \Longleftrightarrow P \models P \Rightarrow Q$ is valid, as the following truth-table shows:

P	Q	(P∧Q)	⟺	P	⊨	P⇒Q
t	t	t	t	t		t
t	f	f	f	t		f
f	t	f	t	f		t
f	f	f	t	f		t

e) The sequent $Q \Rightarrow R \models (P \vee Q) \Rightarrow (P \vee R)$ is valid, as the following truth-table shows:

P	Q	R	Q⇒R	⊨	(P∨Q)	⇒	(P∨R)
t	t	t	t		t	t	t
t	t	f	f		t	t	t
t	f	t	t		t	t	t
t	f	f	t		t	t	t
f	t	t	t		t	t	t
f	t	f	f		t	f	f
f	f	t	t		f	t	t
f	f	f	t		f	t	f

f) The sequent $P_1 \Rightarrow P_2, P_3 \Rightarrow P_4 \models (P_1 \vee P_3) \Rightarrow (P_2 \vee P_4)$ is valid, as the following truth-table shows:

P_1	P_2	P_3	P_4	$P_1 \Rightarrow P_2$	$P_3 \Rightarrow P_4$	⊨	$(P_1 \vee P_3)$	⇒	$(P_2 \vee P_4)$
t	t	t	t	t	t		t	t	t
t	t	t	f	t	f		t	t	t
t	t	f	t	t	t		t	t	t
t	t	f	f	t	t		t	t	t
t	f	t	t	f	t		t	t	t
t	f	t	f	f	f		t	f	f
t	f	f	t	f	t		t	t	t
t	f	f	f	f	t		t	f	f
f	t	t	t	t	t		t	t	t
f	t	t	f	t	f		t	t	t
f	t	f	t	t	t		f	t	t
f	t	f	f	t	t		f	t	t
f	f	t	t	t	t		t	t	t
f	f	t	f	t	f		t	f	f
f	f	f	t	t	t		f	t	t
f	f	f	f	t	t		f	t	f

2.3)
$$P \vee Q == \neg(\neg P \wedge \neg Q),$$

$$P \Rightarrow Q == \neg P \vee Q,$$
$$== \neg(P \wedge \neg Q),$$

$$P \Longleftrightarrow Q == (P \Rightarrow Q) \wedge (Q \Rightarrow P),$$
$$== (\neg(P \wedge \neg Q)) \wedge (\neg(Q \wedge \neg P)).$$

2.4) First, we define $\neg P$ and $P \wedge Q$ as follows:

$$\neg P == P \downarrow P,$$
$$P \wedge Q == (P \downarrow P) \downarrow (Q \downarrow Q).$$

Then, we use the definitions given in the previous answer.

2.5) a) $\forall i: \mathbf{N} \mid i \in \{4, 5, 7, 19\} \bullet 2 + 3 = i.$

  b) $\exists i: \mathbf{N} \mid i \in \{4, 5, 7, 19\} \bullet 2 + 3 = i.$

2.6) a) $\forall i: \mathbf{N} \mid i < 3 \bullet i \neq 7.$

  b) $\exists i: \mathbf{N} \mid i < 3 \bullet i \neq 7.$

  c) $\forall i: \mathbf{N} \mid even\ i \wedge i < 9 \bullet \neg(odd\ i).$

  d) $\exists x: Europe \mid ec\ x \bullet x\ borders\ belgium.$

  e) $\forall x: Europe \mid ec\ x \bullet \neg(pact\ x).$

where the following key is used:

ec _	_ is a member of the EC
pact _	_ is a member of the Warsaw Pact
_ borders _	_ borders _

Chapter 3

3.1) a) $\{1, 3, 5, 7, 9, 19, 21, 23, 25, 27\}.$

  b) $\{2, 4, 6, 8, 10, 11, 13, 15, 17, 20, 22, 24, 26, 28\}.$

  c) $\{11, 13, 15, 17, 29, 31, 33, 35\}.$

  d) $\{1, 2, 3, 4, 5, 6, 7, 8, 9, 10, 19, 20, 21, 22, 23, 24, 25, 26, 27, 28\}.$

  e) $\{2, 4, 6, 8, 10\}.$

  f) 18/37.

g) 27/37.

h) 36/37.

i) 5/37.

j) 20/37.

3.2) a)
$$U \cup V = \{0,1,2,3,4,5,7,11,13,17\},$$
$$U \cap V = \{2,3,5\},$$
$$U \setminus V = \{7,11,13,17\}.$$

b)
$$10 \mathinner{\ldotp\ldotp} 15 \cup 12 \mathinner{\ldotp\ldotp} 18 = 10 \mathinner{\ldotp\ldotp} 18 = \{10,11,12,13,14,15,16,17,18\},$$
$$10 \mathinner{\ldotp\ldotp} 15 \cap 12 \mathinner{\ldotp\ldotp} 18 = 12 \mathinner{\ldotp\ldotp} 15 = \{12,13,14,15\},$$
$$10 \mathinner{\ldotp\ldotp} 15 \setminus 12 \mathinner{\ldotp\ldotp} 18 = 10 \mathinner{\ldotp\ldotp} 11 = \{10,11\}.$$

c)
$$U \cap \{x\colon \mathbf{N} \mid x \bmod 3 = 1\} = \{1,4,7,10,13,16,19,22,25\},$$
$$U \cap \{x\colon \mathbf{N} \mid x \operatorname{div} 7 = 2\} = \{2,9,16,23\}.$$

d)
$$\{\{\ \}, \{england\}, \{france\}, \{spain\},$$
$$\{england, france\}, \{england, spain\}, \{france, spain\},$$
$$\{england, france, spain\}\}.$$

3.3) a) $\{n\colon \mathbf{N} \mid (1900 \le n \le 2100) \wedge ((n \bmod 4 = 0 \wedge n \bmod 100 \ne 0) \vee n \bmod 400 = 0)\}$.
As Rohl (1983), p. 7, writes, 'A year n is a leap year if it is divisible by 4, but not by 100, unless it is also divisible by 400'.

b) $\{x\colon Europe \mid ec\ x\}$ and $\{x\colon Europe \mid pact\ x\}$.

Chapter 5

5.1) a)

$$
\begin{array}{|l}
\hline
brother\colon Person \leftrightarrow Person \\
\hline
\forall x, y\colon Person \bullet \\
\quad x \mapsto y \in brother \iff \\
\qquad \exists z_1, z_2\colon Person \bullet \\
\qquad\quad x \mapsto z_1 \in father \wedge \\
\qquad\quad y \mapsto z_1 \in father \wedge \\
\qquad\quad x \mapsto z_2 \in mother \wedge \\
\qquad\quad y \mapsto z_2 \in mother \wedge \\
\qquad\quad \{x, y\} \subseteq male \\
\end{array}
$$

b)

$$\boxed{\begin{array}{l} firstcousin: Person \leftrightarrow Person \\ \hline \forall x, y: Person \bullet \\ \quad x \mapsto y \in firstcousin \Longleftrightarrow \\ \qquad \exists z: Person \bullet \\ \qquad\qquad x \mapsto z \in (father \cup mother) \,\raisebox{0.2ex}{\scriptsize$\circ$}\!\raisebox{-0.4ex}{\scriptsize$\circ$}\, (father \cup mother) \land \\ \qquad\qquad y \mapsto z \in (father \cup mother) \,\raisebox{0.2ex}{\scriptsize$\circ$}\!\raisebox{-0.4ex}{\scriptsize$\circ$}\, (father \cup mother) \end{array}}$$

c)

$$\boxed{\begin{array}{l} grandfather: Person \leftrightarrow Person \\ \hline \forall x, y: Person \bullet \\ \quad x \mapsto y \in grandfather \Longleftrightarrow \\ \qquad \exists z: Person \bullet \\ \qquad\qquad (x \mapsto z \in father \cup mother) \land \\ \qquad\qquad z \mapsto y \in father \end{array}}$$

$$\boxed{\begin{array}{l} grandfather: Person \leftrightarrow Person \\ \hline grandfather = (father \cup mother) \,\raisebox{0.2ex}{\scriptsize$\circ$}\!\raisebox{-0.4ex}{\scriptsize$\circ$}\, father \end{array}}$$

d) The expression $grandfather(\!|\{x\}|\!)$ denotes the set of all of x's grandfathers and $grandfather^{-1}(\!|\{x\}|\!)$ is the set of all of x's grandchildren.

e)

$$\boxed{\begin{array}{l} greatgrandmother: Person \leftrightarrow Person \\ \hline \forall x, y: Person \bullet \\ \quad x \mapsto y \in greatgrandmother \Longleftrightarrow \\ \qquad \exists z_1, z_2: Person \bullet \\ \qquad\qquad x \mapsto z_1 \in father \cup mother \land \\ \qquad\qquad z_1 \mapsto z_2 \in father \cup mother \land \\ \qquad\qquad z_2 \mapsto y \in mother \end{array}}$$

$$\boxed{\begin{array}{l} greatgrandmother: Person \leftrightarrow Person \\ \hline greatgrandmother = (father \cup mother) \,\raisebox{0.2ex}{\scriptsize$\circ$}\!\raisebox{-0.4ex}{\scriptsize$\circ$}\, (father \cup mother) \,\raisebox{0.2ex}{\scriptsize$\circ$}\!\raisebox{-0.4ex}{\scriptsize$\circ$}\, mother \end{array}}$$

f) $(father \cup mother)^{+}(\!|\{x\}|\!)$.

5.2) First, we work out what the schema *Alpha* is. This is defined as being equivalent to the schema $AddMember[members^+/members'][telephones^+/telephones']$.

Alpha

$members, members^+: \mathbb{P}\ Person$
$telephones, telephones^+: Person \leftrightarrow Phone$
$name?: Person$

$\mathrm{dom}\ telephones \subseteq members$
$\mathrm{dom}\ telephones^+ \subseteq members^+$
$name? \notin members$
$members^+ = members \cup \{name?\}$
$telephones^+ = telephones$

Then, we form the schema *Beta*, which is defined to be the conjunction of the schema $AddMember[members^+/members'][telephones^+/telephones']$ and the schema $AddEntry[members^+/members'][telephones^+/telephones']$.

Beta

$members, members^+, members': \mathbb{P}\ Person$
$telephones, telephones^+, telephones': Person \leftrightarrow Phone$
$newnumber?: Phone$
$name?: Person$

$\mathrm{dom}\ telephones \subseteq members$
$\mathrm{dom}\ telephones^+ \subseteq members^+$
$\mathrm{dom}\ telephones' \subseteq members'$
$name? \notin members$
$members^+ = members \cup \{name?\}$
$telephones^+ = telephones$
$name? \in members^+$
$name? \mapsto newnumber? \notin telephones^+$
$telephones' = telephones^+ \cup \{name? \mapsto newnumber?\}$
$members' = members^+$

The schema $Gamma \mathrel{\hat=} AddMember \,\mathbin{\raise.2ex\hbox{$;$}}\, AddEntry$ is obtained by existentially quantifying over the variables $members^+$ and $telephones^+$ in the schema *Beta*.

```
┌─ Gamma ──────────────────────────────────────────────────────
│ ΔPhoneDB
│ newnumber?: Phone
│ name?: Person
├──────────────────────────────────────────────────────────────
│ name? ∉ members
│ ∃members⁺: P Person; telephones⁺: Person ↔ Phone •
│     dom telephones⁺ ⊆ members⁺ ∧
│     members⁺ = members ∪ {name?} ∧
│     telephones⁺ = telephones ∧
│     name? ∈ members⁺ ∧
│     name? ↦ newnumber? ∉ telephones⁺ ∧
│     telephones' = telephones⁺ ∪ {name? ↦ newnumber?} ∧
│     members' = members⁺
└──────────────────────────────────────────────────────────────
```

Gamma simplifies to the following schema:

```
┌─ Gamma ──────────────────────────────────────────────────────
│ ΔPhoneDB
│ name?: Person
│ newnumber?: Phone
├──────────────────────────────────────────────────────────────
│ name? ∉ members
│ name? ↦ newnumber? ∉ telephones
│ members' = members ∪ {name?}
│ telephones' = telephones ∪ {name? ↦ newnumber?}
└──────────────────────────────────────────────────────────────
```

5.3) The given types for this specification are:

$$[Person, Film]$$

where *Person* is the set of all people and *Film* is the set of all films, both those that have already been made and also all those that will ever be made in the future.

The state of the filmic database is given by the schema *Films*:

```
┌─ Films ──────────────────────────────────────────────────────
│ directedby, writtenby: Person ↔ Film
├──────────────────────────────────────────────────────────────
│ ran directedby = ran writtenby
└──────────────────────────────────────────────────────────────
```

The schemas Δ*Films*, Ξ*Films* and *InitFilms'* are defined in the usual way:

$$\Delta Films \; \hat{=} \; Films \land Films',$$

$$\Xi Films \; \hat{=} \; \Delta Films \mid directedby' = directedby \land writtenby = writtenby',$$

$$InitFilms' \; \hat{=} \; Films' \mid directedby' = \{\,\} \land writtenby = \{\,\}.$$

273

The schema *AddFilm* adds information to the database concerning a film with only one director and only one writer. The film is represented by the identifier $f?$ and the director and writer are represented, respectively, by the identifiers $d?$ and $w?$.

```
┌─ AddFilm ─────────────────────────────────────────
│ Δ Films
│ d?, w?: Person
│ f?: Film
├───────────────────────────────────────────────────
│ f? ∉ ran directedby
│ directedby' = directedby ∪ {d? ↦ f?}
│ writtenby' = writtenby ∪ {w? ↦ f?}
└───────────────────────────────────────────────────
```

The schema *AddFilm* specifies the successful carrying out of the operation of adding information to the database. The schema *Success* just makes this explicit.

```
┌─ Success ─────────────────────────────────────────
│ rep!: Report
├───────────────────────────────────────────────────
│ rep! = 'Okay'
└───────────────────────────────────────────────────
```

The operation *AddFilm* can only go wrong in one way, namely if the film $f?$ is already in the database. This possibility is captured by means of the schema *AlreadyPresent*. Recall that the film we are adding has only one director and only one writer.

```
┌─ AlreadyPresent ──────────────────────────────────
│ Ξ Films
│ f?: Film
│ rep!: Report
├───────────────────────────────────────────────────
│ f? ∈ ran directedby
│ rep! = 'Already in database'
└───────────────────────────────────────────────────
```

The total operation of adding a film to the database is captured by means of the schema *DoAddFilm*.

$$DoAddFilm \,\hat{=}\, AddFilm \land Success$$
$$\lor$$
$$AlreadyPresent$$

The schema *FindFilmsD* interrogates the database using a person $d?$ as input. The output *oeuvre!* is the set of all the films he has had a hand in directing. It is totalized in the standard way.

```
┌─ FindFilmsD ──────────────────────────────────────────────
│ Ξ Films
│ d?: Person
│ oeuvre!: F Film
│ ──────────────────────────────────────────────────────────
│ d? ∈ dom directedby
│ oeuvre! = directedby(|{d?}|)
└────────────────────────────────────────────────────────────
```

```
┌─ UnknownDirector ─────────────────────────────────────────
│ Ξ Films
│ d?: Person
│ rep!: Report
│ ──────────────────────────────────────────────────────────
│ d? ∉ dom directedby
│ rep! = 'Unknown director'
└────────────────────────────────────────────────────────────
```

$$DoFindFilmsD \ \hat{=}\ FindFilmsD \wedge Success$$
$$\vee$$
$$UnknownDirector$$

The schema *FindFilmsW* interrogates the database using a person *w?* as input. The output *oeuvre!* is the set of all the films he has had a hand in writing. It is totalized in the standard way.

```
┌─ FindFilmsW ──────────────────────────────────────────────
│ Ξ Films
│ w?: Person
│ oeuvre!: F Film
│ ──────────────────────────────────────────────────────────
│ w? ∈ dom writtenby
│ oeuvre! = writtenby(|{w?}|)
└────────────────────────────────────────────────────────────
```

```
┌─ UnknownWriter ───────────────────────────────────────────
│ Ξ Films
│ w?: Person
│ rep!: Report
│ ──────────────────────────────────────────────────────────
│ d? ∉ dom writtenby
│ rep! = 'Unknown writer'
└────────────────────────────────────────────────────────────
```

$$DoFindFilmsW \ \hat{=}\ FindFilmsW \wedge Success$$
$$\vee$$
$$UnknownWriter$$

Chapter 7

7.1) a) $\langle B, L, A, C, K, J, A, C, K \rangle$.

b) B.

c) C.

d) $\langle L, A, C \rangle$.

e) $\langle A, C, K, B, L \rangle$.

f) $\langle L, B, K, C, A \rangle$.

g) $\{1, 2, 3, 4, 5\}$.

h) $\{B, L, A, C, K\}$.

i) $\{A \mapsto 1, C \mapsto 2, K \mapsto 3, B \mapsto 4, L \mapsto 5\}$.

j) $\{C \mapsto A, K \mapsto C, B \mapsto K, L \mapsto B\}$.

k) $\langle A, C, K, E, R \rangle$.

l) $\{2 \mapsto C, 3 \mapsto K, 4 \mapsto B, 5 \mapsto L\}$.

m) $\{B, L, O, C, K\}$.

n) $\{C, A, B, L, E\}$.

Chapter 10

10.1) a) First, I prove $P \wedge (Q \wedge R) \vdash (P \wedge Q) \wedge R$:

1	(1)	$P \wedge (Q \wedge R)$	ass
1	(2)	P	1 $\wedge$-$elim_1$
1	(3)	$Q \wedge R$	1 $\wedge$-$elim_2$
1	(4)	Q	3 $\wedge$-$elim_1$
1	(5)	R	3 $\wedge$-$elim_2$
1	(6)	$P \wedge Q$	2,4 $\wedge$-int
1	(7)	$(P \wedge Q) \wedge R$	6,5 $\wedge$-int

Next, I prove $(P \wedge Q) \wedge R \vdash P \wedge (Q \wedge R)$:

1	(1)	$(P \wedge Q) \wedge R$	ass
1	(2)	$P \wedge Q$	1 $\wedge$-$elim_1$
1	(3)	P	2 $\wedge$-$elim_1$
1	(4)	Q	2 $\wedge$-$elim_2$
1	(5)	R	1 $\wedge$-$elim_2$
1	(6)	$Q \wedge R$	4,5 $\wedge$-int
1	(7)	$P \wedge (Q \wedge R)$	3,6 $\wedge$-int

b) First, I prove $P \vee (Q \vee R) \vdash (P \vee Q) \vee R$:

1	(1)	$P \vee (Q \vee R)$	ass
2	(2)	$Q \vee R$	ass
3	(3)	Q	ass
3	(4)	$P \vee Q$	3 $\vee$-int_i
3	(5)	$(P \vee Q) \vee R$	4 $\vee$-int_i
6	(6)	R	ass
6	(7)	$(P \vee Q) \vee R$	6 $\vee$-int_i
2	(8)	$(P \vee Q) \vee R$	2,5,7 $\vee$-$elim$
9	(9)	P	ass
9	(10)	$P \vee Q$	9 $\vee$-int_i
9	(11)	$(P \vee Q) \vee R$	10 $\vee$-int_i
1	(12)	$(P \vee Q) \vee R$	1,8,11 $\vee$-$elim$

Next, I prove $(P \vee Q) \vee R \vdash P \vee (Q \vee R)$:

1	(1)	$(P \vee Q) \vee R$	ass
2	(2)	$P \vee Q$	ass
3	(3)	P	ass
3	(4)	$P \vee (Q \vee R)$	3 $\vee$-int_i
5	(5)	Q	ass
5	(6)	$Q \vee R$	5 $\vee$-int_i
5	(7)	$P \vee (Q \vee R)$	6 $\vee$-int_i
2	(8)	$P \vee (Q \vee R)$	2,4,7 $\vee$-$elim$
9	(9)	R	ass
9	(10)	$Q \vee R$	9 $\vee$-int_i
9	(11)	$P \vee (Q \vee R)$	10 $\vee$-int_i
1	(12)	$P \vee (Q \vee R)$	1,8,11 $\vee$-$elim$

c) First, I prove $P \wedge Q \vdash (P \vee \neg Q) \wedge Q$:

1	(1)	$P \wedge Q$	ass
1	(2)	P	1 $\wedge$-$elim_1$
1	(3)	$P \vee \neg Q$	2 $\vee$-int_i
1	(4)	Q	1 $\wedge$-$elim_2$
1	(5)	$(P \vee \neg Q) \wedge Q$	3,4 $\wedge$-int

Next, I prove $(P \vee \neg Q) \wedge Q \vdash P \wedge Q$:

1	(1)	$(P \vee \neg Q) \wedge Q$	ass
1	(2)	$(P \vee \neg Q)$	1 $\wedge$-$elim_1$
3	(3)	P	ass
1	(4)	Q	1 $\wedge$-$elim_2$
1,3	(5)	$P \wedge Q$	3,4 $\wedge$-int
6	(6)	$\neg Q$	ass
1,6	(7)	$false$	4,6 $\neg$-$elim$
1,6	(8)	$P \wedge Q$	7 $false$-$elim$
1	(9)	$P \wedge Q$	2,5,8 $\vee$-$elim$

277

d) First, I prove $P \Rightarrow Q \vdash \neg P \vee Q$:

1	(1)	$P \Rightarrow Q$	ass
2	(2)	$\neg(\neg P \vee Q)$	ass
2	(3)	$\neg\neg P \wedge \neg Q$	2 de Morgan
2	(4)	$\neg\neg P$	3 $\wedge$-elim$_1$
2	(5)	P	4 $\neg\neg$-elim
1,2	(6)	Q	1,5 $\Rightarrow$-elim
2	(7)	$\neg Q$	3 $\wedge$-elim$_2$
1,2	(8)	false	6,7 $\neg$-elim
1	(9)	$\neg\neg(\neg P \vee Q)$	8 $\neg$-int
1	(10)	$\neg P \vee Q$	9 $\neg\neg$-elim

Next, I prove $\neg P \vee Q \vdash P \Rightarrow Q$:

1	(1)	$\neg P \vee Q$	ass
2	(2)	$\neg P$	ass
3	(3)	P	ass
2,3	(4)	false	2,3 $\neg$-elim
2,3	(5)	Q	4 false-elim
2	(6)	$P \Rightarrow Q$	5 $\Rightarrow$-int
7	(7)	Q	ass
7	(8)	$P \Rightarrow Q$	7 $\Rightarrow$-int
1	(9)	$P \Rightarrow Q$	1,2,7 $\vee$-elim

e) $Q \Rightarrow R \vdash (P \vee Q) \Rightarrow (P \vee R)$ is proved as follows:

1	(1)	$Q \Rightarrow R$	ass
2	(2)	$P \vee Q$	ass
3	(3)	P	ass
3	(4)	$P \vee R$	3 $\vee$-int$_i$
5	(5)	Q	ass
1,5	(6)	R	1,5 $\Rightarrow$-elim
1,5	(7)	$P \vee R$	6 $\vee$-int$_i$
1,2	(8)	$P \vee R$	2,4,7 $\vee$-elim
1	(9)	$(P \vee Q) \Rightarrow (P \vee R)$	8 $\Rightarrow$-int

f) $P_1 \Rightarrow P_2, P_3 \Rightarrow P_4 \vdash (P_1 \vee P_3) \Rightarrow (P_2 \vee P_4)$ is proved as follows:

1	(1)	$P_1 \Rightarrow P_2$	ass
2	(2)	$P_3 \Rightarrow P_4$	ass
3	(3)	$P_1 \vee P_3$	ass
4	(4)	P_1	ass
1,4	(5)	P_2	$1,4 \Rightarrow$-elim
1,4	(6)	$P_2 \vee P_4$	5 $\vee$-int;
7	(7)	P_3	ass
2,7	(8)	P_4	$2,7 \Rightarrow$-elim
2,7	(9)	$P_2 \vee P_4$	8 $\vee$-int;
1,3,2	(10)	$P_2 \vee P_4$	3,6,9 $\vee$-elim
1,2	(11)	$P_1 \vee P_3 \Rightarrow P_2 \vee P_4$	10 $\Rightarrow$-int

10.2)   a) First, I prove $\forall x\!: X \bullet (Px \wedge Qx) \vdash (\forall x\!: X \bullet Px) \wedge (\forall x\!: X \bullet Qx)$.

1	(1)	$\forall x\!: X \bullet (Px \wedge Qx)$	ass
1	(2)	$Pa \wedge Qa$	1 $\forall$-elim
1	(3)	Pa	2 $\wedge$-elim$_1$
1	(4)	$\forall x\!: X \bullet Px$	3 $\forall$-int
1	(5)	Qa	2 $\wedge$-elim$_2$
1	(6)	$\forall x\!: X \bullet Qx$	5 $\forall$-int
1	(7)	$(\forall x\!: X \bullet Px) \wedge (\forall x\!: X \bullet Qx)$	4,6 $\wedge$-int

Next, I prove $(\forall x\!: X \bullet Px) \wedge (\forall x\!: X \bullet Qx) \vdash \forall x\!: X \bullet (Px \wedge Qx)$.

1	(1)	$(\forall x\!: X \bullet Px) \wedge (\forall x\!: X \bullet Qx)$	ass
1	(2)	$\forall x\!: X \bullet Px$	1 $\wedge$-elim$_1$
1	(3)	Pa	2 $\forall$-elim
1	(4)	$\forall x\!: X \bullet Qx$	1 $\wedge$-elim$_2$
1	(5)	Qa	4 $\forall$-elim
1	(6)	$Pa \wedge Qa$	3,5 $\wedge$-int
1	(7)	$\forall x\!: X \bullet (Px \wedge Qx)$	6 $\forall$-int

b) First, I prove $\exists x\!: X \bullet (Px \vee Qx) \vdash (\exists x\!: X \bullet Px) \vee (\exists x\!: X \bullet Qx)$.

1	(1)	$\exists x\!: X \bullet (Px \vee Qx)$	ass
2	(2)	$Pa \vee Qa$	ass
3	(3)	Pa	ass
3	(4)	$\exists x\!: X \bullet Px$	3 $\exists$-int
3	(5)	$(\exists x\!: X \bullet Px) \vee (\exists x\!: X \bullet Qx)$	4 $\vee$-int;
6	(6)	Qa	ass
6	(7)	$\exists x\!: X \bullet Qx$	6 $\exists$-int
6	(8)	$(\exists x\!: X \bullet Px) \vee (\exists x\!: X \bullet Qx)$	7 $\vee$-int;
2	(9)	$(\exists x\!: X \bullet Px) \vee (\exists x\!: X \bullet Qx)$	2,5,8 $\vee$-elim
1	(10)	$(\exists x\!: X \bullet Px) \vee (\exists x\!: X \bullet Qx)$	1,9 $\exists$-elim

Next, I prove $(\exists x\colon X \bullet Px) \vee (\exists x\colon X \bullet Qx) \vdash \exists x\colon X \bullet (Px \vee Qx)$.

1	(1)	$(\exists x\colon X \bullet Px) \vee (\exists x\colon X \bullet Qx)$	ass
2	(2)	$\exists x\colon X \bullet Px$	ass
3	(3)	Pa	ass
3	(4)	$Pa \vee Qa$	3 $\vee$-int$_i$
3	(5)	$\exists x\colon X \bullet (Px \vee Qx)$	4 $\exists$-int
2	(6)	$\exists x\colon X \bullet (Px \vee Qx)$	2,5 $\exists$-elim
7	(7)	$\exists x\colon X \bullet Qx$	ass
8	(8)	Qa	ass
8	(9)	$Pa \vee Qa$	8 $\vee$-int$_i$
8	(10)	$\exists x\colon X \bullet (Px \vee Qx)$	9 $\exists$-int
7	(11)	$\exists x\colon X \bullet (Px \vee Qx)$	7,10 $\exists$-elim
1	(12)	$\exists x\colon X \bullet (Px \vee Qx)$	1,6,11 $\vee$-elim

c) $\forall x\colon X \bullet Px \vdash \neg \exists x\colon X \bullet \neg Px$ is proved as follows:

1	(1)	$\forall x\colon X \bullet Px$	ass
2	(2)	$\exists x\colon X \bullet \neg Px$	ass
3	(3)	$\neg Pa$	ass
1	(4)	Pa	1 $\forall$-elim
1,3	(5)	$false$	3,4 $\neg$-elim
3	(6)	$\neg \forall x\colon X \bullet Px$	5 $\neg$-int
2	(7)	$\neg \forall x\colon X \bullet Px$	2,6 $\exists$-elim
1,2	(8)	$false$	1,7 $\neg$-elim
1	(9)	$\neg \exists x\colon X \bullet \neg Px$	8 $\neg$-int

$\neg \exists x\colon X \bullet \neg Px \vdash \forall x\colon X \bullet Px$ is proved as follows:

1	(1)	$\neg \exists x\colon X \bullet \neg Px$	ass
2	(2)	$\neg Pa$	ass
2	(3)	$\exists x\colon X \bullet \neg Px$	2 $\exists$-int
1,2	(4)	$false$	1,3 $\neg$-elim
1	(5)	$\neg\neg Pa$	4 $\neg$-int
1	(6)	Pa	5 $\neg\neg$-elim
1	(7)	$\forall x\colon X \bullet Px$	6 $\forall$-int

d) $\forall x\colon X \bullet (Px \Rightarrow Qx), \forall x\colon X \bullet Px \vdash \forall x\colon X \bullet Qx$ is proved as follows:

1	(1)	$\forall x\colon X \bullet (Px \Rightarrow Qx)$	ass
2	(2)	$\forall x\colon X \bullet Px$	ass
1	(3)	$Pa \Rightarrow Qa$	1 $\forall$-elim
2	(4)	Pa	2 $\forall$-elim
1,2	(5)	Qa	3,4 $\Rightarrow$-elim
1,2	(6)	$\forall x\colon X \bullet Qx$	5 $\forall$-int

e) $\exists x \colon X \bullet (Px \wedge Qx) \vdash (\exists x \colon X \bullet Px) \wedge (\exists x \colon X \bullet Qx)$ is proved as follows:

1	(1)	$\exists x \colon X \bullet (Px \wedge Qx)$	ass
2	(2)	$Pa \wedge Qa$	ass
2	(3)	Pa	2 $\wedge$-$elim_1$
2	(4)	$\exists x \colon X \bullet Px$	3 $\exists$-int
2	(5)	Qa	2 $\wedge$-$elim_2$
2	(6)	$\exists x \colon X \bullet Qx$	5 $\exists$-int
2	(7)	$(\exists x \colon X \bullet Px) \wedge (\exists x \colon X \bullet Qx)$	4, 6 $\wedge$-int
1	(8)	$(\exists x \colon X \bullet Px) \wedge (\exists x \colon X \bullet Qx)$	1, 7 $\exists$-elim

Chapter 11

11.1) a) Apart from the fundamental property of set difference, the following proof also uses a number of properties of the propositional calculus, namely one of de Morgan's laws, double negation, the fact that $\wedge$ distributes forwards through $\vee$ and the laws $P \wedge \neg P \dashv\vdash false$ and $false \vee P \dashv\vdash P$.

$$x \in X \setminus (X \setminus U) \Longleftrightarrow x \in X \wedge x \notin X \setminus U,$$
$$\Longleftrightarrow x \in X \wedge \neg(x \in X \wedge x \notin U),$$
$$\Longleftrightarrow x \in X \wedge (x \notin X \vee x \in U),$$
$$\Longleftrightarrow (x \in X \wedge x \notin X) \vee (x \in X \wedge x \in U),$$
$$\Longleftrightarrow x \in U.$$

b) Apart from the definitions of set difference, intersection and union, the following proof also uses a number of properties of the propositional calculus, namely one of de Morgan's laws and the fact that $\wedge$ distributes forwards through $\vee$.

$$x \in X \setminus (U \cap V) \Longleftrightarrow x \in X \wedge x \notin U \cap V,$$
$$\Longleftrightarrow x \in X \wedge \neg(x \in U \wedge x \in V),$$
$$\Longleftrightarrow x \in X \wedge (x \notin U \vee x \notin V),$$
$$\Longleftrightarrow (x \in X \wedge x \notin U) \vee (x \in X \wedge x \notin V),$$
$$\Longleftrightarrow x \in X \setminus U \vee x \in X \setminus V,$$
$$\Longleftrightarrow x \in (X \setminus U) \cup (X \setminus V).$$

11.2) a) We want to prove that:

$$\sum_{i=0}^{i=n} i = \frac{n(n+1)}{2}, \tag{B.1}$$

holds for all non-negative natural numbers n.

Base Case When $n = 0$, then:

$$LHS \text{ of (B.1)} = \sum_{i=0}^{i=0} i = 0.$$

Similarly, when $n = 0$, then:

$$RHS \text{ of (B.1)} = \frac{0(0+1)}{2} = 0.$$

As both the *LHS* and *RHS* of (B.1) are equal to 0, the base case is established.

Inductive Step We have to prove that:

$$\sum_{i=0}^{i=n+1} i = \frac{(n+1)(n+2)}{2}, \tag{B.2}$$

on the assumption that:

$$\sum_{i=0}^{i=n} i = \frac{n(n+1)}{2}, \tag{B.3}$$

is true. This is proved as follows:

$$LHS \text{ of (B.2)} = \sum_{i=0}^{i=n} i + (n+1),$$

$$= \frac{n(n+1)}{2} + (n+1),$$

by the inductive hypothesis (B.3),

$$= \frac{n(n+1) + 2(n+1)}{2},$$

$$= \frac{(n+1)(n+2)}{2},$$

$$= RHS \text{ of (B.2)}.$$

Thus, the inductive step has been established. As both the base case and the inductive step have been established, the proof of (B.1) for all natural numbers follows by mathematical induction.

b) We want to prove that:

$$\sum_{i=0}^{i=n} i^3 = \left(\frac{n(n+1)}{2} \right)^2, \tag{B.4}$$

holds for all non-negative natural numbers n.

Base Case When $n = 0$, then:

$$LHS \text{ of (B.4)} = \sum_{i=0}^{i=0} i^3 = 0.$$

Similarly, when $n = 0$, then:

$$RHS \text{ of (B.4)} = \left(\frac{0(0+1)}{2}\right)^2 = 0.$$

As both the LHS and RHS of (B.4) are equal to 0, the base case is established.

Inductive Step We have to prove that:

$$\sum_{i=0}^{i=n+1} i^3 = \left(\frac{(n+1)(n+2)}{2}\right)^2, \tag{B.5}$$

on the assumption that:

$$\sum_{i=0}^{i=n} i^3 = \left(\frac{n(n+1)}{2}\right)^2, \tag{B.6}$$

is true. This is proved like this:

$$LHS \text{ of (B.5)} = \sum_{i=0}^{i=n} i^3 + (n+1)^3,$$

$$= \left(\frac{n(n+1)}{2}\right)^2 + (n+1)^3,$$

by the inductive hypothesis (B.6),

$$= \left(\frac{n+1}{2}\right)^2 (n^2 + 4n + 4),$$

$$= \left(\frac{(n+1)(n+2)}{2}\right)^2,$$

$$= RHS \text{ of (B.5)}.$$

Thus, the inductive step has been established. As both the base case and the inductive step have been established, the proof of (B.4) for all natural numbers follows by mathematical induction.

Annotated Bibliography

Annotations

Part I: The Philosophy of Formal Methods

Chapter 1: What is Z?

Abrial is always mentioned as one of the founding fathers of **Z**, but his own work is very idiosyncratic. See, for example, the papers Abrial (1983, 1984, 1985). More recently he has been working on a tool called B, which is a very interesting proof-assistant—amongst other things! This is described in Abrial (1986) and Vickers and Gardiner (1988). The fundamental abstraction methods used in **Z**, namely operational and representational abstraction, are frequently mentioned. A good account of them is found, for example, in the introduction to Sufrin (1981). Ince has written the best "propaganda" for **Z**. The first two chapters of Ince (1988a) and the article (1989) are typical examples. Clarke (1988), Cohen (1989a, 1989b), Davies (1988) and Gibbins (1988) are also useful.

Part II: Tutorial Introduction

Chapter 2: First-order Logic

For a discussion of books about logic see the comments for chapter 10 on "Formal Proof".

Chapter 3: Set Theory

There are lots of books about set theory. For example, Enderton (1977), Halmos (1960), Hamilton (1978) and Suppes (1957). Unfortunately, the vast majority of books on set theory deal with *Zermelo–Fraenkel* set theory, whereas **Z** is based on *the theory of types*. Theses two approaches to set theory are radically different. Quine (1969) discusses both and compares them, and Hatcher (1982) contains a detailed look at the theory of types. Both of these accounts are based on the presentation found in Gödel (1931). Copi (1971) is a very readable account of the theory of types. The theory of types has its origin in Whitehead and Russell (1910, 1912, 1913).

Chapter 4: Relations and Schemas

Some of the notations used in **Z** for operations associated with relations are standard mathematical symbols, but many are not. The best accounts of the **Z** notation are to be found in Spivey (1989b) and Woodcock and Loomes (1989b).

Chapter 5: More about Relations and Schemas

The schema notation is one of **Z**'s characteristic features. Originally, it was just an abbreviatory device to succinctly capture the common pattern $D \mid P$, where D is a declaration and P a predicate, found in restricted universal and existential quantifications, set comprehensions, λ-terms and μ-terms, but now it has taken on a life and a meaning all of its own.[1] The first published use of schemas was in Sufrin (1982b).

Chapter 6: Functions

Hayes (1987c) contains a good introduction to how functions can be used in specifications, using a symbol table for illustrative purposes. An account of λ-expressions and currying can be found in Ince (1988a), pp. 194–196.

Chapter 7: Sequences

Although a sequence in **Z** is defined to be a function from an initial segment of the non-negative numbers to some arbitrary set, the way sequences are used is very similar to how lists are used in functional programming languages and much about sequences can be learnt from books and articles about functional programming. Bird (1986, 1987, 1988) and Bird and Wadler (1988) are particularly useful.

Chapter 8: Bags

Although bags and bag manipulating functions are included in the standard **Z** notation defined in Spivey (1989b) and King, Sørensen and Woodcock (1988), they are not used very frequently. Woodcock (1989b), pp. 109–123, however, contains a nice specification about bags of money.

Chapter 9: Free Types

Spivey (1989b), pp. 81–85, is a good account of free types in **Z** and shows how they do not strengthen the language in any way, since any use of a free type can be replaced with suitably defined constants and functions.

---

[1] For the meaning of schemas see section 3.6, p. 72, of Spivey (1988).

Part III: Methods of Reasoning

Chapter 10: Formal Proof

There are hundreds of books about logic. By far the most popular proof-architecture for logic *users*, that is to say, for people who actually construct formal proofs, is the linear notation I introduced on pp. 111ff. of chapter 10. This is presented in many textbooks, for example, Suppes (1957), Lemmon (1965), Mates (1972) and Newton-Smith (1985). A much less popular proof-architecture is that of Fitch. This is presented in a small number of books, namely Fitch (1952), Thomason (1970) and Simpson (1988).[2] Apparently, it is being re-invented by Woodcock, since a similar proof-architecture appears in Woodcock and Loomes (1988) and Woodcock (1989b). This is unfortunate as the Lemmon type of presentation has many advantages. I argue for this in Diller (1990b). Other interesting books about logic are Hamilton (1978), Hunter (1971), Prior (1962), Quine (1962) and Tennant (1978).

All the books on logic mentioned above deal thoroughly with both the propositional and the predicate calculuses. Unfortunately, none of them presents a *typed* predicate calculus, which is what is used in **Z**. In order to cope with types you need what is known as a *many-sorted logic*.[3] Such logics are studied in Gallier (1985) and Monk (1976).

Chapter 11: Rigorous Proof

Several books have been published recently which introduce the idea of a rigorous, but not fully formal, mathematical proof. See, for example, Morash (1987), Franklin and Daoud (1988) and Cupillari (1989). It is also a good idea to read Lakatos (1976) to get an idea of the real role of proofs in mathematics. If you think Lakatos is too reactionary, then read Feyerabend (1982,1987,1988).

Chapter 12: Immanent Reasoning

The best accounts of reasoning about **Z** specifications are to be found in Woodcock and Loomes (1988) and Woodcock (1989b).

Chapter 13: Reification and Decomposition

The best presentations of reification and decomposition are to be found in Jones (1980, 1986a); unfortunately these are expressed using VDM. Neilson (1988), Morgan, Robinson and Gardiner (1988) and Wordsworth (1988) deal with refinement in **Z**, though their methods have not yet become universally accepted.

---

[2]These comments on the relative popularity of these two proof-architectures is based on my reading of the *Computerised Logic Teaching Bulletin* and from attending workshops on the teaching of logic.

[3]This was pointed out many years ago by Wang (1952).

Part IV: Case Studies

Jones (1980) extensively discusses the bill of materials problem and my colleague Tom Axford suggested the route planning problem to me as one which might prove to be a good example of the use of **Z**.

King and Sørensen (1988) present another **Z** specification of Wing's library problem. The specification contained in chapter 15 of the present book was produced independently and the reader is encouraged to compare them. The problem is given in Wing (1988) and is a slightly modified version of one to be found in Kemmerer (1985). A VDM specification of this problem is contained in Bjørner (1988b).

Sufrin's specification of the VED and QED editors—to be found in Sufrin (1981, 1982a)—rightly holds a place in the folklore of **Z**. The specification contained here owes a great deal to Sufrin and also to Neilson (1988) and the reader is strongly urged to read all those papers.

Quite a large number of case studies of the use of **Z** have been published. Some of the more recent ones are included here, namely Alexander (1988), Barrett (1987), Bowen (1987, 1988, 1989), Bowen, Gimson and Topp-Jørgensen (1987, 1988), Burns and Morrison (1989), Chi (1985), Clement (1983), Earl, Whittington, Hitchcock and Hall (1986), Fenton and Mole (1988), Froome and Monahan (1988), Gimson (1987), Gimson and Morgan (1985), Hayes (1985a, 1985b, 1985c, 1987d), Nicholl (1988), Sufrin and Woodcock (1987), Teruel (1982), Todd (1987) and Took (1986a, 1986b).

Part V: Specification Animation

The functional programming language Miranda is described in Turner (1985a, 1985b, 1986) and in Bird and Wadler (1988). There are numerous books on Prolog. I have found Coelho, Cotta and Pereira (1985) and Covington, Nute and Vellino (1988) to be helpful, since I am not a hard-core Prolog person. Stepney and Lord (1987) present a **Z** specification of an access control system and then briefly describe how it can be animated using Prolog. Knott and Krause (1988a, 1988b) present a far from satisfactory approach to the problem of animating **Z** using Prolog.

Part VI: Reference Manual

Several very thorough reference manuals have been produced for the **Z** notation. I think that Sufrin (1986b) is an excellent document, superior in many ways to Spivey (1989b), which is now the *de facto* standard for writing **Z** specifications. I have not deliberately used a notation in this book that is inconsistent with Spivey's recommendations. King, Sørensen and Woodcock (1988) presents a grammar of **Z**. Morgan and Sanders (1989) present a collection of classical predicate calculus laws that they have found useful in specification work.

References

Abelson, H., and G.J. Sussman, (1985), *Structure and Interpretation of Computer Programs*, Cambridge (MA), MIT Press.

Abrial, J.-R., (1983), "Specification and Construction of Machines", in Elphick (1983), pp. 5–40.

Abrial, J.-R., (1984), "The Mathematical Construction of a Program", *Science of Computer Programming*, vol. 4, pp. 45–86.

Abrial, J.-R., (1985), "Programming as a Mathematical Exercise", in Hoare and Shepherdson (1985), pp. 113–139.

Abrial, J.-R., (1986), *B User Manual*, BP Project Report, Programming Research Group, University of Oxford.

Alexander, H., (1988), "Comments on 'Formal Specification of User Interfaces: A Comparison and Evaluation of Four Axiomatic Approaches' by U.H. Chi", *IEEE Trans. Softw. Eng.*, vol. SE-14, pp. 438–439.

Baber, R.L., (1987), *The Spine of Software: Designing Provably Correct Software: Theory and Practice, or a Mathematical Introduction to the Semantics of Computer Programs*, Chichester, Wiley.

Backhouse, R.C., (1986), *Program Construction and Verification*, Hemel Hempstead, Prentice Hall.

Barrett, G., (1987), *Formal Methods Applied to a Floating Point Number System*, Technical Monograph PRG–58, Oxford University Computing Laboratory. Also published in *IEEE Trans. Softw. Eng.*, vol. SE-15 (1989), pp. 611–621.

Bird, R.S., (1986), *An Introduction to the Theory of Lists*, Technical Monograph PRG–56, Oxford University Computing Laboratory.

Bird, R.S., (1987), *A Calculus of Functions for Program Derivation*, Technical Monograph PRG–64, Oxford University Computing Laboratory.

Bird, R.S., (1988), *Lectures on Constructive Functional Programming*, Technical Monograph PRG–69, Oxford University Computing Laboratory.

Bird, R., and P. Wadler, (1988), *Introduction to Functional Programming*, Hemel Hempstead, Prentice Hall.

Bjørner, D., (1988a), *Software Architectures and Programming Systems Design*, vol. I, *Foundations*, preprint, Department of Computer Science, Technical University of Denmark.

Bjørner, D., (1988b), *Software Architectures and Programming Systems Design*, vol. II, *Basic Abstraction Principles*, preprint, Department of Computer Science, Technical University of Denmark.

Bjørner, D., C.B. Jones, M. Mac an Airchinnigh and E.J. Neuhold, (eds.), (1987), *VDM '87: VDM—A Formal Method at Work, Lecture Notes in Computer Science*, vol. 252, London, Springer-Verlag.

Bowen, J., (1987), *The Formal Specification of a Microprocessor Instruction Set*, Technical Monograph PRG–60, Oxford University Computing Laboratory.

Bowen, J., (1988), "Formal Specification in **Z** as a Design and Documentation Tool", *Second IEE/BCS Conference: Software Engineering 88*, London, IEE, pp. 164–168.

Bowen, J., (1989), "POS—Formal Specification of a UNIX Tool", *Software Engineering Journal*, vol. 4, pp. 67–72.

Bowen, J., R. Gimson and S. Topp-Jørgensen, (1987), *The Specification of Network Services*, Technical Monograph PRG–61, Oxford University Computing Laboratory.

Bowen, J., R. Gimson and S. Topp-Jørgensen, (1988), *Specifying System Implementations in **Z***, Technical Monograph PRG–63, Oxford University Computing Laboratory.

Boyer, R.S., and J.S. Moore, (eds.), (1981), *The Correctness Problem in Computer Science*, London, Academic Press.

Burns, A., and I.W. Morrison, (1989), "A Formal Description of the Structure Attribute Model for Tool Interfacing", *Software Engineering Journal*, vol. 4, pp. 74–78.

Cheng, J.H., (1986), *A Logic for Partial Functions*, Technical Report UMCS–86–7–1, Department of Computer Science, University of Manchester.

Chi, U.H., (1985), "Formal Specification of User Interfaces: A Comparison and Evaluation of Four Axiomatic Approaches" *IEEE Trans. Softw. Eng.*, vol. 11, pp. 671–688.

Clarke, S., (1988), "The Increasing Importance of Formal Methods", *Computer Bulletin*, vol. 4, pp. 22–23 and 26.

Clement, T., (1983), *The Formal Specification of a Conference Organizing System*, Technical Monograph PRG–36, Oxford University Computing Laboratory.

Coelho, H., J.C. Cotta and L.M. Pereira, (1985), *How to Solve it with Prolog*, Lisbon, Laboratório Nacional de Engenharia Civil, fourth edition.

Cohen, B., (1989a), "Justification of Formal Methods for System Specification", *Software Engineering Journal*, vol. 4, pp. 26–35.

Cohen, B., (1989b), "A Rejustification of Formal Notations", *Software Engineering Journal*, vol. 4, pp. 36–38.

Copi, I.M., (1971), *The Theory of Logical Types*, London, Routledge & Kegan Paul.

Covington, M.A., D. Nute and A. Vellino, (1988), *Prolog Programming in Depth*, London, Scott, Foresman and Company.

Cupillari, A., (1989), *The Nuts and Bolts of Proofs*, Belmont (California), Wadsworth Publishing Company.

Darlington, (1987), "Software Development in Declarative Languages", in Eisenbach (1987), pp. 71–85.

Davies, A.C., (1988), "Introduction to Formal Methods of Software Design", *Microprocess. Microsyst.*, vol. 12, pp. 547–553.

Dijkstra, E.W., (1981), "Why Correctness must be a Mathematical Concern", in Boyer and Moore (1981), pp. 1–8.

Dijkstra, E.W., and W.H.J. Feijen, (1988), *A Method of Programming*, Wokingham, Addison-Wesley.

Diller, A., (1989), "Towards a Formal Specification of the Leeds Logic System", *Computerised Logic Teaching Bulletin*, vol. 2 (1989), pp. 2–15.

Diller, A., (1990a) "Specifying Interactive Programs in **Z**", preprint, School of Computer Science, University of Birmingham.

Diller, A., (1990b) "A **Z** Specification of Three Notions of Proof", preprint, School of Computer Science, University of Birmingham.

Dodgson, C.L., (1895), "What the Tortoise said to Achilles", *Mind*, vol. 4, pp. 278–280. Reprinted in Hofstadter (1979), pp. 43–45.

Dromey, R.G., (1982), *How to Solve it by Computer*, Hemel Hempstead, Prentice Hall.

Dromey, R.G., (1989), *Program Derivation: The Development of Programs from Specifications*, Wokingham, Addison-Wesley.

Dummett, M., (1975), "The Justification of Deduction", *Proceedings of the British Academy*, vol. LIX, pp. 201–232. Reprinted in Dummett (1978), pp. 290–318.

Dummett, M., (1977), *Elements of Intuitionism, Oxford Logic Guides*, Oxford, Oxford University Press.

Dummett, M., (1978), *Truth and Other Enigmas*, London, Duckworth.

Earl, A.N., R.P. Whittington, P. Hitchcock and A. Hall, (1986), "Specifying a Semantic Model for use in an Integrated Project Support Environment", in Sommerville (1986), pp. 202–219.

Eisenbach, S., (ed.), (1987), *Functional Programming: Languages, Tools and Architectures*, Chichester, Ellis Horwood.

Elphick, M.J., (ed.), (1983), *Formal Specification, Proceedings of the Joint IBM/University of Newcastle upon Tyne Seminar*, University of Newcastle upon Tyne Computing Laboratory.

Enderton, H.B., (1977), *Elements of Set Theory*, London, Academic Press.

Fenton, N.E., and P.D.A. Mole, (1988), "A Note on the use of Z to Specify Flowgraph Decomposition", *Inf. Softw. Technol.*, vol. 30, pp. 432–437.

Feyerabend, P., (1982), *Science in a Free Society*, London, Verso. This was first published in 1978.

Feyerabend, P., (1987), *Farewell to Reason*, London, Verso.

Feyerabend, P., (1988), *Against Method*, London, Verso, revised edition. This was first published in 1975.

Fitch, F., (1952), *Symbolic Logic*, New York, Ronald.

Franklin, J., and A. Daoud, (1988), *Introduction to Proofs in Mathematics*, Sydney, Prentice Hall.

Froome, P., and B. Monahan, (1988), "The Role of Mathematically Formal Methods in the Development and Assessment of Safety-critical Systems", *Microprocess. Microsyst.*, vol. 12, pp. 539–546.

Gabbay, D., and F. Guenthner (eds.), (1983), *Handbook of Philosophical Logic*, vol. I, *Elements of Classical Logic*, Dordrecht, Reidel.

Gallier, J.H., (1985), *Logic for Computer Science*, Chichester, Wiley.

Gibbins, P.F., (1988), "What are Formal Methods?", *Inf. Softw. Technol.*, vol. 30, pp. 131–137.

Gimson, R., (1987), *The Formal Documentation of a Block Storage System*, Technical Monograph PRG–62, Oxford University Computing Laboratory.

Gimson, R., and C. Morgan, (1985), *The Distributed Computing Software Project*, Technical Monograph PRG–50, Oxford University Computing Laboratory.

Gödel, K., (1931), "Ueber formal unentscheidbare Sätze der Principia Mathematica und verwandter Systeme I", *Monatshefte für Mathematik und Physik*, vol. 38, pp. 173–198.

Gödel, K., (1967), "On Formally Undecidable Propositions of *Principia Mathematics and Related Systems I*", in van Heijenoort (1967), pp. 596–616. This is an English translation by J. van Heijenoort of Gödel (1931).

Gordon, M.J.C., (1988), *Programming Language Theory and its Implementation: Applicative and Imperative Paradigms*, Hemel Hempstead, Prentice Hall.

Green, T.R.G., "Cognitive Ergonomic Research at SAPU, Sheffield", in van der Veer, Tauber, Green and Gorny (1984), pp. 102–113.

Gries, D., (1981), *The Science of Programming*, Berlin, Springer-Verlag.

Gumb, R.D., (1989), *Programming Logics: An Introduction to Verification and Semantics*, Chichester, Wiley.

Hall, P.A.V., (1988), "Towards Testing with Respect to Formal Specification", *Second IEE/BCS Conference: Software Engineering 88*, London, IEE, pp. 159–163.

Halmos, P.R., (1960), *Naive Set Theory*, London, Van Nostrand Reinhold.

Hamilton, A.G., (1978), *Logic for Mathematicians*, Cambridge, Cambridge University Press.

Harrison, M.D., and A.F. Monk, (eds.), (1986), *People and Computers: Designing for Usability: Proceedings of the Second Conference of the British Computer Society Human Computer Interaction Specialist Group*, Cambridge, Cambridge University Press.

Hatcher, W.S., (1982), *The Logical Foundations of Mathematics*, Oxford, Pergamon.

Hayes, I., (1985a), "Applying Formal Specification to Software Development in Industry", *IEEE Transactions on Software Engineering*, vol. SE-11, pp. 169–178. Also in Hayes (1987d), pp. 285–310.

Hayes, I., (1985b), *Specification Directed Module Testing*, Technical Monograph PRG–49, Oxford University Computing Laboratory.

Hayes, I., (1985c), *Specifying the CICS Application Programmer's Interface*, Technical Monograph PRG–47, Oxford University Computing Laboratory.

Hayes, I., (1987a), "CICS Message System", in Hayes (1987d), pp. 325–332.

Hayes, I., (1987b), "CICS Temporary Storage", in Hayes (1987d), pp. 311–324.

Hayes, I., (1987c), "Examples of Specification using Mathematics", in Hayes (1987d), pp. 37–50.

Hayes, I., (ed.), (1987d), *Specification Case Studies*, Hemel Hempstead, Prentice Hall.

Hoare, C.A.R., (1969), "An Axiomatic Basis for Computer Programming", *Communications of the ACM*, vol. 12, pp. 576–580 and 583. Reprinted in Hoare (1989), pp. 45–58.

Hoare, C.A.R., (1983), "Programming is an Engineering Profession", in Wallis (1983), pp. 77–84. Reprinted in Hoare (1989), pp. 315–324.

Hoare, C.A.R., (1985), "A Couple of Novelties in the Propositional Calculus", in *Zeitschr. f. Math. Logik und Grundlagen d. Math.*, vol. 31, pp. 173–178. Reprinted in Hoare (1989), pp. 325–331.

Hoare, C.A.R., (1989), *Essays in Computing Science*, Hemel Hempstead, Prentice Hall.

Hoare, C.A.R., and J.C. Shepherdson, (eds.), (1985), *Mathematical Logic and Programming Languages*, London, Prentice-Hall.

Hofstadter, D.R., (1979), *Gödel, Escher, Bach: An Eternal Golden Braid: A Metaphoric Fugue on Minds and Machines in the Spirit of Lewis Carroll*, Harmondsworth, Penguin.

Hughes, G.E., and M.J. Cresswell, (1968), *An Introduction to Modal Logic*, London, Methuen.

Hughes, G.E., and M.J. Cresswell, (1984), *A Companion to Modal Logic*, London, Methuen.

Hunter, G., (1971), *Metalogic: An Introduction to the Metatheory of Standard First-order Logic*, London, Macmillan.

Ince, D.C., (1988a), *An Introduction to Discrete Mathematics and Formal System Specification*, Oxford, Oxford University Press.

Ince, D.C., (1988b), "Z and System Specification", *Inf. Softw. Technol.*, vol. 30, pp. 138–145.

Ince, D.C., (1989), "Maths Matters", *EXE*, vol. 3, pp. 30, 32 and 34–35.

Jones, C.B., (1980), *Software Development: A Rigorous Approach*, Hemel Hempstead, Prentice Hall.

Jones, C.B., (1986a), *Systematic Software Development Using VDM*, Hemel Hempstead, Prentice Hall.

Jones, C.B., (1986b), *Teaching Notes for Systematic Software Development Using VDM*, Technical Report UMCS–86–4–2, Department of Computer Science, University of Manchester.

Jouannaud, J.–P., (ed.), (1985), *Functional Programming Languages and Computer Architecture, Lecture Notes in Computer Science*, vol. 201, London, Springer-Verlag.

Kemmerer, R.A., (1985), "Testing Formal Specifications to Detect Design Errors", *IEEE Transactions on Software Engineering*, pp. 32–43.

King, S., and I.H. Sørensen, (1988), "Specification and Design of a Library System", paper presented at the Refinement Workshop held at the University of York in January 1988.

King, S., I.H. Sørensen and J.C.P. Woodcock, (1988), **Z**: *Grammar and Concrete and Abstract Syntaxes*, version 2.0, Technical Monograph PRG–68, Oxford University Computing Laboratory.

Knott, R.D., and P.J. Krause, (1988a), "An Approach to Animating **Z** using Prolog", Report No. A1.1 of Alvey Project SE/065, Department of Mathematics, University of Surrey.

Knott, R.D., and P.J. Krause, (1988b), "An Example of the Rapid Prototyping of a **Z** Specification in Prolog", Report No. A1.2 of Alvey Project SE/065, Department of Mathematics, University of Surrey.

Knuth, D.E., (1973), *The Art of Computer Programming*, vol. 1, *Fundamental Algorithms*, Wokingham, Addison-Wesley, 1968[1], 1973[2].

Lakatos, I., (1976), *Proofs and Refutations: The Logic of Mathematical Discovery*, Cambridge, Cambridge University Press.

Lemmon, E.J., (1965), *Beginning Logic*, London, Nelson.

Lewis, C.I., and C.H. Langford, (1959), *Symbolic Logic*, New York, Dover Publications, second edition.

Martin-Löf, P., (1984), *Intuitionistic Type Theory, Studies in Proof Theory Lecture Notes*, Napoli, Bibliopolis.

Mates, B., (1972), *Elementary Logic*, Oxford, Oxford University Press, 1965[1], 1972[2].

Monk, J.D., (1976), *Mathematical Logic*, Berlin, Springer-Verlag.

Morash, R.P., (1987), *Bridge to Abstract Mathematics: Mathematical Proof and Structures*, New York, Random House.

Morgan, C., K. Robinson and P. Gardiner, (1988), *On the Refinement Calculus*, Technical Monograph PRG–70, Oxford University Computing Laboratory.

Morgan, C., and J.W. Sanders, (1989), *Laws of the Logical Calculi*, Technical Monograph PRG–78, Oxford University Computing Laboratory.

Néel, D., (1982), *Tools and Notions for Program Construction: An Advanced Course*, Cambridge, Cambridge University Press.

Neilson, D., (1988), "Hierarchical Refinement of a **Z** Specification", paper delivered at the Refinement Workshop held at the University of York in January 1988.

Newton-Smith, W.H., (1985), *Logic: An Introductory Course*, London, Routledge & Kegan Paul.

Nicholl, R.A., (1988), "A Specification of Modula-2 Process (Coroutine) Management", *J. Pascal Ada Modula-2*, vol. 7, pp. 16–22.

Polimeni, A.D., and H.J. Straight, (1985), *Foundations of Discrete Mathematics*, Belmont (California), Wadsworth.

Prior, M.L., and A.N. Prior, (1955), "Erotetic Logic", *Philosophical Review*, pp. 43–59.

Prior, A.N., (1962), *Formal Logic*, Oxford, Oxford University Press, 1955[1], 1962[2].

Quine, W.V.O., (1962), *Methods of Logic*, London, Routledge & Kegan Paul, 1952[1], 1962[2].

Quine, W.V.O., (1969), *Set Theory and its Logic*, Cambridge (MA), Harvard University Press, revised edition.

Rohl, J.S., (1983), *Writing Pascal Programs*, Cambridge, Cambridge University Press.

Scharbach, P.N., (ed.), (1989), *Formal Methods: Theory and Practice*, Oxford, Blackwell.

Shoesmith, D.J., and T.J. Smiley, (1978), *Multiple-conclusion Logic*, Cambridge, Cambridge University Press.

Simpson, R.L., (1988), *Elements of Symbolic Logic*, London, Routledge.

Sommerville, I., (ed.), (1986), *Software Engineering Environments*, London, Peter Peregrinus.

Stepney, S., and S.P. Lord, (1987), "Formal Specification of an Access Control System", *Software—Practice and Experience*, vol. 17, pp. 575–593.

Spivey, J.M., (1988), *Understanding Z: A Specification Language and its Formal Semantics*, Cambridge, Cambridge University Press.

Spivey, J.M., (1989a), "An Introduction to Z and Formal Specifications", *Software Engineering Journal*, vol. 4, pp. 40–50.

Spivey, J.M., (1989b), *The Z Notation: A Reference Manual*, Hemel Hempstead, Prentice Hall.

Stewart, I., and D. Tall, (1977), *The Foundations of Mathematics*, Oxford, Oxford University Press.

Sufrin, B.A, (1981), *Formal Specification of a Display Editor*, Technical Monograph PRG–21, Oxford University Computing Laboratory.

Sufrin, B.A, (1982a), "Formal Specification of a Display-oriented Text Editor", *Science of Computer Programming*, vol. 1, pp. 157–202.

Sufrin, B.A, (1982b), "Formal System Specifications, Notation and Examples", in Néel (1982), pp. 27–74.

Sufrin, B.A, (1986a), "Formal Methods and the Design of Effective User Interfaces", in Harrison and Monk (1986), pp. 24–43.

Sufrin, B.A, (ed.), (1986b), *Z Handbook*, Programming Research Group, Oxford University Computing Laboratory.

Sufrin, B.A., and J.C.P. Woodcock, (1987), "Towards the Formal Specification of a Simple Programming Support Environment", *Software Engineering Journal*, vol. 2, pp. 86–94.

Sundholm, G., (1983), "Systems of Deduction", in Gabbay and Guenthner (1983), pp. 133–188.

Suppes, P., (1957), *Introduction to Logic*, London, van Nostrand.

Suppes, P., (1960), *Axiomatic Set Theory*, London, van Nostrand.

Tennant, N., (1978), *Natural Logic*, Edinburgh, Edinburgh University Press.

Teruel, A., (1982), *Case Studies in Specification: Four Games*, Technical Monograph PRG–30, Oxford University Computing Laboratory.

Thomason, R.H., (1970), *Symbolic Logic*, London, Collier–Macmillan.

Todd, B.S., (1987), "A Model-Based Diagnostic Program", *Software Engineering Journal*, vol. 2, pp. 54–63.

Took, R., (1986a), "The Presenter—A Formal Design for an Autonomous Display Manager", in Sommerville (1986), pp. 151–169.

Took, R., (1986b), "Text Representation and Manipulation in a Mouse-driven Interface", in Harrison and Monk (1986), pp. 386–401.

Turner, D.A., (1985a), "Functional Programs as Executable Specifications", in Hoare and Shepherdson (1985), pp. 29–54.

Turner, D.A., (1985b), "Miranda: A Non-Strict Functional Language with Polymorphic Types", in Jouannaud (1985), pp. 1–16.

Turner, D.A., (1986), "An Overview of Miranda", *ACM SIGPLAN Notices*, vol. 21, pp. 158–166.

Turner, R., (1984), *Logics for Artificial Intelligence, Ellis Horwood Series in Artificial Intelligence*, Chichester, Ellis Horwood.

van der Veer, G.C., M.J. Tauber, T.R.G. Green and P. Gorny, (eds.), (1984), *Readings on Cognitive Ergonomics*, Berlin, Springer-Verlag.

van Heijenoort, J., (1967), *From Frege to Gödel: A Source Book in Mathematical Logic, 1879–1931*, Cambridge (MA), Harvard University Press.

Vickers, T., and P. Gardiner, (1988), *A Tutorial on B: A Theorem Proving Assistant*, BP Project Report, Programming Research Group, University of Oxford.

Wallis, P.J.L., (ed.), (1983), *Software Engineering*, State of the Art Report, vol. 11.

Wang, H., (1952), "Logic of Many-sorted Theories", *Journal of Symbolic Logic*, vol. 17, pp. 105–116.

Whitehead, A.N., and B. Russell, (1910), *Principia Mathematica*, vol. 1, Cambridge, Cambridge University Press.

Whitehead, A.N., and B. Russell, (1912), *Principia Mathematica*, vol. 2, Cambridge, Cambridge University Press.

Whitehead, A.N., and B. Russell, (1913), *Principia Mathematica*, vol. 3, Cambridge, Cambridge University Press.

Wilson, R.J., (1975), *Introduction to Graph Theory*, London, Longman.

Wing, J.M., (1988), "A Study of 12 Specifications of the Library Problem", *IEEE Software*, July, pp. 66–76.

Woodcock, J.C.P., (1989a), "Structuring Specifications in **Z**", *Software Engineering Journal*, vol. 4, pp. 51–66.

Woodcock, J.C.P., (1989b), *Using **Z**: Specification, Refinement and Proof*, preprint, Programming Research Group, Oxford University Computing Laboratory.

Woodcock, J.C.P., and M. Loomes, (1988), *Software Engineering Mathematics: Formal Methods Demystified*, London, Pitnam.

Wordsworth, J.B., (1988), "Specifying and Refining Programs with **Z**", *Second IEE/BCS Conference: Software Engineering 88*, London, IEE, pp. 8–16.

Index

Standard Z Notation

Every symbol included in this part of the index is standard **Z** notation as defined in Spivey (1989b). I have tried to organize this index logically, first presenting syntactic constructs, then those dealing with logical notions, then arithmetical symbols, then set theoretic ones, and then those concerned with relations, functions, sequences, bags and finally schemas.

Additionally Defined Symbols

Z is an extendible language in that it contains ways of defining new symbols, viz. abbreviation definition, axiomatic description and generic constant introduction. Here I list all symbols defined using these, as well as some common meta-linguistic symbols, namely ⊨, ⫤⊨, ⊢ , ⊣⊢ and schema renaming [x/y].

Names and Concepts

λ-calculus, 75

Abrial, Jean-Raymond, 3
abbreviation definition, xvii, 20, 231, 302
abstraction, 22
    lambda, 247
    operational, 4, 6
    procedural, 4, 6, 100
    representational, 7
adequacy, 116
animation, of a specification, 211, 221
antecedent, 14
anti-restriction,
    domain, 242
    range, 68, 243
anti-symmetric relation, 87
apodosis, 15
application,
    function, 246
    generalized, 244
argument,
    logical, 11
    of a function, 71
associativity,
    of conjunction, 235
    of disjunction, 235
axiom, 12
    extensionality, 29
    schema, 98
axiomatic description, xvii, 76, 231, 302

B (proof-assistant), 285
bag, 85, 253
    sum, 254
    union, 86, 254
base name, 63
bi-implication, 15, 233
    elimination rules for, 107, 256
    introduction rule for, 107, 256
    truth-table for, 15, 233
bijection, 100, 246
bijective function, 100
bivalence, law of, 12

calculating preconditions, 137
car (Lisp), 79
cardinality, of a set, 32, 240
case studies, *see* specification case studies
categorical imperative, 264
cdr (Lisp), 80
chain, of relationships, 170
CICS, 3
classroom specification, 133
closure,
    reflexive-transitive, 57, 62, 244
    transitive, 57, 62, 244
commands, 12
commutativity,
    of conjunction, 235
    of disjunction, 235
commuting diagram, 146, 159
completeness, 116
complexity, management of, 7
composition,
    forward relational, 57
    backward relational, 61
    schema, 63
comprehension, set, 27, 28
computer scientists, demented, 202
concatenation,
    distributed, 81
    sequence, 78
conclusion, 18, 105
conditional, 14
conjunct, 13
conjunction, 13, 233
    elimination rules for, 106, 255
    introduction rule for, 106, 255
    truth-table for, 13, 233
connective,
    propositional, 13
        two-place, 233
    truth-functional, 13
consequent, 15
conventions, variable, 263–264
corestriction,
    domain, 242

303

functional description, 4

generalized application, 244
generic definition, xvii, 79, 231, 302
given set, 54

heterogeneous relation, 62
hiding, schema, 63
homogeneous relation, 57, 62

IBM, 3
identifier, decoration of, 5
identity, 237
    as a relation, 242
    elimination rule for, 119, 258
    introduction rule for, 119, 258
    relation, 57, 62
    of sets, 29
iff (abbreviation), 13
image, of a relation, 48, 244
imperative, 12
    categorical, 264
implementation, 7
implication, 14, 233
    elimination rule for, 107, 256
    introduction rule for, 107, 256
    material, 15
    truth-table for, 14, 233
induction,
    mathematical, 129, 258
    sequence, 130, 146, 259
inference, 11
    rule of, 12, *see also* rule of inference
infinite sequence, 82
initial state, 54
initialization, proof-obligation, 135
injection, 100
    partial, 245
injective function, 100, 245
    finite, 246
    partial, 245
    total, 246
injective sequence 144, 249
inputs in $\mathbf{Z}$, 5, 41
interactive process, specification of, 211

interpretation, 12
interrogatives, 12
intersection,
    generalized, 32, 238
    set, 31, 238
inverse, of a relation, 50, 242

lambda abstraction, 247
language, typed, 21
Lisp, 96
list, 95
logic, 11
    classical, 12
    erotetic, 13
    first-order, 233
    Floyd–Hoare, 5
    Hilbert-style, 95
    intuitionistic, 108
    n-valued, 12

maplet, 241
mapping, 71
mathematical induction, 129
mathematics, discrete, 8
maximal type, 43, 74
membership, set, 29
meta-language, 18
model, 144
    software, 8
    model-theory, 12, 105
modelling, correctness criterion for, 146
modus ponendo ponens, 98, 107
modus ponens, 107
modus tollendo tollens, 115
morphism, 71
multi-set, 85

name, base, 63
negation, 13, 233
    elimination rule for, 108, 256
    introduction rule for, 108, 257
    truth-table for, 13, 233
non-contradiction, law of, 235
normalization, schema, 43
number range, 27, 240